HESIOD

HESIOD

Theogony, Works and Days, Shield

Translation, Introduction, and Notes
by Apostolos N. Athanassakis

THIRD EDITION

 Johns Hopkins University Press : Baltimore

The first edition of this book was published with the generous assistance
of the David M. Robinson Publication Fund.

Johns Hopkins University Press
2715 North Charles Street
Baltimore, Maryland 21218–4363
www.press.jhu.edu

Library of Congress Cataloging-in-Publication Data

Names: Hesiod, author. | Athanassakis, Apostolos N., translator, writer of supplementary
    textual content. | Hesiod. Theogony. English (Athanassakis) | Hesiod. Works and days.
    English (Athanassakis) | Hesiod. Shield of Heracles. English (Athanassakis)
Title: Theogony ; Works and days ; Shield / Hesiod ; translation, introduction,
    and notes by Apostolos N. Athanassakis.
Description: Third edition. | Baltimore : Johns Hopkins University Press, 2022. |
    Includes bibliographical references and index.
Identifiers: LCCN 2021039602 | ISBN 9781421443942 (paperback) | ISBN 9781421443959 (ebook)
Subjects: LCSH: Heracles (Greek mythological character)—Poetry. | Religious poetry,
    Greek—Translations into English. | Didactic poetry, Greek—Translations into English. |
    Agriculture—Greece—Poetry. | Gods, Greek—Poetry. | LCGFT: Poetry. | Religious poetry. |
    Didactic poetry.
Classification: LCC PA4010.E5 T5 2022 | DDC 881/.01—dc23
LC record available at https://lccn.loc.gov/2021039602

A catalog record for this book is available from the British Library.

*Special discounts are available for bulk purchases of this book. For more information, please contact Special Sales
at specialsales@jh.edu.*

To Lloyd W. Daly, teacher and friend, with gratitude

Contents

Preface   ix

Introduction   xi

List of Abbreviations   xix

The *Theogony*   1

    Theogony   11
    Notes   37

The *Works and Days*   57

    Works and Days   65
    Notes   87

The *Shield*   113

    Shield   121
    Notes   145

    Select Bibliography   151

    Index   157

Preface

The Greek text I have used in translating the *Theogony*, the *Works and Days*, and the *Shield* is that of Friedrich Solmsen (Oxford, 1970). The translation of the *Theogony* and the *Works and Days* follows the original line by line. Few exceptions have been made for cases in which this practice would result in ambiguous or hardly comprehensible English. I have followed this strict translation probably at great cost. I know that a freer translation would be more elegant, and even more dynamic and moving. These two poems, however, are primary sources for Greek religion and mythology, and for the history of the development of Greek thought. My aim is to provide especially the Greekless student of these subjects with a dependable translation to which convenient reference may be made for academic discussion and writing. In the translation of the *Shield*, I felt that I could afford the luxury of departing from this practice because the poem is not frequently studied as a primary source for Greek mythology and religion and because its structure and tempo made a freer rendition into English imperative. In the present third edition the reader is provided with notes. Let me assure my readers that I consider all three poems beautiful, and I hope that my departures from the literal meaning of the original do not make my translations unfaithful. I have tried to let Hesiod speak for himself and not to use his poetry as a springboard for fanciful rhapsodizing of my own making. Classical texts of such importance and pristine dignity are only distorted and tarnished when they are made relevant to each passing fad.

The first person to whom I wish to record gratitude is Professor Lloyd W. Daly, who was an inspiring and patient teacher when I studied Hesiod as a graduate student at the University of Pennsylvania. My debt to M. L. West for his masterful commentaries to the *Theogony* and the *Works and Days* is great. Carlo F. Russo is the only scholar who has treated the *Shield* with the seriousness and insightfulness it deserves, and the excellent introduction to his critical edition and commentary has been of inestimable value to me.

In my notes, there is considerable material from the beliefs and practices of the people of rural Greece. Classicists usually have such an attachment to pre-classical and classical Greece that they resent the intrusion of modern Greek survivals and instructive analogues. It is high time for this elitist trend to reverse itself, especially now that the tide of mass communications threatens to destroy in one or two generations what millennia have preserved. Relevant details from oral tradition and folk culture are every bit as important as the shards archaeologists conscientiously collect and evaluate. To spurn them is to turn one's eyes away from what frequently might be useful evidence.

Johns Hopkins University Press published the first edition of my translation of Hesiod's works in 1983, almost forty years ago. Both the first edition and the second edition in 2004 have been received very warmly. Poetry is untranslatable. Yet, the love of the ancient originals and the imperative need to share them with others, both as poetic achievements and as precious sources of information and knowledge, drive us to do the impossible. The present revision is a gentle one. Its principal aim is greater accuracy, the removal of words that are strikingly obsolete, and the reduction of overly long lines. The additions to the notes are lean, offering the reader critical information and fresh perspectives born of new research.

Once more, I wish to thank Timothy S. Heckenlively, a UC Santa Barbara PhD now teaching at Baylor University, for the preparation of the genealogical charts and the bibliography. Benjamin M. Wolkow, also a UCSB PhD, now teaching at the University of Georgia, helped me a great deal in incorporating changes in translation and additions to the notes of the second edition. His patience, enthusiasm, and razor-sharp editorial and philological skills are memorable. Both Timothy S. Heckenlively's and Benjamin M. Wolkow's contributions enhanced the second edition and continue to live on in the third edition. For this third edition, I have been very competently assisted by Paschalia Mitskidou, doctoral candidate in the Department of American Literature and Culture at the Aristotle University of Thessaloniki. Her editorial and philological skills have protected against the intrusion of errors.

Introduction

There is no agreement among modern scholars as to Hesiod's exact date. The best we can do is place him somewhere between the second half of the eighth century BC and the first quarter of the seventh BC. The prevalent opinion among Greeks of the classical period was that Hesiod was among the earliest poets and teachers of the race. They usually placed him after the mythical Orpheus and Mousaios and before Homer. By the fifth century BC, the memory of what had happened three centuries earlier was blurred, and, despite the anecdotal poetic contest between Homer and Hesiod, there is no compelling reason for the assumption that Hesiod either preceded Homer or even that he was his contemporary. As for details concerning his life, it should be said that we ought to rely only on what Hesiod himself tells in the poems, either directly or by inference. Even if the information that he supplies is scant, it is better than all fanciful conjecture. Hesiod is Hesiod's best biographer.

From *Works and Days* 27–41, 63–68, and *Theogony* 22–35, we gather that Hesiod was the son of an immigrant from Aeolian Kyme (Cyme) in Asia Minor. His father settled in Boeotian Askre, close to the slopes of Mt. Helikon. He tells us that he tended sheep in the foothills of this mountain, and that one day, while tending his sheep, he had a profound experience: he met the Muses and they gave him the gift of song. Given the pastoral character of the region and the intense religiosity and vivid imagination of the Greeks, neither claim can be refuted by scientific inquiry. Indeed, there is no reason to assume that either Hesiod's shepherding or his vision is fiction or pure literary convention. As is clear from the *Works and Days,* Hesiod's less enterprising brother, Perses, tried to cheat him of his rightful portion of the patrimony by resorting to lies and bribery. We do not know how the strife was settled, but Hesiod at some point turned his poetic ability to the composition of a poem that would teach his brother and others like him how to pursue their own well-being without harming others, how to work, and when to work. The poet became a moral and practical preceptor to his greedy brother, and thus, it seems, the *Works and Days* was born. The dispute may also have preceded the composition of his more ambitious *Theogony*, which in its present form antedates the *Works and Days*. It was probably composed sometime in the last quarter of the eighth century BC.

The date of the composition of Hesiod's poems, especially of the *Theogony*, roughly coincided with the introduction of the alphabet to Greece. We do not know how long it took until the alphabet was first used in literary composition. Hesiod definitely belongs to that transitional period when the oral tradition was slowly coming to an end, and the written one was taking its first, timid steps. If the Homeric epics were composed without the aid of writing, it follows a fortiori that the much shorter Hesiodic poems could have also been composed without the aid of writing. There is little or nothing in the poems of Hesiod that proves or disproves oral composition. Large sections of the poems were definitely part of traditional didactic lore. If Hesiod employed writing, he did so not in the way we usually think of writing. It is entirely possible that he operated like a traditional oral poet except for some minimal use of the new art, perhaps as a sort of crude stenographic device, at least until later in his life when the finished poems could be committed to writing in their final form.

There is no doubt that the *Theogony* and the *Works and Days* were Hesiod's major poems. Although most modern scholars question the authenticity of the *Shield*, all standard editions include it, thus paying homage to the weight of ancient tradition. There is an excellent edition of the fragments of Hesiod's poetry, the *Fragmenta Hesiodea*, by R. Merkelbach and M. L. West (Oxford University Press, 1966). The bulk of the fragments comes from the *Catalogue of Women*, from which the first fifty-four or fifty-six lines of the *Shield* were borrowed by the rhapsode who composed the poem. Of his lost *Ornithomanteia* (Bird Divination) nothing survives, except perhaps what is now line 828 of the *Works and Days*. There are also fragments from such works as *Astronomy*, *Idaean Dactyls*, *Aigimios*, the *Marriage of Keyx*, the *Divinations of Melampus*, the *Precepts of Cheiron*, the *Great Eoiai*, and the *Great Works*. Many of these are of doubtful authenticity, and their number indicates that, much as in the case of Homer and Hippocrates, tradition tended to ascribe to one consecrated master both works that seemed to be thematically connected with his oeuvre and impressive imitations by anonymous rhapsodes.

The poetry of Hesiod has attracted political and sociological interest. He is, after all, the oldest repository of Western culture when it comes to the origin of the cosmos and the many divinities in it, as well as to the social values and practices that make human culture and human survival possible.

A. R. Burn's influential book *The World of Hesiod* was published in 1936. Burn ignored entirely the great German scholar Wilamowitz for reasons that could have been only political. To Burn, Hesiod was an anomaly, an un-Homer whose gift of poetry raised him above the miseries of the peasant underclass to which he was born, an underclass that consisted of racially inferior Greeks steeped in the mire of magic and superstition. It would be interesting to know how great scholars like Werner Jaeger, Bruno Snell, and Hermann Fränkel would have judged Hesiod's poetry if Hesiod himself had been born to wealth and high privilege. It seems to me that his humble origin cast a shadow on his work, even on his *Theogony*, which has nothing to do with the backbreaking work and unheroic thrift necessary to keep the specter of famine at bay. In all fairness to the scholars just mentioned as examples of mainstream views of Hesiod during most of the twentieth century, it must be said that the discipline of classics itself was, and to some extent continues to be, very elitist. Hesiod is simply a test case. Class-linked prejudice has contributed to a warped view of the poet as a monumental failure. Despite the majestic portions of the *Theogony* and the very fundamental quest for the norms and dynamics that make work and justice interdependent conditions of civilized life in the *Works and Days,* for many classicists Hesiod remained a lesser poet.

Three scholars paved the way for a much wider acceptance of Hesiod's poetic worth by arguing that the *Works and Days* is a great poem. They were F. R. Earp, Paul Mazon, and M. L. West. The basic tenets of the theory of oral composition have not convinced West, especially with regard to Hesiod. However, his books *Hesiod: Theogony* and *Hesiod: Works and Days* will dominate the field of Hesiodic studies for a very long time. Pietro Pucci and Mark Griffith have done much to elevate the discourse on Hesiod and to introduce new approaches to the study of his poetry. The most prominent interpreters of Hesiod have been, directly or indirectly, influenced by structuralism, especially by Claude Lévi-Strauss and his disciples. Classicists who have benefited from the advances made by such cultural anthropologists as Campbell, Walcot, Gernet, and Girard will read Hesiod from a perspective that simply did not exist two to three generations ago. From among the many influential French thinkers, P. Vernant and M. Detienne deserve special mention for their highly original contributions to the study of archaic Greece. The American scholars Milman Parry and A. B. Lord applied what they had learned from the study of Serbo-Croatian epic to the study of Homeric verse. The pathbreaking work by Parry and Lord supported entirely novel and revolutionary ideas about the birth and transmission of heroic epic.

Genuine heroic song is composed and transmitted orally by singers who do not write their compositions down and do not depend on any kind of written text put together by others. Apprenticeship with great singers at a very young age, creative performance, and powerful memory help the singer compose in a style that is largely formulaic. The set expression, the formula, is his building block. Meter helps him fuse formulaic and nonformulaic language into an acceptable poetic entity. Each performance is unique. The use of writing usually signals the death knell of true oral epic poetry. It is clear even from this extremely oversimplified and brief description of the theory of oral composition that no discussion of Hesiod can any longer be entirely constructive if it ignores the implications of oral composition for his poetry. The most powerful support, at least within the anglophone world, for the proposition that Hesiod was an oral poet has come from Gregory Nagy. Indeed, in his lengthy article "Hesiod," Nagy writes that for Hesiod and Homer performance was the medium of transmitting, not reading. Composition in oral poetry becomes a reality only in performance, and rhapsodes were much more than mere memorizers of texts (Nagy, "Hesiod," especially 45–46). My own opinion is not so entirely unwavering. There are questions about the oral or non-oral aspects of Hesiodic poetry that cannot be settled. Hesiod certainly inherited oral poetry, and he produced oral poetry in a way that was more self-conscious and more deliberate than that of his teachers and his ancestors.

By Hesiod's time, the alphabet must have reached Boeotia. Some might think that, because Hesiod was born in the backwoods of Boeotia, he had no idea of innovations that may have taken place in the great and not too distant city of Thebes. Why would Hesiod not make use of the alphabet? Could it be that he, being an oral poet, saw a threat to his profession in the new invention? Hesiod does not mention the alphabet anywhere in his poems. Not much can be concluded from this omission. Cheese and olives must have been very important in the diet of the society Hesiod addresses. Yet, they are nowhere to be found in his works. Then again, we do have deliberate omissions. For all of Hesiod's elaborate description of the underworld and its gloomy prisoners, the souls of the dead (the *psychai*) are given neither space nor mention. Hesiod the materialist excluded them from his thorough account of the underworld because he may have considered the traditional belief in the existence of the soul naive and no longer tenable.

The ideological orientation of Hesiod's arguments, his persistently didactic intent, and his purposeful and politically expedient use of myth and religion do not seem to be the product of spontaneous creativity. Perhaps, like Prometheus, the "Fore-Thinker," Hesiod was a premeditative revolutionary. His trysts with Mnemosyne and her nine daughters, the Muses, of whom he speaks so movingly in both the *Theogony* and in the *Works and Days*, were not chance encounters, but rather complex arrangements that involved the mind more than they involved the heart.

In Hesiod's extant works, spontaneous impulse yields to an obsessive pre-occupation with the imperative need for tracing origins and accounting for results. Homer delights in life and in the excellence to which man can attain. He revels in the nuances and stratifications of glory inherited and glory be-queathed. Hesiod chose to ignore *kleos,* a warrior's reputation and fame, both in his own generation and in ages to come. He did so consciously and in a way that his audiences may or may not have found enthralling or immedi-ately acceptable. How could an oral poet, one that was an heir to the heroic tradition, dismiss the saga of Troy and the great heroes who fought to re-cover the beautiful Helen and the honor of the Greeks in the terse and dis-approving manner of *Works and Days* 160–67:

> They were the divine race of heroes, who are called
> demigods; they preceded us on this boundless earth.
> Evil war and dreadful battle wiped them all out,
> some fighting over the flocks of Oedipus
> at seven-gated Thebes, in the land of Kadmos,
> others over the great gulf of the sea in ships
> that had sailed to Troy for the sake of lovely-haired Helen;
> there death threw his dark mantle over them.

Catalogues are very important. The Catalogue of Ships in the second book of the *Iliad* is an unrivaled record of memory of oral poetic performance at work, testing the limits of human ability to remember names and places and to put them next to each other in ways that preserve and declare hierarchy and meaningful interconnection of kingdoms, nations, families, and outstanding indi-viduals. Hesiod's impressive catalogue of the daughters of Nereus (*Theogony* 240–64) as well as his catalogue of the daughters of Okeanos (*Theogony* 346–61) required no ordinary mnemonic ability. Both catalogues of these marvelous daughters of the great waters could just as well belong to the performative dynam-ics of competing oral singers. Yet, elsewhere I find it difficult, if not impossible, to imagine Hesiod as an oral poet of an entirely preliterate age. His reflections on Eris (Strife) in the *Works and Days* seem to be the product of a retrospective mind. In this poem, which is so very different from the *Theogony,* the poet in an almost conversational tone recalls that he had mentioned Eris in the *Theogony* as being only of one kind, a single entity. He conveys the impression that years of reflection have taught him otherwise. So he proceeds to demonstrate its duality. There is the competitive and productive Eris as opposed to the destructive Eris. Work and justice are interdependent moral imperatives. Their interdependence is supported through details of life as well as through major themes of social collaboration that can rise to the level of systemic synergy. The potential for violence lurks in every corner. Human imperfection cannot only flaw our every step to social, indeed political, excellence, it can make it difficult and even painful. The path to virtue (*aretê*) is a steep one, a laborious climb. The threading through of kernel concepts, the plaiting and weaving of argument, and the navigation of complexities are not of a piece with the directness, the swiftness, and the limpidity of Homeric heroic narrative.

Hesiod is a driven man. In his world, everything must occupy its proper place. It is because of this that he becomes the genealogist of the cosmic elements, of the divine persons and powers, and then, fervidly, of physical and social realities. We have to ask ourselves what sort of audience could be amused or captivated by contortions, omissions, and abstruse leaps of the imagination. I know there are huge gaps in our evidence. Yet the fact is that, in terms of the evidence we do have, Hesiod is unprecedented. Formulaic composition is not an adequate criterion by which to judge his poetry as oral. For this, I think, our matrix must expand to include narratological formulae. Inescapably, the question of mixed composition, oral for some themes, not so oral for other themes, must claim the attention it deserves.

Hesiod knew and could easily recite stretches of set text of oral literature. He knew proverbs and folk tales that were not unlike the parables of the New Testament. Most certainly, he knew folk songs. Moral commandments like "Give to those who give to you, never to those who do not" or "No shame in work but plenty of it in sloth" sound more like collective social utterances born of collective social experience than like sudden strokes of individual poetic inspiration.

One thing is certain: Hesiod was a great poet. He crossed from mainland Greece over to Euboea to take part in a song contest in honor of Amphidamas, a local nobleman, perhaps even a king. He won a great prize, an eared tripod, which he brought back to Askre, his birthplace, and dedicated it to the Muses of Helikon on the very spot where they taught him "flowing song" (*Works and Days* 646–59). I have no doubt that Hesiod was an oral poet, but I have no way of knowing that all of the text of the *Theogony* and of the *Works and Days* was oral in the strictest sense of the word as it is commonly understood by all who have followed the discourse on oral poetry.

The poetry of Hesiod is eternal. Its value increases as time passes. There was nothing trendy about it when he composed it; and there is nothing trendy about it now. Hesiod peers through the darkness to discover such primal elements as Chaos, Gaia, and Tartaros floating in the immensity of the cosmos. The principle of attraction, Eros, is the power that holds these elements together.

This retrogressive journey into the mystery of creation is awesome. Yet, no mistake should be made. For Hesiod, this is neither a spiritual journey nor the product of detached meditation. Rather, it is his singer's way of explaining the tangible, the visible, and the imaginable material universe in terms of matter. Darkness of one kind and darkness of another kind unite, perhaps collide, to produce light. The incredibly appealing divine command known to all of us from the beginning of Genesis is absent here. The word, the command, does not produce a physical entity. Few, I think, could understand Hesiod in his own age. Parallels from the modern world abound. Milman Parry himself made little or no sense to his compatriots more than fifty years ago. Hesiod sang of primitive yet very bold physics. His song must have been as lost on his audience as some aspects of modern physics are lost on the average citizen.

Hesiod the cosmologist, the hierarch of genealogy, pedigree, and order of the vastness that surrounds man, can reduce the scale to fit human society and the dynamics that determine balance, sanity, and productivity in it. In so many ways, Hesiod is a capitalist and a Marxist at the same time. He gives prescriptions for the ideal age of the plowman and of the oxen that pull his plow. He also prescribes fair rations of food for workers. One must not lose inherited land at any cost. He must have children so that he is not inherited by kinsmen who may have done nothing for him. No matter what the problem is, work is the answer! Ideological trappings aside, somehow both capitalists and Marxists will find some common element in Hesiod's ideology. His thought, his ruminations and obsessions, as well as his flights of the imagination, cross many barriers, walk past many millennia to deliver important messages. In the beginning, Chaos came into being. Work is no shame. Marry when you are close to the age of thirty (this advice is for men). Home is safer. Then complex ideas: If Olympian gods lie, they can be put to a test. Iris will fetch water for them from the infernal waters of Styx. Awful things will happen to them if, as they swear a false oath, they pour a libation of the water of the dread river Styx. Here, the shepherd boy who was given the gift of song by the Muses must be speaking to himself. Styx is a goddess of the defeated old order. Her water can be lethal to those gods of the new order who are guilty of perjury. The new truth of the supremacy of Zeus must be proclaimed by all. Conspirators will pay a heavy price. The Muses are powerful. They can speak to a shepherd boy who knows only the streams and the hills at the foot of Helikon and grant him the power to recollect the past, to see the present, and to peer into the future. The Muses can teach him that gods come and go and that, in the larger scheme of things, power determines the truth. Power determines who lies and who tells the truth. If the poet is like his teachers, the Muses, he has a choice, and he can be a power broker.

ABBREVIATIONS

AJA	*American Journal of Archaeology*
Ant.R.	*Antioch Review*
C & M	*Classica et Mediaevalia*
CJ	*Classical Journal*
CP	*Classical Philology*
CQ	*Classical Quarterly*
CR	*Classical Review*
EMC	*Échos du Monde Classique*
GRBS	*Greek, Roman, and Byzantine Studies*
JHI	*Journal of the History of Ideas*
JHS	*Journal of Hellenic Studies*
KFLQ	*Kentucky Foreign Language Quarterly*
OCD	*Oxford Classical Dictionary*
REG	*Revue des Études Grecques*
SO	*Symbolae Osloenses*
TAPA	*Transactions and Proceedings of the American Philological Association*
WS	*Wiener Studien*

I. Primeval Origins

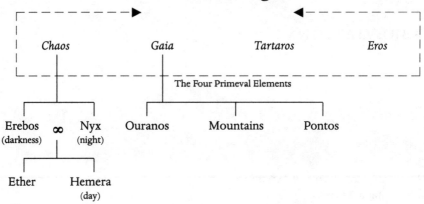

II. Genealogy of the Gods

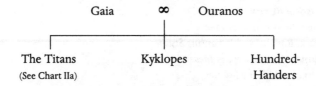

IIa. The Titans and their Offspring

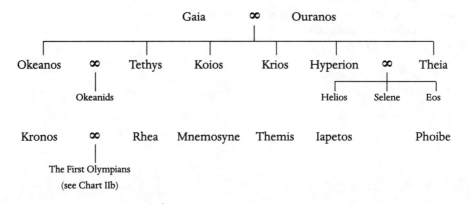

Readers may wish to consult the index for more details.

IIb. The Olympian Gods*

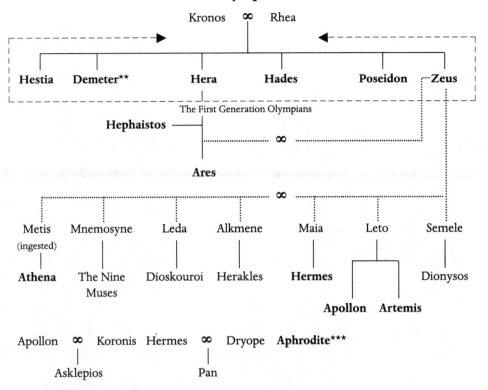

Kronos ∞ Rhea

Hestia **Demeter**** **Hera** **Hades** **Poseidon** **Zeus**

The First Generation Olympians

Hephaistos ———

∞

Ares

∞

Metis (ingested)	Mnemosyne	Leda	Alkmene	Maia	Leto	Semele
Athena	The Nine Muses	Dioskouroi	Herakles	**Hermes**		Dionysos

Apollon Artemis

Apollon ∞ Koronis   Hermes ∞ Dryope   **Aphrodite*****

Asklepios   Pan

* Olympian gods are indicated in bold. The gods born of Kronos and Rhea are the older Olympians. The canon of the twelve Olympians came to include Athena, born of Zeus's own head; Hephaistos, the parthenogenetic son of Hera; and Hermes, son of Zeus and Maia. An incestuous union of Zeus and Hera produced Ares, while the Titaness Leto bore to Zeus Apollon and Artemis.

** Earth Mother of All (not to be confused with Gaia), Rhea, Kybele, and also the Mother of the Gods share a great deal with Demeter.

*** Aphrodite was born of the sea fecundated by the blood drops of the severed genitals of Ouranos.

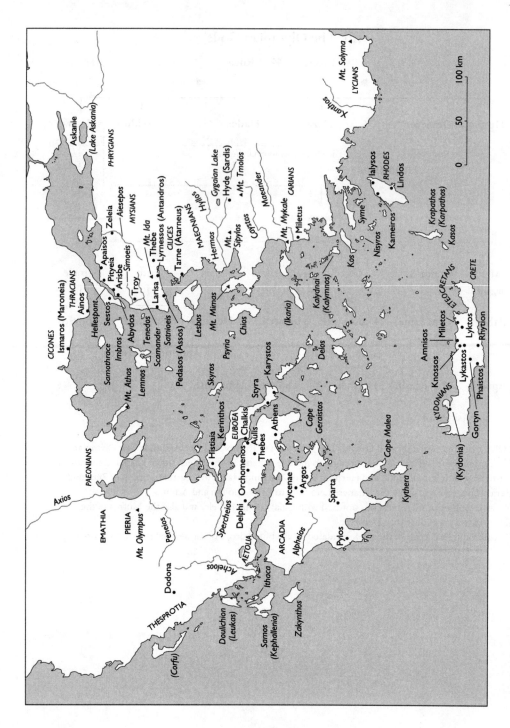

Preclassical Greece and Asia Minor. Drawn by William L. Nelson; adapted from J. D. Falconer and E. J. Owens in *Atlas of Classical History*, ed. R. J. A. Talbert, 9, 10 (London: Routledge, 1985).

HESIOD

The *Theogony*

To Hesiod, Earth (Gaia), Sky (Ouranos), and Sea (Pontos) are not mere elements, but gods. Thus, when Hesiod sets out to compose a poem on the birth of the gods, a *Theogony*, he is prepared to give his listeners—and eventually his readers—not only an account of the birth of the Olympian gods, so familiar to us mostly through Homer, but also an account of the birth of the *kosmos* and of all the divinities that move within it. The *Theogony* then is partly a cosmogony, that is, a poem not only about the birth of the gods and the various divine powers but also about the birth of the multifarious divine universe.

The most familiar type of theogonic literature—I use the word in the Hesiodic sense, which includes cosmogonic elements as well—comes to us from the opening chapters of Genesis. The Hebrew tradition, however, because of its monotheistic character, is bound to be less instructive. Although the subject of theogonic literature is such that one may study all similar accounts with profit, from Japan's *Ko-Ji-Ki* to the rich material from the indigenous American Indian religious and mythological lore, it is in traditions ethnolinguistically or geographically closer to the Greek that one must search for more instructive analogues.

A lengthy account of theogonic literature is indeed outside the scope of this short introduction. Therefore, I choose to refer eclectically and briefly to some examples from the Near East, from India, and from Iceland. The story of Kumarbi comes to us in Hittite texts but is doubtless of Hurrian origin. In one text, the sky-god Anu defeated Alalu and forced him to flee to the earth. After Anu reigned in the sky for nine years, he was threatened by Kumarbi and fled up to his own element, the sky, but Kumarbi pursued him, caught him, and then bit off and swallowed his genitals. The river Tigris and the god Tasmisu are born from what Kumarbi disgorges when warned by Anu about the potential danger from "the three gods" he has swallowed. The third god is still inside him. With the aid of a fabulous emetic and after considerable

I

travail, his body is rid of the third god, who turns out to be the weather-god. What follows is fragmentary and unclear, but in a longer text called the *Song of Ullikummi*, Kumarbi gives birth to a mighty child of monstrous size. This child eventually threatens all the gods, but his feet are cut off and he is finally subdued by the gods.

Another epic of creation, the Babylonian *Enûma Eliš*, is a poem whose length is roughly the same as that of the *Theogony*, but whose composition antedates that of the *Theogony* probably by as much as five hundred years. In this account, Apsû and Tiamât unite by mingling their waters. (Apsû seems to approximate the earth and its waters, and Tiamât the sea.) Of the gods born of this union, the male god Ea is the most important. Apsû decides to destroy these gods because they are restless and noisy. Ea contrives to have Apsû fall into a coma, and then strips him of his regalia and kills him. Ea's son, Marduk, causes fear among the elder gods. In their apprehension, they persuade Tiamât to make war on the new gods. Ea feels powerless, and even Anu (Sky) proves ineffective. Only Marduk, the youngest god, dares confront her after the younger gods agree to make him their king. Marduk is armed with such conventional weapons as bow and club, but also with lightning and the four winds. In the final confrontation, Tiamât opens her mouth to swallow her grandson, but his four winds inflate her belly so much that she is unable to close her mouth again. He then cleaves her carcass into two pieces and makes the heavens from the one and the earth from the other. Then he proceeds to set up the moon and the constellations, and to create man from the blood of one of the vanquished gods. Details do differ, and the Hittite-Hurrian story may in some ways, especially in the castration motif, be somewhat closer to the Hesiodic account, but both the Hittite-Hurrian and the Babylonian theogonies show, in overall terms and patterns, an astounding similarity to the Hesiodic *Theogony*.

The *Ṛgveda* contains substantial passages of a theogonic character, and the creation of heaven and earth by Indra as well as his victory over the primeval serpent (ii, 12) will strike familiar notes in the minds of Hesiod's readers. Likewise, the monumental *Mahābhārata* contains a theogonic excursus that starts with the birth of Brahma and Prajāpati from the primeval egg. More, however, is to be found in one of eighteen long poems (the *Purāṇas*), the *Viṣṇu Purāṇa*, which contains a full cosmogony, divine and human (royal) genealogies as well as genealogies of animals and plants. The material is vast, diffuse, and diverse. Parallels between it and the *Theogony* can be found in detail but not in the overall scheme.

The reader of the *Elder Edda* and of the *Snorra Edda* will find that Norse literature offers tempting analogues that are too numerous to list here. The thunder-god Thor, the cunning schemer Loki, Hel the region of the dead, are relevant here. Also, the three Norns who rule the destinies of man, the primeval serpent that lives at the root of the Yggdrasil, the World Tree, and will confront Thor in the final battle of the gods, and the Spring of Fate—to mention only a few points—force us to a comparison not just with the Hesiodic *Theogony* but with Greek religion in general. Here we definitely deal with the inherited similarities of common Indo-European origin, and even if the succession motif is not the same, we should not fail to note that in the final battle of the gods (*Ragnarök*) Thor kills the serpent, even if he is overcome by its venom. That the ruling gods and men will perish in a final blaze after the dread confrontation of gods and monsters is an element eschatologically so reminiscent of Judaeo-Christian doomsday beliefs that we should, at least tentatively, assume in this account the probability of extraneous influence. In the more original kernel of the myth, the older gods were the ancestors of the ruling gods who came to power after subduing the older gods and their monstrous allies in a battle in which Thor slew the serpent without dying. The new faith that the Norsemen adopted may have started to adulterate their heathen beliefs in extremely subtle ways.

Much like Homer's epics, Hesiod's *Theogony* must stand not at the beginning but at the apex of a tradition. How much this tradition, not in terms of poetic craft but in terms of content, owes to Near Eastern models will always be a moot point. One thing is clear: the underlying concepts and the execution of the poem are Hellenic. The Near Eastern material was probably already assimilated into the religion of the indigenous population of Greece before the arrival of the Zeus-worshiping Indo-Europeans. The syncretism then is old and concerns not so much the historical Greeks and the peoples of the Near East as it does the Indo-European invaders of Greece and the peoples they subdued and assimilated.

The *Theogony* is a digressive poem with a unifying theme. The poem begins with the invocation of the Muses (1–115), but the theogonic-cosmogonic process commences with the first beings—Chaos, Gaia, and Eros (Void, Earth, and Love)—and an account of the progeny of Chaos and the progeny of Gaia (116–53). With the birth of Ouranos (Sky) begins the lineage of Zeus. In this section, we are told of the birth of the mountains and of Pontos (Sea) by Gaia alone and again—by her through incestuous union with her son Ouranos—of the Titans, of whom Kronos is the last one. The next section (154–210) relates the castration of Ouranos by his son Kronos and the birth of Aphrodite. Then follows a large section divided into subsections in which we are given an account of the progeny of Nyx (Night), Nereus, Thaumas, Phorkys, Okeanos and Thetis, and so forth (211–413). This is the section that deals with the birth of such monstrous children as the brood of Nyx and of Echidna, as well as with the birth of the lovely Nereids and Okeanids. Then comes the interesting "Hymn to Hekate" (412–52). The poet is now roughly in the middle of his composition, and so he sees fit to introduce the birth of the first Olympian generation (Hestia, Demeter, Hera, Hades, Poseidon, Zeus) and the deception and overthrow of Kronos (453–506). From here on, the poem is dominated by Zeus. In lines 507–616, we are told how Zeus's first challenger, Prometheus, was born and how Zeus dealt with him and with mankind. Then follows the crushing of the other threats to his supremacy, first of the Titans (617–731) and—after the interlude on the description of the underworld (732–819)—of Typhoeus (820–68). The rest of the poem is a genealogical appendage dealing chiefly with the progeny of Zeus and other gods.

The trunk of Hesiod's genealogical tree is the succession myth of the four divine generations: Gaia—Ouranos—Kronos—Zeus. Other myths are attached to the succession myth, and what emerges is a tree with many primary and secondary branches. Hesiod must have adopted the myths selectively, but the genealogies as we have them are probably his own work. There is nothing in Hesiod's world, bad or good, that is not divine. Divine personages or powers are not only the ones man must worship, but also the ones he must appease or at least come to terms with.

Even though Hesiod leaves the genealogy of man outside the *Theogony*, once the transition from the natural to the anthropomorphic is completed, the chief gods and many of the lesser ones are made in man's image. Thus, we have anthropomorphic gods of the cult, such as Zeus, Apollon, Artemis, and gods of myth, such as the Titans. Then we also have teratomorphic creatures, such as Echidna and Chimaira, and elements of nature, such as Sky, Sea, Night, Mountains. Within these elements dwell certain groups of mostly benign divinities, such as the Nereids, the Okeanids, the Muses, the Fates, and so forth, and within them move certain personified powers, such as Death, Sleep, Strife, Victory, and so forth.

Hesiod proceeds to explain the divine genealogy in the way in which he might have explained genealogical trees and relationships in his village. A marries B and begets children who resemble at least one of the parents. Chaos and Earth never mate with each other. They separately become progenitors of all beings. Chaos begets children like herself: dark and gloomy and intangible. Earth, too, begets children like herself: visible and solid and tangible. Kinsmen are alike and so are neighbors. The Muses are all lovely. The Furies are all dreadful. The brood that dwells in the netherworld of Tartarean darkness consists of hideous creatures. Principles of causation, association, or sequence are decisive factors in the formation of Hesiod's genealogical trees. Thus

Strife (Eris) is mother of War; Night is mother of Dreams—Dreams come at night—and also mother of Day because Day follows Night.

Much of what Hesiod did was predetermined by already existing myth. It is more than probable that he invented the progeny of Night and, more important, of Chaos. It is also next to certain that the lists of the Okeanids, the Nereids, and the Muses are his. Such pluralities surely antedate him, but they most likely were groups without individual names. A study of the lists shows that the names are suggested by the activities of the group, as in the case of the Muses, or by the nature of the element in which it dwells, as in the case of the Nereids.

For most of the poem, it is the mother who matters. The male partner is much less prominent or altogether obscure. Given the fiercely patriarchal character of Hesiod's own society, this is a remarkable departure from his familiar world and an equally remarkable testimony to the tenacity of the substructure of the mythological pattern. It is after the defeat of Typhoeus, when Zeus is left as supreme master of the world, that in the sexual unions the male god, Zeus in this case, is more than an instrument of procreation. Since Zeus, the male sky-god, is ultimately descended from Mother Earth, we have here the record of an evolutionary process that takes us from the physical to the non-physical, and from feminine dominance to male dominance. This male dominance Hesiod equates with law and order. Indeed, Zeus's first children by his second wife, Themis, are the Seasons, who stand for regularity: Eunomia (Law), Dike (Justice), and Eirene (Peace).

The genealogical appendage that concludes the *Theogony* starts with line 901, in which we are told that Zeus takes Themis (Established Custom) as his wife. Zeus himself is born in the middle of the poem (457), a poem of which he is the unquestionable center, and properly begins with Chaos but ends with Law. The procreative process goes on, but Zeus proceeds to introduce Peace and Law and Justice into a world where polarities exist but are controlled and where all the dark forces and monsters of yore have been confined once and for all to the gloomy Tartaros. The theme of the poem is, of course, the birth of the gods but much more so the saga of the establishment of Zeus's supremacy.

Hesiod had a formidable task to perform. He had to explain the origin of the world and of the gods who rule it, and even though scientific thought as we know it did not exist in his day, his genealogical method and mythopoetic reasoning constitute a speculation that is rational in its own terms. All true poets are innovators, and Hesiod is no exception. Since we do not possess something like a canon of Greek religious beliefs either before or after Hesiod, it is not easy for us to tell how Hesiod varied tradition in order to articulate whatever personal beliefs he himself had. We can be quite sure that he did not change the core of traditional myths but rather the detail and the schematic arrangement.

Since his poem is concerned with the birth of the world and the birth of the myriad gods who inhabit it like major and minor officials in a complex system of government, Hesiod, unlike Homer, displays little interest in the Olympians and the capricious side of their behavior. He is more interested in the gradual evolution of the order that was finally established by Zeus and in the conflict of a world that is not static but dynamic. The myths of the past not only explain past conflict; they also account for present polarity and tension. Zeus as lord of the sky stands in antithesis to his vanquished but still living enemies, the Titans and Typhoeus, whom he banished to the gloomy Tartaros.

Zeus won the battle against the Titans with the help of thunder and lightning, which the Kyklopes gave him, and with the aid of the monstrous Hundred-Handers. He needed superior weaponry and brute force. He won because he had these, not because some abstract figure like Justice was on his side. It will be remembered that the Titans were older gods and that his duped father, Kronos, was one of them. There is an implication that Zeus triumphs over brute force with a combination of intelligence and force and that the order he establishes is based on some principles of fairness. Thus after the defeat of Typhoeus, Zeus was "urged" to be king and he made a fair division of titles and power among the gods (881–86). If Zeus is a despot, he is an enlightened one, and his rule is not based on blind force. There is in the myths of succession the gradual emergence of something that by small degrees each time departs from the supremacy of power and slowly begins to resemble civilized order.

> Chaos was born first and after it came Gaia
> the broad-breasted. . . .

Then Chaos gives birth to Nyx (Night), Nyx to Day, and Gaia to the Sky, "equal to herself . . . that it might envelop all of her." Here we have the beginnings of the physical and the divine cosmos. It should be observed that the yawning abyss, Chaos, is not the Void into which the world (universe) is born but rather a *chásma méga* (740–43), a great chasm—more like the Norse *ginnunga gap*. It seems to be below Tartaros, the darkest part of the netherworld, which in turn lies below Hades, the subterranean realm of gloom proper. The earth is born not so much to fill this chasm but to be the secure seat of the immortals (117–18); the roots, the sources, and the ends of Tartaros itself, as well as of Earth, Sky, and Sea, are vaguely placed within Tartarean darkness. We have then the idea of some sort of tree of creation whose top is the Sky, a Sky that rests on the Earth and whose highest point corresponds to the lowest point of Tartaros. If one compares line 116 with lines 736–819, one can, only by a very long stretch of the imagination, attribute to Hesiod an idea of primeval void into which the universe is born. Emptiness is presumed and implied by the very fact that before Chaos there was nothing, and it is this implied emptiness into which Chaos itself is born. Unable at this point to postulate some sort of divine *nous,* an incorporeal creative intelligence, Hesiod begins with concrete entities, which have a definite place within the world itself and the world of myth. He does not start with Chaos in order to explain the birth of the Earth but rather with two entities of unknown origin, Earth and Chaos, because the genealogical trees that he is about to construct will make better sense if he postulates two separate progenitors, one ultimately a progenitor of the physical universe (Sky, Sea, and so forth), in which man lives, and of the gods who rule it and its destiny, and the other a progenitor of darkness (Night) and of the host of negative forces that plague man.

Hesiod's idea of the birth of the world has no truly metaphysical dimension. It is a physical world born not *ex nihilo* but *ex ignoto,* "from the unknown." Here, mingled with the inability to go beyond the limits, is a great deal of fierce intellectual honesty and by implication the stubborn refusal to believe that anything, including Chaos, can be born of nothing. "In the beginning Chaos was born and then the earth" means just what it says, and it implies that we really do not know how these two were born. Hesiod in a way does not explain the creation of the primal elements but the creation of everything else through a process of procreation in which Eros (Love) is the ever-present catalyst. He does not elaborate on Eros as a cosmic force but, since most of the *Theogony* is an account of birth that follows attraction and copulation, the conclusion that Eros is a silent partner to every fruitful union is inescapable.

Although the *Theogony* is a man's account of the birth of the world and of the gods, it is a theocentric poem in which man plays an insignificant role. There is the Prometheus myth, which explains how man and his divine champion were punished, but there is no myth that accounts for the creation of man. Since woman is viewed as an evil visited upon man and since man as a male being perforce antedated the creation of the source of his woes, Hesiod implies that there was a time when human society was womanless. There is no attempt to go beyond this and to tell us how man himself came into being. It is well-nigh impossible that one of the myths explaining the origin of humankind was unknown to Hesiod. Such myths exist even in the most primitive societies. Woman, it will be remembered, was fashioned by Hephaistos from earth (571–72). Hesiod may have faced a dilemma. The evil nature of woman and her punitive origin prevented him from admitting her into his genealogical scheme as one of the two ultimate progenitors of man. Observation of the procreative process in the human race prevented him from postulating the birth of male by male. The fashioning of man by the gods from clay may also have presented him with too humble an alternative. Although it may have been inability to settle on an acceptable progenitor, it is also possible that the genealogy of man lay outside the scope of the *Theogony,* a poem whose objective clearly is cosmogonic and theogonic. That Hesiod envisaged a nobler birth for man is clear from the *Works and Days,* where he does not tell us exactly how man came into being, but he does tell us that the gods fashioned the first generation of men from gold (109ff.).

There is an evolution in the physical and divine universe of Hesiod, but there is also a polarity. Earth is Mother Earth, the mother of all. The Sky (Ouranos) and the Sea (Pontos) are born of her parthenogenetically. The Sky mates with his mother to become the founder of the line of the gods, which in the fourth generation culminates with the birth of Zeus. The elements do not need a begetter, but the divine pantheon does. Since Earth in the beginning needs no male partner to produce Sky and Sea and since the birth of Zeus, ruler of all, is the result of union of male with female divinity, we are clearly dealing with an evolutionary process that begins with a supreme matriarch and ends with a supreme patriarch. The final triumph of male supremacy is reached gradually. Both Ouranos and Kronos are plagued by conspiring wives and rebellious sons. The pattern consists of an alliance between mother and youngest son. In the first case, Gaia conspires with Kronos and achieves the castration of her husband. In the second one, Rhea, the wife of Kronos, is unable to frustrate her husband's plans without the help of Gaia, who becomes the primary conspirator again. The gradual increase of male authority is mirrored in the inability of the female spouse to find a solution by herself. The process ends when Zeus decides to swallow Metis, his first wife. Since Metis was destined to give birth to a powerful son who might do to him what he had done to his father, by swallowing Metis Zeus assimilated both conspiratorial agents and brought an end to the very process that put him in power. Once Metis and by extension her unborn son are lodged inside his belly, Zeus gives birth to the helmeted war-goddess Athena from his head. This daughter is powerful and potentially dangerous, but, father-born as she is, she owes allegiance to no mother. By carrying out a function that properly belongs to the female partner, Zeus breaks the chain of female supremacy. In the battle against the Titans, Zeus secured the alliance of the Kyklopes and the Hundred-Handers, an alliance that together with his abiding link with Glory, Victory, Power, and Strength—all children of Styx—was guaranteed to prove invincible. After the battle, the Kyklopes and the Hundred-Handers become guards at the prison that holds his enemies, but the four children of Styx stay with him as indispensable companions. The new ruler, however, does not depend on force alone. His primary source of power is the resourcefulness that he acquired by swallowing and thereby assimilating Metis.

It should be emphasized again that Zeus triumphs over his adversaries through might and intelligence. His actions are not based on some abstract or concrete principle of law. Zeus does what he has to do in order not to fall prey to the same predicament that bedeviled his male predecessors. Although he is by no means savage, he is single-minded in the pursuit and establishment of his own supremacy. It is after he is king of the gods that he sanctions established custom, Themis, by marrying her in order to beget Good Law (Eunomia) and Peace. This is Hesiod's way of saying that Zeus founded law—he laid it down, as it were; and by begetting it, he implicitly retained paternal supremacy over it. By being the father of law, Zeus may be above it but not outside it. He rules over the other gods and over men the way a benevolent king rules over his princes and subjects. In this new rule in which the powers are concentrated in the hands of an anthropomorphic god, man does not feel a stranger; all the more, since this god chose to mate with noble women in order to beget a race of heroes, which magnanimously links the wretched mortals with the blissful immortals. From the amorphousness of Chaos and the unruliness of the elements the world graduates to a three-tiered pyramid in which man has a definite place within a framework that does not make his life a meaningless accident.

THEOGONY

I begin my song with the Helikonian Muses; they live on
Helikon, the great god-haunted mountain.
On soft feet they move in the dance that rings
the violet-dark spring and the altar of mighty Zeus.
5   They bathe their lithe bodies in the water of Permessos
or of Hippokrene or of god-haunted Olmeios.
On Helikon's peak they join hands in lovely dances
and their pounding feet awaken desire.
From there they set out and, veiled in mist,
10   glide through the night and raise enchanting voices
to exalt aegis-bearing Zeus and queenly Hera,
the lady of Argos who walks in golden sandals,
also gray-eyed Athena, daughter of aegis-bearing Zeus,
and Phoibos Apollon and arrow-shooting Artemis.
15   They exalt Poseidon, holder and shaker of the earth,
stately Themis and Aphrodite of the fluttering eyelids,
and gold-wreathed Hebe and fair Dione.
Then they turn their song to Eos, Helios, and bright Selene,
to Leto, Iapetos, and cunning Kronos,
20   to Gaia, great Okeanos, and black Night,
and to the holy race of the other deathless gods.
It was they who taught Hesiod beautiful song
as he tended his sheep at the foothills of god-haunted Helikon.
Here are the words the daughters of aegis-bearing Zeus,
25   the Muses of Olympos, first spoke to me:
"Listen, you country bumpkins, you pot-bellied blockheads,
we know how to tell many lies that pass for truth,
and when we wish, we know to tell the truth itself."
So spoke Zeus's daughters, masters of word-craft,

30 and from a laurel in full bloom they plucked a branch,
and gave it to me as a staff, and then breathed into me
divine song, that I might spread the fame of past and future,
and commanded me to hymn the race of the deathless gods,
but always begin and end my song with them.

35 Yet, trees and rocks are not my theme. Let me sing on!
Ah, my heart, begin with the Muses who hymn father Zeus
and in the realm of Olympos gladden his great heart;
with sweet voices they speak of things that are
and things that were and will be, and with effortless smoothness

40 the song flows from their mouths. The halls of father Zeus
the thunderer shine with glee and ring, filled with voices
lily-soft and heavenly, and the peaks of snowy Olympos
and the dwellings of the gods resound. With their divine voices
they first sing the glory of the sublime race of the gods

45 from the beginning, the children born to Gaia and vast Ouranos
and of their offspring, the gods who give blessings.
Then they sing of Zeus, father of gods and men—
they begin and end their song with him
and tell of how he surpasses the other gods in rank and might.

50 Then again the Olympian Muses and daughters of aegis-bearing Zeus
hymn the races of men and of the brawny Giants,
and thrill the heart of Zeus in the realm of Olympos.
Mnemosyne, mistress of the Eleutherian hills,
lay with father Zeus and in Pieria gave birth to the Muses

55 who soothe men's troubles and make them forget their sorrows.
Zeus the counselor, far from the other immortals, leaped
into her sacred bed and lay with her for nine nights.
When, as the seasons turned, the moons waned,
many many days passed and a year was completed,

60 she gave birth to nine daughters of harmonious mind,
carefree maidens whose hearts yearn for song;
this was close beneath the highest peak of snowy Olympos,
the very place of their splendid dances and elegant homes.
The Graces and Desire dwell near them and take part

65 in their feasts. Lovely are their voices when they sing
and extol for the whole world the laws
and wise customs of all the immortals.
Then they went to Olympos, delighting in their beautiful voices
and their heavenly song. The black earth resounded with hymns,

HESIOD

70 and a lovely beat arose as they pounded their feet
and advanced toward their father, the king of the sky
who holds the thunderbolt that roars and flames.
He subdued his father, Kronos, by might and for the gods
made a fair settlement and gave each his domain.
75 All this was sung by the Olympian Muses,
great Zeus's nine daughters whose names are
Kleio, Euterpe, Thaleia, Melpomene,
Terpsichore, Erato, Polymnia, Ourania,
and Kalliope, preeminent by far,
80 the singers' pride in the company of noble kings.
And if the daughters of great Zeus honor a king
cherished by Zeus and look upon him when he is born,
they pour on his tongue sweet dew
and make the words that flow from his mouth honey-sweet,
85 and all the people look up to him as with straight justice
he gives his verdict and with unerring firmness
and wisdom brings some great strife to a swift end.
This is why kings are prudent, and when in the assembly
injustice is done, wrongs are righted
90 by the kings with ease and gentle persuasion.
When such a king comes to the assembly he stands out;
yes, he is revered like a god and treated with cheerful respect.
Such is the holy gift the Muses give men.
The singers and lyre players of this earth
95 are descended from the Muses and far-shooting Apollon,
but kings are from the line of Zeus. Blessed is the man
whom the Muses love; sweet song flows from his mouth.
A man may have some fresh grief over which to mourn,
and sorrow may have left him no more tears, but if a singer,
100 a servant of the Muses, sings the glories of ancient men
and hymns the blessed gods who dwell on Olympos,
the heavy-hearted man soon shakes off his dark mood, and oblivion
soothes his grief, for this gift of the gods diverts his mind.
Hail, daughters of Zeus! Grant me the gift of lovely song!
105 Sing the glories of the holy gods to whom death never comes,
the gods born of Gaia and starry Ouranos,
and of those whom dark Night bore, or briny Pontos fostered.
Speak first of how the gods and the earth came into being
and of how the rivers, the boundless sea with its raging swell,

Theogony

110   the gleaming stars, and the wide sky above were created.
Tell of the gods born of them, the givers of blessings,
how they divided wealth, and each was given his realm,
and how they first gained possession of many-folded Olympos.
Tell me, O Muses who dwell on Olympos, and observe proper order
115   for each thing as it first came into being.
Chaos was born first and after it came Gaia
the broad-breasted, the firm seat of all
the immortals who hold the peaks of snowy Olympos,
and the misty Tartaros in the depths of broad-pathed earth
120   and Eros, the fairest of the deathless gods;
he unstrings the limbs and subdues both mind
and sensible thought in the breasts of all gods and all men.
Chaos gave birth to Erebos and black Night;
then Erebos mated with Night and made her pregnant
125   and she in turn gave birth to Ether and Day.
Gaia now first gave birth to starry Ouranos,
her match in size, to encompass all of her,
and be the firm seat of all the blessed gods.
She gave birth to the tall mountains, enchanting haunts
130   of the divine nymphs who dwell in the woodlands;
and then she bore Pontos, the barren sea with its raging swell.
All these she bore without mating in sweet love. But then
she did couple with Ouranos to bear deep-eddying Okeanos,
Koios and Kreios, Hyperion and Iapetos,
135   Theia and Rheia, Themis and Mnemosyne,
as well as gold-wreathed Phoibe and lovely Tethys.
Kronos, ever so cunning, was her last-born,
a most fearful child who hated his mighty father.
Then she bore the Kyklopes, haughty in their might,
140   Brontes, Steropes, and Arges of the strong spirit,
who made and gave to Zeus the crushing thunder.
In all other respects they were like gods,
but they had one eye in the middle of their foreheads;
their name was Kyklopes because of this single
145   round eye that leered from their foreheads,
and inventive skill and strength and power were in their deeds.
Gaia and Ouranos had three other sons, so great
and mighty that their names are best left unspoken,
Kottos, Briareos, and Gyges, brazen sons all three.

                                                                  HESIOD

150 From each one's shoulders a hundred invincible arms
sprang forth, and from each one's shoulders atop the sturdy trunk
there grew no fewer than fifty heads;
and there was matchless strength in their hulking frames.
All these awesome children born of Ouranos and Gaia
155 hated their own father from the day they were born,
for as soon as each one came out of the womb,
Ouranos, with joy in his wicked work, hid it
in Gaia's womb and did not let it return to the light.
Huge Gaia groaned within herself
160 and in her distress she devised a crafty and evil scheme.
With great haste she produced gray iron
and made a huge sickle and showed it to her children;
then, her heart filled with grief, she rallied them with these words:
"Yours is a reckless father; obey me, if you will,
165 that we may all punish your father's outrageous deed,
for he was first to plot shameful actions."
So she spoke, and fear gripped them all; not one of them
uttered a sound. Then great, cunning Kronos
without delay spoke to his prudent mother:
170 "Mother, this deed I promise you will be done,
since I loathe my dread-named father.
It was he who first plotted shameful actions."
So he spoke, and the heart of giant Earth was cheered.
She made him sit in ambush and placed in his hands
175 the sharp-toothed sickle and confided in him her entire scheme.
Ouranos came dragging with him the night, longing for Gaia's love,
and he embraced her and lay stretched out upon her.
Then his son reached out from his hiding place and seized him
with his left hand, while with his right he grasped
180 the huge, long, and sharp-toothed sickle and swiftly hacked off
his father's genitals and tossed them behind him—
and they were not flung from his hand in vain.
Gaia took in all the bloody drops that spattered off,
and as the seasons of the year turned round
185 she bore the potent Furies and the Giants, immense,
dazzling in their armor, holding long spears in their hands,
and then she bore the Ash Tree Nymphs of the boundless earth.
As soon as Kronos had lopped off the genitals with the sickle
he tossed them from the land into the stormy sea.

190 And as they were carried by the sea a long time, all around them
white foam rose from the god's flesh, and in this foam a maiden
was nurtured. First she came close to god-haunted
Kythera and from there she went on to reach sea-girt Cyprus.
There this majestic and fair goddess came out, and soft grass
195 grew all around her tender feet. Both gods and men
call her Aphrodite, foam-born goddess, and fair-wreathed Kythereia;
Aphrodite because she grew out of *aphros*, foam, that is,
and Kythereia because she touched land at Kythera.
She is called Kyprogenes, because she was born
200 in sea-girt Cyprus, and Philommedes, fond of a man's genitals,
because to them she owed her birth. Fair Himeros and Eros
became her companions when she was born and when she joined the gods.
And here is the power she has had from the start
and her share in the lives of men and deathless gods:
205 from her come young girls' whispers and smiles and deception
and honey-sweet love and its joyful pleasures.
The great father Ouranos railed at his own children
and named them Titans, Overreachers,
because he said they had, with reckless power, overreached him
210 to do a monstrous thing that would be avenged someday.
Night gave birth to hideous Moros and black Ker
and then to Death and Sleep and to the brood of Dreams.
After them dark Night, having lain with no one,
gave birth to Momos and painful Oizys
215 and to the Hesperides, who live beyond renowned Okeanos
and keep the golden apples and the fruit-bearing trees.
She also bore the ruthless Keres and the Moirai,
Klotho, Lachesis, and Atropos, who when men are born
give them their share of things good and bad.
220 They watch for the transgressions of men and gods,
and the dreadful anger of these goddesses never abates
until wrongdoers are punished with harshness.
Baneful Night bore Nemesis, too, a woe for mortals,
and after her Deception and the Passion of lovers
225 and destructive Old Age and capricious Strife.
Then loathsome Strife bore Ponos, the bringer of pains,
Oblivion and Famine and the tearful Sorrows,
the Clashes and the Battles and the Manslaughters,
the Quarrels and the Lies and Argument and Counter-Argument,

230 Lawlessness and Ruin whose ways are all alike,
and Oath, who, more than any other, brings pains to mortals
who of their own accord swear false oaths.
Pontos sired truthful Nereus, his oldest son,
who tells no lies; they call him the old man
235 because he is honest and gentle and never forgetful
of right, but ever mindful of just and genial thought.
Then Pontos lay with Gaia and sired great Thaumas,
Phorkys the overbearing, and fair-cheeked Keto,
and Eurybie, who in her breast has a heart of iron.
240 To Nereus and Doris of the lovely hair,
the daughter of Okeanos, the stream surrounding the earth,
a host of godly daughters was born in the barren sea:
Proto, Eukrante, Amphitrite, and Sao,
Eudora, Thetis, Galene, and Glauke,
245 Kymothoe, Speio, Thoe, and lovely Halia,
Pasithea, Erato, and Eunike of the rosy arms,
graceful Melite, Eulimene, and Agaue,
Doto, Proto, Pherousa, and Dynamene,
Nesaia, Aktaia, and Protomedeia,
250 Doris, Panope, and beautiful Galateia,
Hippothoe the lovely and Hipponoe of the rosy arms,
Kymodoke, who, with Kymatolege and Amphitrite
the fair-ankled, easily calms the waves
in the misty sea and the gusts of stormy winds,
255 Kymo, Eione, and fair-wreathed Halimede,
laughter-loving Glaukonome and Pontoporeia,
Leiagora, Euagora, and Laomedeia,
Poulynoe, Autonoe, and Lysianassa,
Euarne of the lovely body and unblemished face,
260 Psamathe of the graceful build, and splendid Menippe,
Nesso, Eupompe, Themisto, and Pronoe,
and Nemertes, whose mind is like that of her immortal father.
These were the daughters born to blameless Nereus,
fifty of them, all wise in deeds of perfection.
265 Thaumas took as his wife Elektra, daughter of Okeanos,
whose stream is deep, and she bore swift Iris
and the lovely-haired Harpies, Aello and Okypete,
who, with fast wings, trail flying birds and windy breezes
as they soar and swoop from high up in the air.

Theogony

270 To Phorkys Keto bore the fair-cheeked Graiai,
  gray from birth, who are given this name
  both by the immortal gods and by men who tread the earth,
  well-robed Pemphredo and saffron-cloaked Enyo;
  then the Gorgons, who dwell beyond glorious Okeanos
275 at earth's end, toward night, by the clear-voiced Hesperides,
  Sthenno, Euryale, and ill-fated Medousa,
  who was mortal; the other two were ageless and immortal.
  Dark-maned Poseidon lay with one of these, Medousa,
  on a soft meadow strewn with spring flowers.
280 When Perseus cut off Medousa's head, immense Chrysaor
  and the horse Pegasos sprang forth.
  His name came from the springs of Okeanos by which he was born,
  but Chrysaor's from the golden sword he carried in his hand.
  Pegasos left the earth, mother of flocks, and flew away
285 and reached the immortals; he lives in the palace
  of Zeus the counselor, to whom he brings thunder and lightning.
  Chrysaor then lay with Kallirhoe, daughter of glorious Okeanos,
  and sired the three-headed Geryones
  whom the might of Herakles slew
290 beside his shambling oxen at sea-girt Erytheia
  on the very day he crossed the stream of Okeanos
  and drove the broad-browed cattle to holy Tiryns.
  Then he also slew Orthos and the oxherd Eurytion
  out at that misty place, beyond glorious Okeanos.
295 Then Keto bore another invincible monster,
  in no way like mortal men or the deathless gods;
  yes, in a hollow cave she bore Echidna, divine
  and iron-hearted, half fair-cheeked and bright-eyed nymph
  and half huge and monstrous snake inside the holy earth,
300 a snake that strikes swiftly and feeds on living flesh.
  Her lair is a cave under a hollow rock,
  far from immortal gods and mortal men;
  the gods decreed for her a glorious dwelling there.
  Arima, beneath the earth, is the stronghold of the grisly Echidna,
305 the nymph who is immortal and ageless for ever.
  They say that this bright-eyed maiden lay in love
  with Typhaon, that lawless and dreadful ravisher,
  and impregnated by him she bore a harsh-tempered brood.
  First she gave birth to Orthos, the dog of Geryones,

310 and then she bore a stubborn and unspeakable creature,
     Kerberos, the fifty-headed dog of Hades, that mighty
     and shameless eater of raw flesh, whose bark resounds like bronze.
     Her third child was the loathsome Hydra of Lerna,
     that was nurtured by white-armed Hera
315 whose wrath at mighty Herakles was implacable.
     But Herakles, born to Amphitryon as son of Zeus,
     together with Iolaos slew her with the merciless bronze blade,
     for Athena, leader of the war host, willed it so.
     She bore Chimaira, mighty, dreadful, huge,
320 and fleet-footed, who breathed forth a ceaseless stream of fire.
     She had three heads, one of a glowering lion,
     another of a goat, and yet another of a savage dragon;
     her front was a lion, her back a dragon, and her middle a goat,
     and she breathed forth an awesome stream of gleaming fire.
325 Pegasos and noble Bellerophon slew her.
     Orthos covered her, and she bore the destructive Sphinx,
     a scourge for the Kadmeans, and then the Lion of Nemea,
     who was reared by Hera, the glorious wife of Zeus,
     and settled on the hills of Nemea, a scourge to mankind.
330 There was his abode and from there he preyed on the tribes of men
     and lorded it over Apesas and Nemean Tretos,
     but the strength of mighty Herakles subdued him.
     Keto then lay in love with Phorkys and bore her youngest,
     a ghastly snake that guards the all-golden apples,
335 lurking in his lair in the gloom of earth's vast limits.
     This is the brood born of Phorkys and Keto.
     Tethys bore to Okeanos the whirling rivers,
     Neilos and Alpheios and deep-eddying Eridanos,
     Strymon and Maiandros and fair-flowing Istros,
340 Phasis and Rhesos and Acheloios of the silver swirls,
     Nessos, Rhodios, Heptaporos, and Haliakmon,
     Grenikos, Aisepos, and divine Simoeis,
     Peneios, Hermos, and fair-flowing Kaikos,
     great Sangarios, Ladon, and Parthenios,
345 Euenos, Ardeskos, and divine Skamandros.
     She gave birth to a throng of holy daughters, who with the Rivers
     and lord Apollon nurture men throughout the earth,
     for this is the task that Zeus has given them.
     They are Peitho, Admete, Ianthe, and Elektra,

Theogony

350 Doris, Prymno, and godlike Ourania,
Hippo, Klymene, Rhodeia, and Kallirhoe,
Zeuxo, Klytia, Idyia, and Peisithoe,
Plexaura, Galaxaura, and lovely Dione,
Melobosis, Thoe, and beautiful Polydora,
355 shapely Kerkeis and cow-eyed Plouto,
Perseis, Ianeira, Akaste, and Xanthe,
lovely Petraia, Menestho, and Europe,
Metis, Eurynome, and saffron-robed Telesto,
Chryseis, Asia, and enchanting Kalypso,
360 Eudora, Tyche, Amphiro, and Okyrhoe,
and Styx, who holds the highest rank.
These are the eldest daughters born to Tethys
and Okeanos. But there are many others.
Okeanos has three thousand slender-ankled daughters—
365 splendid children of goddesses—who roam in bevies
and haunt the earth and the depths of the waters alike.
There are as many tumbling and rushing rivers,
all sons of Okeanos and queenly Tethys.
It is hard for a mortal to recite the names of all,
370 but those who live by them know each of their names.
Theia yielded to Hyperion's love and gave birth
to great Helios and bright Selene and Eos,
who brings light to all the mortals of this earth
and to the immortal gods who rule the wide sky.
375 Eurybia, the radiant goddess, lay in love with Kreios
and gave birth to great Astraios and to Pallas
and then to Perses, who surpassed all in wisdom.
Eos shared love's bed with Astraios
and bore him the mighty-spirited winds,
380 bright Zephyros and gusty Boreas and Notos.
After them Eos the early-born brought forth the dawn star,
Eosphoros, and the glittering stars that crown the heavens;
Styx, the daughter of Okeanos, lay in love with Pallas
and in his mansion gave birth to Zelos and fair-ankled Nike,
385 and then she bore two illustrious children, Kratos and Bia.
These two have no home apart from Zeus, nor seat
nor path, except the one to which he leads them,
but their place is with Zeus of the roaring thunder.
For this was the will of Styx, the deathless daughter of Okeanos,

HESIOD

390   on the day the Olympian hurler of lightning
      called all the immortals to lofty Olympos
      and said that he would not wrest away the rights
      of those who would fight with him against the Titans
      and that each god would retain his previous honors.
395   He said that those deprived of rights and honors
      by Kronos could now lay just claim to them.
      On her own father's advice the immortal Styx
      and her children were first to come to Olympos.
      Zeus granted her honor and countless gifts
400   and decreed that the gods should swear great oaths by her
      and that her children should dwell with him for ever.
      He fulfilled with exactness the promises made to all;
      and yet, he is sovereign lord and his power is unchallenged.
      Phoibe went to the much longed-for bed of Koios,
405   and she, a goddess loved by a god, conceived
      and gave birth to dark-robed Leto, ever sweet,
      gentle to men and to gods who never die,
      sweet from the beginning, gentlest of all the Olympians.
      She also bore Asteria, whose name brings good luck;
410   Perses brought her to his great house, to be his dear wife.
      There she conceived and bore Hekate, whom Zeus
      honored above all others; he gave her dazzling gifts,
      a share of the earth and a share of the barren sea.
      She was given a place of honor in the starry sky,
415   and among the deathless gods her rank is high.
      For even now, when a mortal propitiates the gods
      and, following custom, sacrifices well-chosen victims,
      he invokes Hekate, and if she receives his prayers
      with favor, then honor goes to him with great ease,
420   and he is given blessings, because she has power
      and a share in all the rights once granted
      to the offspring born to Ouranos and Gaia.
      The son of Kronos did not use force on her and took away
      none of the rights she held under the Titans, those older gods.
425   The distribution made in the beginning is still the same.
      Nor does the goddess have less honor for being an only child;
      in fact, she has much more because Zeus honors her,
      and her domain extends over land and sky and sea,
      and she can greatly aid a man—if this is her wish.

430 In trials her seat is at the side of illustrious kings,
     and in assemblies the man she favors gains distinction.
     And when men arm themselves for man-destroying battle,
     the goddess always stands beside those she prefers
     and gladly grants them victory and glory.
435 Again, she is a noble goddess when men compete
     for athletic prizes, because she stands by them and helps,
     and whoever, by force and strength, wins a fair prize,
     carries it away with ease and joy and brings his parents glory.
     To horsemen, as well, when she wishes, she is a noble helper
440 and to those working out on the stormy and gray sea
     who pray to Hekate and to the rumbling Earthshaker.
     With ease this glorious goddess grants a great catch of fish
     and with ease, if that is her wish, she makes it vanish.
     When she wishes from the heart, she can be noble
445 and, with Hermes, help livestock breed in the stalls,
     and swell or thin out herds of cattle and wide-ranging
     flocks of goats and thick-wooled sheep.
     And even though she was her mother's only child
     she has her share of honors among all the gods.
450 The son of Kronos made her the fostering goddess for all youths
     who after her birth saw the light of wakeful Dawn.
     A nurturer of youths from the beginning, she holds these honors.
     Rheia succumbed to Kronos's love and bore him illustrious children,
     Hestia and Demeter and Hera, who walks in golden sandals,
455 imperious Hades, whose heart knows no mercy
     in his subterranean dwelling, and the rumbling Earthshaker,
     and Zeus the counselor and father of gods and men,
     Zeus under whose thunder the wide earth quivers.
     But majestic Kronos swallowed each child
460 as it moved from the holy womb toward the knees;
     his purpose was to prevent any other child of the Sky Dwellers
     from holding the kingly office among immortals.
     He had learned from Gaia and starry Ouranos
     that he, despite his power, was fated
465 to be subdued by his own son, a victim of his own schemes.
     Therefore, he kept no blind watch, but ever wary
     he gulped down his own children to Rhea's endless grief.
     Yet as she was about to bear Zeus, father of gods
     and men, she begged her own parents,

470 Gaia, that is, and starry Ouranos,
to contrive such a plan that the birth of her dear child
would go unnoticed and her father's Erinys would take revenge
for the children swallowed by majestic, cunning Kronos.
They listened to their dear daughter and granted her wish
475 and let her know what fate had in store
for King Kronos and his bold-spirited son.
So they sent her to Lyktos, in the rich land of Crete,
just as she was about to bear the last of her children,
great Zeus, whom huge Gaia would take into her care
480 on broad Crete, to nourish and foster with tender love.
She carried him swiftly in the darkness of night, and Lyktos was
the first place she reached; she took him in her arms
and hid him inside the god-haunted earth in a cave
lodged deep within a sheer cliff of densely wooded Mount Aigaion.
485 But to the great lord Kronos, king of the older gods,
she handed a huge stone wrapped in swaddling clothes.
He took it in his hands and stuffed it into his belly—
the great fool! It never crossed his mind that the stone
was given in place of his son thus saved to become
490 carefree and invincible, destined to crush him by might of hand,
drive him out of his rule, and become king of the immortals.
The lord's strength and splendid limbs grew swiftly
and, as the year followed its revolving course,
cunning Kronos was deceived by Gaia's
495 crafty suggestions to disgorge his own offspring—
overpowered also by the craft and brawn of his own son.
The stone last swallowed was first to come out,
and Zeus set it up on the broad-pathed earth,
at sacred Pytho, under the rocky folds of Parnassos,
500 forever to be a marvel and a portent for mortal men.
He freed from their wretched bonds his father's brothers,
Brontes and Steropes and Arges of the bold spirit,
whom Ouranos, their father, had thrown into chains;
they did not forget the favors he had done them,
and they gave him the thunder and the smoky thunderbolt
505 and lightning, all of which had lain hidden in the earth.
Trusting in these, he ruled over mortals and immortals.
Iapetos took as his wife the fair-ankled Klymene,
daughter of Okeanos; he shared her bed
and she bore him Atlas, a son of invincible spirit,

Theogony

510　also Menoitios of the towering pride, and Prometheus,
　　　whose mind was labyrinthine and swift, and foolish Epimetheus,
　　　who from the start brought harm to men who toil for bread;
　　　he was first to accept the virgin woman fashioned by far-seeing Zeus,
　　　who with flaming thunderbolt struck Menoitios
515　and cast him into murky Erebos
　　　for his folly and reckless flaunting of manliness.
　　　By harsh necessity, Atlas supports the broad sky
　　　on his head and unwearying arms,
　　　at the earth's limits, near the clear-voiced Hesperides,
520　for this is the doom decreed for him by Zeus the counselor.
　　　With shackles and inescapable fetters Zeus riveted Prometheus
　　　on a pillar—Prometheus of the labyrinthine mind;
　　　and he sent a long-winged eagle to swoop down on him
　　　and devour his immortal liver; but what the long-winged bird ate
525　in the course of each day grew back and was restored to its full size
　　　during the night. Herakles, the mighty son of fair-ankled Alkmene,
　　　killed the eagle, drove the evil scourge away
　　　from the son of Iapetos, and freed him from his sorry plight,
　　　and did all this obeying the will of Olympian Zeus,
530　who rules on high, to make the glory of Herakles, child of Thebes,
　　　greater than before over the earth that nurtures many.
　　　Zeus so respected these things and honored his illustrious son
　　　that he quelled the wrath he had nursed against Prometheus,
　　　who had opposed the counsels of Kronos's mighty son.
535　When the gods and mortal men were settling their accounts
　　　at Mekone, Prometheus cheerfully took a great ox,
　　　carved it up, and set it before Zeus to trick his mind.
　　　He placed meat, entrails, and fat within a hide
　　　and covered them with the ox's tripe,
540　but with guile he arranged the white bones of the ox,
　　　wrapped them with glistening fat, and laid them down as an offer.
　　　Then indeed the father of gods and men said to him:
　　　"Son of Iapetos, you outshine all other kings,
　　　but, friend, you have divided with self-serving zeal."
545　These were the sarcastic words of Zeus, whose counsels never perish,
　　　but Prometheus was a skillful crook and he smiled faintly,
　　　all the while mindful of his cunning scheme,
　　　and said: "Sublime Zeus, highest among the everlasting gods,
　　　choose of the two portions whichever your heart desires."

550 He spoke with guileful intent, and Zeus, whose counsels never perish,
knew the guile and took note of it; so he pondered evils in his mind
for mortal men, evils he meant to bring on them.
With both hands he took up the white fat,
and spiteful anger rushed through his mind and heart
555 when he saw the white bones of the ox laid out in deceit.
From that time on the tribes of mortal men on earth
have burned the white bones for the gods on smoky altars.
Then Zeus the cloud-gatherer angrily said:
"Son of Iapetos, no one matches your resourceful wits,
560 but, friend, your mind is clinging stubbornly to guile."
So Zeus, whose counsels never perish, spoke in anger
and thereafter never forgot that he had been beguiled
and never gave to ash trees the power of unwearying fire
for the good of men who live on this earth,
565 but the noble son of Iapetos deceived him again
and within a hollowed fennel stalk stole the far-flashing
unwearying fire. This stung the depths of Zeus's mind,
Zeus who roars on high, and filled his heart with anger,
when he saw among mortal men the far-seen flash of fire;
570 so straightway because of the stolen fire he contrived evil for men.
The famous lame smith took clay and, through Zeus's counsels,
gave it the shape of a modest maiden.
Athena, the gray-eyed goddess, clothed her and decked her out
with a flashy garment and then with her hands
575 she hung over her head a fine draping veil, a marvel to behold;
Pallas Athena crowned her head with lovely wreaths
of fresh flowers that had just bloomed in the green meadows.
The famous lame smith placed on her head a crown of gold
fashioned by the skill of his own hands
580 to please the heart of Zeus the father.
It was a wondrous thing with many intricate designs
of all the dreaded beasts nurtured by land and sea.
Such grace he breathed into the many marvels therein
that they seemed endowed with life and voice.
585 Once he had finished—not something good but a mixture
of good and bad—he took the maiden before gods and men,
and she delighted in the finery given her by gray-eyed Athena,
daughter of a mighty father. Immortal gods and mortal men
were amazed when they saw this tempting snare

Theogony

590   from which men cannot escape. From her comes the fair sex;
      yes, wicked womenfolk are her descendants.
      They live among mortal men as a nagging burden
      and are no good sharers of abject want, but only of wealth.
      Men are like swarms of bees clinging to cave roofs
595   to feed drones that contribute only to malicious deeds;
      the bees themselves all day long until sundown
      are busy carrying and storing the white wax,
      but the drones stay inside in their roofed hives
      and cram their bellies full of what others harvest.
600   So, too, Zeus who roars on high made women
      to be an evil for mortal men, helpmates in deeds of harshness.
      He bestowed another gift, evil in place of good:
      whoever does not wish to marry, fleeing the malice of women,
      reaches harsh old age with no one to care for him;
605   then even if he is well-provided,
      he dies at the end only to have his livelihood shared
      by distant kin. And even the man who does marry
      and has a wife of sound and prudent mind
      spends his life ever trying to balance the bad
610   and the good in her. But he who marries into a foul brood
      lives plagued by unabating trouble in his heart
      and in his mind, and there is no cure for his plight.
      So there is no way to deceive or hide from the mind of Zeus,
      for not even noble Prometheus, son of Iapetos,
615   escaped the heavy wrath of Zeus, indeed, despite his many skills,
      succumbed to force and was bound in mighty chains.
      First father Ouranos nursed anger in his heart
      against Briareos, Kottos, and Gyges, and bound them in chains
      and then settled them under the earth of the wide paths,
620   awed at their size, their shape, and their towering vigor.
      There they stayed and suffered great pains,
      sitting at the utmost limits of the boundless earth,
      their hearts stung by endless grief and mourning.
      But the son of Kronos and the other immortal gods
625   born of the love of Kronos and lovely-haired Rheia
      brought them into the light again, following Gaia's instructions,
      for she kept on reminding them that in alliance
      with those three they would win victory and dazzling glory.
      The divine Titans and the gods Kronos sired

630　struggled for a long time against one another
　　　and did fierce battle, heartsore with strife,
　　　the noble Titans from the peak of lofty Othrys,
　　　and the gods born of Kronos and lovely-haired Rheia
　　　—the very gods who give blessings—from Olympos.
635　With heavy hearts, they did battle against one another
　　　and fought incessantly for ten full years;
　　　their strife was harsh and there was no end and no resolution
　　　for either side, and the outcome was indecisive.
　　　But when Zeus gave the three gods what strengthens the body,
640　the very nectar and ambrosia of the gods,
　　　and they drank nectar and ate exquisite ambrosia,
　　　then the spirit rose bold in the hearts of all,
　　　and Zeus, the father of gods and men, spoke and said:
　　　"Listen to me, noble sons of Ouranos and Gaia,
645　for I wish to speak out what spirit and heart command.
　　　So far the divine Titans and the gods Kronos sired
　　　have fought against one another every day
　　　and far too long for victory and power.
　　　Now in this bitter battle give the Titans proof
650　of the unyielding strength in your invincible arms.
　　　Remember our noble friendship and the pains you suffered
　　　until, through plans we conceived, you came up to the light again
　　　out of cruel chains and murky darkness."
　　　So he spoke, and blameless Kottos gave this answer:
655　"Lord Zeus, you speak of things that are not unknown,
　　　for we know full well that your mind is sharp
　　　and that you defended the gods against dread disaster.
　　　O lord and son of Kronos, it is through plans
　　　conceived by you that we, sore from unexpected pains,
660　came back up again out of cruel chains and murky darkness.
　　　For this, with unbending mind and shrewd resolve,
　　　we shall battle the Titans with might and main,
　　　to defend your power in the savage clash."
　　　So he spoke, and the gods, givers of blessings,
665　heard and acclaimed his words. Then more than ever before
　　　they yearned for war and they fought a fierce battle
　　　on that day, all of them, both male and female:
　　　the divine Titans and the gods Kronos sired,
　　　and those whom Zeus from Erebos brought up into the light,

　　　　　　　　　　　　　　　　　　　　Theogony

670 the dread and mighty ones, whose strength was matchless.
From each one's shoulders a hundred arms sprang forth
and from each one's shoulders and sturdy trunk
there grew no fewer than fifty heads.
They pitted themselves against the Titans in relentless battle,
675 with huge boulders in their stout hands.
The Titans, for their part, strengthened their ranks
and both sides eagerly gave proof of mettle and might of hand.
The deep and boundless sea resounded all around,
the earth boomed and the wide sky above shook
680 and groaned while lofty Olympos heaved from its foundation
in the whirl of missiles flung by the immortals. A heavy din
and the ear-splitting sound of feet in merciless pursuit
and of hefty missiles reached gloomy Tartaros.
They hurled whining missiles at one another
685 and the rousing shouts when both sides clashed
with deafening clamor reached the starry heavens.
Zeus could no longer hold back his fighting spirit,
which straightway surged to fill his heart
and showed all his strength, as from the sky and from Olympos
690 he advanced with steady pace amid flashes of lightning
and from his stout hand let fly thunderbolts
that crashed and spewed forth a stream of sacred flames.
The life-giving earth burned and resounded all over
and the vast forest groaned, consumed by fire.
695 The whole earth and the streams of Okeanos seethed,
and so did the barren sea; then the heated vapor engulfed
the earth-born Titans and towering flames licked the bright sky.
For all the might of the Titans, the blazing flash
of thunderbolt and lightning blinded their eyes.
700 Wondrous conflagration spread through Chaos, and to eyes and ears
it seemed as though what they saw and heard
was the collision of the Earth and the wide Sky above.
For so vast a crash could only arise
if earth collapsed under collapsing sky;
705 such was the uproar of the battling gods.
The winds churned quaking land, dust, and thunder,
lightning, too, and glowing thunderbolts, great Zeus's weapons,
and they swept the noise and clamor into the midst
of the warring hosts. Unbearable din hovered above

710 the horrid fray. Both sides gave proof of strength,
and then the scales of conflict tipped, as each side charged
against the other and fought a grisly and stubborn battle.
But now Kottos and Briareos and war-hungry Gyges
in the front lines stirred up bitter battle
715 as from their stout hands they hurled three hundred boulders
in thick-falling volleys that threw a mantle of darkness
over the Titans. The Titans' spirit was bold indeed
and yet they were vanquished and hurled beneath the earth
of the wide paths and bound with racking chains,
720 as deep down below the earth as the sky is high above it;
so deep down into the gloomy Tartaros they were cast.
A bronze anvil falling from the sky would travel
nine days and nine nights to reach the earth on the tenth day
and a bronze anvil falling from the earth would need
725 nine days and nine nights to reach Tartaros on the tenth day.
Tartaros is fenced with bronze and round its gullet
drifts night in triple array, while above it grow
the roots of the earth and of the barren sea.
There, by the decree of Zeus the cloud-gatherer,
730 the divine Titans have been hidden in the misty gloom
in a dank realm at the utmost limits of giant earth.
There is no escape for them; Poseidon built gates of bronze,
and a wall runs all around on every side.
There dwell Gyges, Briareos, and high-mettled Kottos,
735 ever the trusted guards of aegis-bearing Zeus.
There, in proper order, lie the sources and the limits
of the black earth and of mist-wrapped Tartaros,
of the barren sea, too, and of the starry sky—
grim and dank and loathed even by the gods—
740 this chasm is so great that, once past the gates,
one does not reach the bottom in a full year's course,
but is tossed about by stormy gales;
even the gods shudder at this eerie place.
There also stands the gloomy house of Night;
745 ghastly clouds shroud it in darkness.
Before it Atlas stands erect and on his head
and unwearying arms firmly supports the broad sky,
where Night and Day cross a bronze threshold
and then come close and greet each other.

Theogony

750 When one of the two descends the other shrinks away,
　　and the house is never host to both of them,
　　but always one of the two is out and away from it
　　and roams over the earth, while the other inside it
　　awaits the appointed time for its own journey.
755 One brings to mortals the light that sees all,
　　while the other, harmful Night, veiled in dusky fog,
　　carries in her arms Sleep, Death's own brother.
　　There, too, dwell the children of black Night,
　　Sleep and Death, the awesome gods who are never seen
760 by the rays of the blazing sun when it rises
　　on the sky, or moves on its downward path.
　　Of these, one wanders over land and broad-backed sea,
　　ever at peace and ever gentle to mortals,
　　but the other, hated by the immortal gods,
765 has a heart of iron and feelings hard as bronze,
　　and no man gripped by him can free himself again.
　　There, too, stand the echoing halls of Hades,
　　whose sway is great, and of awesome Persephone.
　　A hideous and ruthless hound guards the place
770 skilled in an evil trick: wagging his tail
　　and wriggling his ears he fawns on those who enter,
　　but he does not let them out again;
　　instead, he lies in wait and devours those he catches
　　outside the gates of sovereign Hades and of awesome Persephone.
775 There dwells a goddess loathed by the immortals,
　　dreadful Styx, eldest daughter of Okeanos, whose stream
　　flows back on itself; she dwells apart from the gods
　　in a stately palace roofed by lofty rocks and ringed
　　by silver pillars that tower into the sky.
780 Seldom does fleet-footed Iris, the daughter of Thaumas,
　　roam on the broad-backed sea to bring her a message
　　when strife and quarrel arise among the immortals
　　and when a dweller of Olympos is guilty of lying.
　　Then Zeus sends Iris far away to fetch in a golden jar
785 the legendary cold water by which the gods swear great oaths,
　　water that tumbles down from a steep and soaring rock.
　　This water flows through the black night
　　from a sacred river, far below the earth of the wide paths.
　　It is a branch of Okeanos allotted one-tenth of the water;

790 the other nine parts wind round the earth and the broad-backed sea
and, silver-swirled, cascade into the briny deep,
but this one branch—an affliction for the gods—runs off a cliff.
If one of the gods who hold the peaks of snowy Olympos
pours a libation of this water and then swears a false oath,
795 he lies breathless for no less than a full year's course;
he cannot come close to ambrosia and nectar
for nourishment but, no longer able to speak or breathe,
lies in bed, wrapped in the shroud of evil coma.
When the illness is over at the long year's end,
800 another, even harsher, trial is in store for him.
For nine years he is an outcast to the eternal gods
and does not mingle with them at council or feast
for nine full years, but on the tenth he joins again
the meetings of the gods who call Olympos their home.
805 Such is the oath the gods made of the primeval and immortal
water of Styx that gushes through a rugged place.
There, in proper order, lie the sources and the limits
of black earth and of mist-wrapped Tartaros,
of the barren sea and of the starry sky,
810 and they are grim and dank and loathed even by the gods.
There stand the gates of marble and the threshold of bronze,
unshakable and self-grown from the roots that reach
deep into the ground. In front of these gates, away from all the gods
dwell the Titans, on the other side of murky Chaos.
815 But the renowned allies of Zeus, whose thunder echoes
through the sky, have their houses at the foundations of Okeanos.
These are Kottos and Gyges, and noble Briareos;
to him the deep-rumbling Shaker of the Earth gave Kymopoleia,
his own daughter, and thus made Briareos his son-in-law.
820 When Zeus drove the Titans out of the sky
giant Gaia bore her youngest child, Typhoeus;
goaded by Aphrodite, she lay in love with Tartaros.
The arms of Typhoeus were made for deeds of might,
his legs never wearied, and from his shoulders there leapt up
825 a hundred snake heads, such as fierce dragons have,
and from them licking black tongues darted forth.
The eyes on all the monstrous heads flashed
from under their brows and cast glances of burning fire;
from all the ghastly heads voices were heard,

Theogony

830 weird voices of all kinds. Sometimes they uttered words
     that the gods understood, and then again
     they bellowed like bulls, proud and fierce
     beyond restraint, or they roared like brazen-hearted lions
     or—wondrous to hear—their voices sounded like a whelp's bark,
835 or a strident hiss that echoed through the lofty mountains.
     An irreversible deed would have been done that day,
     and Typhoeus would have become lord over gods and men,
     had not the father of gods and men kept sharp-eyed watch.
     He hurled a mighty bolt and its ear-splitting crash
840 reverberated grimly through the earth and the wide sky above,
     through the sea, the streams of Okeanos, and through the underworld.
     When the lord moved, massive Olympos shook,
     the earth groaned under his indestructible feet,
     and the heat of the duel engulfed the violet-dark sea,
845 heat from Zeus's lightning and thunder, from hurricanes
     and from the fire that raged as thunderbolts struck the monster.
     The whole earth, the sea, and the sky seethed;
     a dread quake arose in the wake of the immortals' charge
     and heaving waves rolled up against the shores.
850 Then Hades, lord of the wasted shades below,
     and the Titans deep down in Tartaros and around Kronos
     shuddered at the unending din and frightful clash.
     As Zeus's strength surged, he grasped his weapons,
     thunder and lightning and glowing thunderbolt,
855 and, lunging from Olympos, he set fire
     to all of the hellish monster's gruesome heads.
     When Zeus's blows had whipped Typhoeus to submission,
     he collapsed, crippled, on the groaning giant earth;
     the flame from the thunder-smitten lord
860 leaped along the dark and rocky woodlands
     of the mountains, and the infernal blast of the flames
     set much of the giant earth on fire until it melted
     like tin that has been heated by craftsmen
     over a well-pierced crucible, or like mighty iron,
865 which in mountain woodlands the scorching fire tames
     and the craft of Hephaistos melts inside the divine earth.
     So melted the earth from the flash of the burning fire,
     Zeus in terrible anger cast Typhoeus into broad Tartaros.
     From Typhoeus come the violent and damp winds,

HESIOD

870   not Notos, Boreas, and bright Zephyros,
      who are descended from the gods, a great boon to mortals,
      but other fitful blasts blow over the sea to bring harm.
      They swoop down on the face of the misty sea,
      a raging and wicked gale, a great scourge to mortals;
875   they blow in all directions, they scatter ships
      and wipe out the sailors, and men who run into such winds
      in the open sea have no way to fend off havoc.
      They fill the flowering and boundless earth
      with harmful and whirling clouds of dust
880   and sweep away the lovely works of earth-born men.
      When the gods achieved their toilsome feat
      and by brute force stripped the Titans of their claim to honor,
      then, through Gaia's advice, they stubbornly urged
      Olympian Zeus, whose thunder is heard far and wide, to rule
885   over the gods, and he divided titles and power justly.
      Zeus, king of the gods, took as his first wife Metis,
      a mate wiser than all gods and mortal men.
      When she was about to bear gray-eyed Athena,
      through the schemes of Gaia and starry Ouranos,
890   he deceived the mind of Metis with guile
      and coaxing words, and lodged her in his belly.
      Such was their advice, so that of the immortals
      none other than Zeus would hold kingly sway.
      It was fated that Metis would bear keen-minded children,
895   first a gray-eyed daughter, Tritogeneia,
      who in strength and wisdom would be her father's match,
      and then a male child, high-mettled
      and destined to rule over gods and men.
      Zeus lodged her in his belly before she did all this,
900   that she might advise him in matters good and bad.
      His second wife was radiant Themis; she bore the Seasons,
      Lawfulness and Justice and blooming Peace,
      who watch over the works of mortal men,
      and also the Fates, to whom wise Zeus allotted high honors.
905   These are Klotho, Lachesis, and Atropos,
      and they give mortals their share of good and evil.
      Then Eurynome, fair daughter of Okeanos,
      bore to Zeus the three Graces, all fair-cheeked,
      Aglaia, Euphrosyne, and shapely Thalia;

Theogony

910   their alluring eyes glance from under their brows,
         and from their eyelids drips desire that unstrings the limbs.
         After Zeus slept with Demeter who nurtures many,
         she bore white-armed Persephone, whom Aidoneus
         snatched away from her mother with the consent of wise Zeus.
915   Then he fell in love with Mnemosyne the lovely-haired,
         who gave birth to the gold-filleted Muses,
         lovers, all nine, of feasts and of enchanting song.
         Leto lay in love with aegis-bearing Zeus
         and gave birth to Apollon and arrow-shooting Artemis,
920   children comelier than all the other sky-dwellers.
         Last of all, Zeus made Hera his buxom bride,
         and she lay in love with the king of gods and men
         and bore Hebe and Ares and Eileithyia.
         Then from his head he himself bore gray-eyed Athena,
925   weariless leader of armies, dreaded and mighty goddess,
         who stirs men to battle and is thrilled by the clash of arms.
         Hera wrangled with her husband and because of anger,
         untouched by him, she bore glorious Hephaistos
         who surpasses all the other gods in craftsmanship.
930   From the union of rumbling Poseidon and Amphitrite
         came the great Triton, whose might is far-flung,
         an awesome god dwelling in a golden house that lies
         at the sea's bottom, near his cherished mother and lordly father.
         Now to shield-shattering Ares Kythereia bore the dreaded twins
935   Fear and Panic who with Ares, sacker of cities,
         force men to flee in disorder from the thick array of battle.
         Harmonia, too, the wife of bold Kadmos, was her daughter.
         Maia, daughter of Atlas, shared the sacred bed of Zeus
         and gave birth to Hermes, renowned herald of the gods.
940   Semele, daughter of Kadmos, yielded to Zeus's lust,
         and she, a mere mortal, is now the divine mother
         of the dazzling and deathless god in whom many exult.
         Alkmene gave birth to invincible Herakles
         after she had lain in love with Zeus the cloud gatherer.
945   Hephaistos, the lame smith of wide renown,
         took as his buxom bride Aglaia, the youngest of the Graces.
         Golden-haired Dionysos took blond Ariadne,
         daughter of Minos, to be his buxom bride,
         and then Zeus made her ageless and immortal.

950   Herakles, mighty son of fair-ankled Alkmene,
      accomplished his grim labors and took Hebe,
      daughter of great Zeus and gold-sandaled Hera,
      to be his noble spouse on snowy Olympos.
      Blessed is he! His exploits all finished,
955   he is now among the gods, griefless and ageless forever.
      Perseis, famous daughter of Okeanos, bore to Helios,
      who never wearies, both Kirke and King Aietes.
      Then Aietes, son of Helios who shines his light on mortals
      through divine decree, married Idyia of the blooming cheeks,
960   daughter of Okeanos, the river whose stream rings the earth;
      under the spell of golden Aphrodite, she yielded
      to her husband's desire and bore fair-ankled Medeia.
      Hail, O gods dwelling on Olympos,
      and hail islands and continents parted by the briny sea!
965   Now Olympian Muses, sweet-voiced daughters of Zeus
      the aegis-bearer, make the theme of your song
      the immortal goddesses who shared the beds of mortals
      and bore them children with divine looks.
      Radiant Demeter, a goddess, and Iasion, a hero,
970   coupled with passion on a field plowed three times,
      in the rich soil of Crete; their child, noble Ploutos,
      wanders everywhere on land and broad-backed sea
      and grants the bliss that comes from great wealth
      when he comes into the hands of those he meets.
975   Harmonia, daughter of golden Aphrodite,
      bore to Kadmos Ino and Semele and fair-cheeked Agaue;
      Autonoe, too, who became the bride of lush-haired Aristaios,
      and then, Polydoros—all in turret-crowned Thebes.
      Kallirhoe, daughter of Okeanos, spell-bound by golden Aphrodite,
980   coupled in love with stout-hearted Chrysaor
      and bore a son surpassing all men in strength,
      Geryones, whom brawny Herakles slew
      in sea-stroked Erytheia, to win the ambling oxen.
      To Tithonos Eos bore bronze-geared Memnon,
985   king of the Ethiopians, and also lord Emathion.
      The blossom of her love for Kephalos was a splendid son,
      high-honored Phaethon, a man of godlike beauty;
      when he was still in the tender blossom of luxuriant youth,
      a child lost in innocent thought, smile-loving Aphrodite

990 swooped down on him and carried him away to her temple
   to be keeper of its holiest part, a luminous demigod.
   Then Jason, through the decrees of the undying gods,
   took as his bride the daughter of Aietes, the Zeus-cherished king,
   after he had accomplished many grim labors on orders from Pelias,
995 the great and brazen king, whose deeds were shameless folly.
   These done, Jason suffered no few hardships
   and then on a swift ship sailed to Iolkos, whence he brought
   a bright-eyed maiden who became his buxom wife.
1000 Jason, shepherd of the people, made her submit
   to his passion, and she bore Medeios, a son fostered on the mountains
   by Philyra's son, Cheiron, and great Zeus's design was fulfilled.
   Then come the daughters of Nereus, old man of the sea:
   the exalted goddess Psamathe, incited by golden Aphrodite,
1005 lay with Aiakos in love and gave birth to Phokos;
   then Thetis, the silver-sandaled goddess, became the wife
   of Peleus and bore lion-hearted Achilleus, breaker of men.
   Fair-wreathed Kythereia gave birth to Aineias,
   after she and the hero Anchises tenderly coupled
1010 on the wind-swept peaks of many-folded Ida.
   Kirke, daughter of Helios Hyperionides,
   took as her lover Odysseus, whose resolve never flagged,
   and bore him Agrios and the blameless and stout Latinos,
   and also Telegonos, under the spell of golden Aphrodite.
1015 The first two ruled over all the glorious Tyrsenians,
   very far away in the inner enclave of the sacred islands.
   Kalypso, the radiant goddess, came to know the charm
   of Odysseus's love, and bore him Nausithoos and Nausinoos.
   These are the immortal goddesses who shared the beds
1020 of mortal men and gave them godlike children.
   But now, O sweet-singing Olympian Muses,
   daughters of aegis-bearing Zeus, sing of mortal women.

Notes

1–115. These lines constitute the proem, a shorter poem that introduces the longer poem, or poem proper, as it were. Although in many ways it resembles the longer Homeric Hymns, its authenticity, much as the authenticity of the proem of the *Works and Days*, was questioned even in antiquity. Yet, Hesiod deploys his introductory piece with singular deftness. He is about to embark on a very difficult and ambitious poetic effort. Therefore, it makes excellent sense to start with a song to the Muses, the givers of song. He tells us who they are, how they were born, and what they do. The poem is not just an invocation or a prayer to the Muses. This Hesiod could have done more briefly. He uses the introduction of the Muses and their concerns to introduce himself and his concerns. By this, I mean that the epiphany of the Muses that Hesiod describes in lines 22–34 is what he is most eager to recount, for with it he links himself directly with the Muses. In my opinion, it is this epiphany that forms the kernel of the introduction.

1–4. In line 34, Hesiod tells us why he begins with the Muses. The epithet *Helikonian* does not distinguish the Muses of Helikon (cf. line 114) from the Muses of any other mountain. The Muses are the same everywhere, even if their shrines and manner of worship differ. Then it is natural for the poet to address the Muses with an epithet that has local connections and reminds him and the world of his initiation into the divine art of poetry and song. The ring dance has deep roots in Greek antiquity and is still a common type of dance in Greece today.

5–8. Permessos and Olmeios have been identified with the streams of Zagará and Kefalári, respectively. Helikon is the largest Boeotian mountain, and it lies between Kopais and the Korinthian Gulf. The sanctuary of the Muses lay on the summit behind Thespiai. The Horse's Spring, Hippokrene, so called for having been created by a kick of the mythical horse Pegasos, is most likely the modern Kriopigádi, a cold spring near the summit of Helikon.

9–21. Hesiod tells us that the Muses set out from the peak of Helikon, and scholars are puzzled because he does not tell us where they go. To him, the important point is not where they go but whence they start. It is tantamount to saying something like "you may see them in many other mountains, but they do set out from Helikon." They start their song with Zeus, who is their father, and with other Olympians, and progress to Titans and older gods and then to primeval forces: Dawn (Eos), Sun (Helios), Moon (Selene), Earth (Gaia), Ocean (Okeanos), and Night. The list is neither complete nor truly progressive; it is retrogressive and partly, at least, haphazard. Thus in the case of the Olympians, it culminates with Hebe, a very minor deity, and Aphrodite's not terribly well-known mother, Dione, who for Hesiod is only a beautiful nymph (353).

22–34. What Hesiod describes in these lines has the appearance of a vision, an awe-inspiring encounter with some concrete manifestation of the divine. Eminent scholars have identified the generic elements that it shares with many other encounters of lawgivers, prophets, and poets with the divine, encounters that gave them special powers and at the same time changed their lives. Hesiod was no doubt aware of similar precedents in his own tradition. Such awareness, however, does not rob his experience of credibility. It goes rather far to suggest that he is treating us to another variant of a literary convention. To me, he seems to be describing a very vivid religious experience, which changed the course of his life by transforming him from shepherd to singer. Testimonies to such experiences abound even in our day, where people still include them in their scheme of what is possible, and one cannot prove or disprove them since to those who believe in them, they are a priori real, whereas to nonbelievers they are—again a priori—aberrant figments of the imagination. To Hesiod, Helikon is god-haunted, as god-haunted as any temple for a person who believes in the deity worshiped in it. Up to the time of the encounter with the Muses, Hesiod was as ignorant as all the other country bumpkins (cf. modern Greek *vlachos*, "shepherd, ignorant and uncouth fellow") around him. His main concern was the concern of every poor peasant, hunger, but from then on he would become the chosen of the Muses. They told him that to some men they lie but to others they tell the truth. The implication is that they will tell him the truth and that he, in turn, unlike those poets who propagated falsehood, will also tell the truth. In my opinion, the somewhat cryptic meaning of lines 27–28 is: "Of course, we can lie to you. We are goddesses; we can do what we wish. But to you we will tell the truth." The granting of the laurel staff is tantamount to an act of ordination. From now on, Hesiod will be their mantic spokesman, carrying a staff plucked from a tree associated with the oracle of Apollon (*Homeric Hymn to Apollon* 3.396). Although Hesiod breaks into prophecy in *Works and Days* 176–201, the claim of line 32, "that I might spread the fame of past and future," is justified only partially. He is mainly a poet of the past. But this, too, is vision, retrogressive vision. The laurel staff is the symbol of the new power, the power of divine song that the Muses breathed into him (31–32). Lau-

rel is a mantic plant; wreaths of laurel were used to crown winners in athletic contests. In *Works and Days,* the laurel wood is used to construct a part of the plow. In a technical or narrow sense, Hesiod does honor the behest of line 34; he begins his song with the Muses but does not end it with them (cf. *Homeric Hymn* 21). This form of honoring a deity may once have been observed, since its basis lay in cultic practice. Thus according to *Homeric Hymn* 29, to Hestia went "the first and last libation of honey-sweet wine" (5–6). By Hesiod's day, the verbal counterpart may have become partly conventional, and the behest may mean no more than "always remember us," "keep us foremost in your mind" (cf. the concluding line of most Homeric Hymns: *Homeric Hymn* 21; lines 1–4 in *Theognis;* and *Theogony* 48).

35. The meaning of this line is very puzzling. Hesiod, after all, has not been talking about "oak and rock" (literal meaning of the original) but about the profoundest experience of his life. In genealogical contexts, not to be of the proverbial "oak and rock" probably means that the person in question, like all other persons, has a genealogy that goes back to people and not to inanimate objects or that he has a decent genealogy, that is, not a savage one, since oaks and rocks are to be associated with the backward and wooded hinterland. Since the mention of his own name and the attribution of his poetic gift to a direct encounter with the Muses are both bold steps that might be looked upon by others as hardly modest, the phrase may be speciously self-effacing and may mean "enough talk of rustic tales and on to more important matters!"

36–52. These lines seem to form a sort of concentric circle, a proem within a proem. This part of the proem describes the theme of the song of the Muses. Beginning and ending as it does with Zeus—the delight felt by him—it somehow justifies the presence of line 48, which on other grounds, including metrical, is most likely spurious. The order within the theme of the song is: (a) the children of Gaia and Ouranos, (b) Zeus, (c) men and giants. Thus, Zeus is sung second and not first. One way to save line

HESIOD

48 might be to suggest that the poet takes the first subtheme (a) merely as the genealogical order of Zeus and, therefore, as part of the praise that belongs to him. This is not very logical, but again much else in the *Theogony* is not strictly logical. The juxtaposition of men and giants also creates difficulties. The reason may be that, although by strength and size they are closer to the gods, their mortality links them with men.

53–55. Mnemosyne is "memory," and Hesiod must be conscious of the semantic implication. It is quite possible that the goddess of *Iliad* 1 and the Muse of *Odyssey* 1 is none other than Mnemosyne herself. In the *Homeric Hymn to Hermes* 4.429–33, when Hermes sings to his lyre, he first pays tribute to Mnemosyne. The Eleutherian hills belong to Kithairon. Pieria lies to the north of Olympos and must have been the principal site of the cult to the Muses.

56–63. The idea that the number of nights a woman sleeps with a man or the number of men with whom she has intercourse influences the number of children she bears occurs outside the Greek mythological tradition as well. The number of nights here may have been influenced by the number of months of pregnancy, the word *eniautós*, "year," of line 59 meaning "due time" or "normal time" (cf. *Odyssey* 11.248).

64–80. In line 201, Himeros (Desire) is an attendant of Aphrodite. In the *Homeric Hymn to Aphrodite* 5.60–64, the Graces are attendants of Aphrodite (for their close connection with this goddess, see Paus. 6.24.7). Line 64 may be Hesiod's way of saying that the Muses are characterized by grace and desire. The Muses and the Graces are mentioned together again in the *Homeric Hymn to Artemis* 27.15. Hesiod speaks of them again and gives their birth and their names in *Theogony* 907–11. Line 911 shows that "Desire" in 64 is a mere personification of one of their properties. The Hesiodic list of the Muses (77–79) became standard in later antiquity (cf. *Orphic Hymn* 76). In the Homeric tradition, they are graceful and benevolent deities who inspire artists and especially poets, and who frequently sing as Apollon plays the lyre (*Iliad* 1.601–4; *Homeric Hymn to Apollon* 3.189–93; and *Homeric Hymn to Hermes*

4.450–52). Their distinction according to field of creative endeavor is late, and Homer never names them individually. It may be that their names were first mentioned by Hesiod in this passage.

80–92. The connection between kings and Muses at first seems contrived, but lines 84 and 97 argue for an unambiguous association. One should remember that kingly power comes from Zeus and that the Muses are his daughters. A persuasive ruler must be eloquent, and much of the traditional wisdom handed down from generation to generation was couched in gnomic verses, which in Hesiod's day, much like all other poetry, were attributed to inspiration from the Muses. Line 96 shows that Hesiod was thinking in quasi-genealogical terms. The Muses give to kings they honor the gift of honey-sweet speech. When they do so, their people obey them and quarrels come to an end. In these cases, people look upon their kings as divine beings. We may recall here that King Nestor was such a speaker.

94–104. This passage offers excellent testimony to the very real social and psychological function of public epic performance, which was not mere amusement, but an experience with healing potential not unlike that offered by folk musicians and storytellers to hard-working country people of all cultures (cf. *Homeric Hymn to Hermes* 4.480–90).

105–15. These lines spell out the subject of Hesiod's poem and determine that it will be both cosmogonic and theogonic.

116–25. We are not told how Chaos came to be, or what existed before it. For Hesiod, Chaos is a dark and gloomy chasm between the Earth and Tartaros (cf. 736–45, 805–13). One wonders whether here Chaos is more like the great void, the *ginnunga gap*, of Norse mythology. Gaia (Earth) and Tartaros simply come into existence. Tartaros is still preserved in modern Greek belief and folklore. Its description is given in 726–819. The position of Eros among such primeval elements as Chaos and Gaia indirectly or tacitly intimates a very important role, that of a demiurgic catalyst, perhaps, within creation. This figure has nothing in common with the winged and cherubic child of Hellenistic and Roman art. His role in the Orphic cosmogonies is more explicit, for in them he is said to have sprung from the primeval egg that Night laid in the bosom of Erebos (Darkness) and to have mingled with Chaos, thereby becoming father even of the gods (Aristophanes *Birds* 693–700). The *Orphic Hymn to Eros* (58) credits him with all-pervasive powers but yields little concrete information. For Hesiod, Eros is the motive force in the generative and procreative processes. The birth of Erebos and Night from Chaos is "automatic" and unexplained. It is quite interesting that Ether, the higher and hence purer stratum of air, and Day are born of the union of Erebos with Night. In the Hebrew Bible, God creates light out of darkness. For Hesiod, light was not a gift of the gods. Light had to come from somewhere. Erebos and Night, being part of an evolving cosmic order, whose energies were governed by attraction (Eros), coupled and produced Ether and Day. We must not for a moment think that Hesiod came to this thought by accident or that, in an abstract way, he suggested that light succeeded darkness as day succeeds night. Hesiod saw lightning flashing on a dark sky. He saw fire produced by a drill and also the iron struck by flint to produce sparks of fire. He knew that, when men and women mate, there is a clashing of bodies, friction, and penetration. Impact is involved in all these productive activities. As two nonluminous objects, like flint and iron, produce sparks when they meet with evident force, so too Erebos and Night could produce Ether (fire) and Day (glow).

126–32. As physical element, Ouranos is a sort of luminous dome that roofs the world. Outside his role as mate of the Earth (Gaia) for the procreation of Okeanos and of the first generation of anthropomorphic divinities, Ouranos is rather insignificant.

133–38. The concept of the mating of Earth and Sky is an almost universal mythological motif, and one that is easy to understand not only because of the very necessity of postulating a male counterpart for Mother Earth but also because of the visibly fecundating role of the rain that comes from the sky. After mating with Ouranos, Gaia gives birth to six sons and six daughters, all of them constituting the generation of the Titans. Judged by what ensues, the list is strikingly heterogeneous, as some of them are peaceful and harmless and others bellicose and violent. Although several of the Titans have names that make sense in Greek, as a group they probably represent older pre-Hellenic divinities, which were subdued by the sky-god of the invading Indo-Europeans and consigned to eternal darkness (cf. 424, 729–36, 813–19). Okeanos as an element is the great river that flows round the world. All other rivers come from him (337–45). Koios, Leto's father, Kreios, and Hyperion, father of Helios (Sun), are obscure figures.

Iapetos is an important Titanic figure and the father of Prometheus (507–12). Theia is obscure, but not so Rheia or Rhea, who is Zeus's mother by Kronos (453). She is later identified with Demeter, Kybele, and quite fittingly with the Mother of the Gods (cf. *Orphic Hymn* 14). Themis is Zeus's second consort and definitely an old earth-goddess. Phoibe is Leto's mother, and Tethys Okeanos's wife. Kronos is Zeus's father and, although the youngest of the Titans, he is not treated like one of them. Most of them are violent and sinister figures imprisoned in the darkness below the earth, but Kronos, after being ousted by his son, rules the Isles of the Blest. In all likelihood, he too is a pre-Hellenic god who gave way to the supremacy of Zeus.

139–53. The Kyklopes and the Hundred-Handers are not Titans, and Zeus frees them before the Titanomachy (501, 624–28). The Kyklopes have little in common with the Kyklopes of the *Odyssey*. They are one-eyed craftsmen, and their chief function is the making of the thunderbolt. Their names, Thunder, Lightning, and Flash, are suggestive of their respective functions. The Hundred-Handers are not only described by Hesiod, but in line 149 they are given names clearly suggestive of their brute strength. In endowing them with so many arms, Hesiod anticipates their decisive assistance in the battle against the Titans in which they serve as what might correspond to a primitive man's idea of a machine gun.

154–82. It has been maintained by several scholars that this castration myth represents primitive man's rationalization of the separation of Earth and Sky, since primitive man observes that the sky stands above the earth without collapsing upon it. I think it is more probable that the myth is a remnant from a pre-Indo-European earth-oriented religion in which a ritual of castration of the earth-goddess's consort signified her supremacy of power and perhaps even corresponded to practice in some aboriginal matriarchal society. After all, the Olympic pantheon, which succeeded the older gods, in terms of practice and structure, mirrored the patriarchal family of the Hellenes. Certain scholars have also seen in the presence of the sickle a remnant of a harvest ritual. It may not be too bold to suggest that such a ritual may have contributed to the making of the myth. Grain comes from the earth, but it is seed and therefore something masculine and as such ultimately attributable to the sky. Man reaps grain, keeps most of it for his sustenance, and then reseeds the earth. Primitive man may have thought that the original grain-seed came from the sky. Earth had to effect the castration of the sky in order to secure the survival of her children. Primitive man may have felt that, in cutting off the grain for his survival, he violated what came from the genitals of Father Sky. It is interesting that certain Indian tribes in Mexico believe that the hallucinogenic mushrooms that they use grow from what thunderbolts plant into the earth.

183–210. The blood drops from Ouranos's severed genitals fecundate both earth and sea. As a result of this fecundation, the earth (Gaia) gives birth to the Erinyes (Furies), the Giants, and the Meliai (Ash Tree Nymphs). The Erinyes are malevolent spirits of retribution for murder, especially murder within the family or clan. In origin, they are either the ghosts of slain persons or personifications of curses that called for revenge (see also *Orphic Hymn* 69). The Giants in Hesiod play no role in the battle against the gods. The Gigantomachy may be as old a motif as the Titanomachy, but this is not evident in literature. For Homer, they are just a savage race of men (*Odyssey* 7.59). It was later mythography and art that developed the theme to its full potential. The myth seems to represent the threat to organized religion or civilized order by savages of superhuman strength (see Apollodoros 1.34–38). It is not clear why the Ash Tree Nymphs are singled out. The birth of nymphs provides a transition from the birth of savage creatures to the birth of someone as lovely as Aphrodite. The explanation of the name *Aphrodite* and of the epithets *Kythereia*, *Kyprogenês*, and *Philommêdês* is pure folk etymology, but folk etymology that is drawn into the mythopoetic process. Aphrodite's normal epithet is *philommeidês*, "smile-loving" (as in 989), but here Hesiod is either punning on the similarity of *meidês* to *mêdea* ("genitals"), or he is indeed preserving a genuine epithet with profounder significance (i.e., *philommêdês*, "fond of genitals").

In the case of the Titans (207–10), Hesiod in similar fashion explains the name *Titan*. Yet, one may be sure that the name *Titan*, probably an old Thracian word, is of much greater antiquity than Hesiod's explanation. The name *Aphrodite* may have nothing to do with *aphrós* ("foam"), and the epithets *Kypris*, of which Kyprogenês is a folk-etymological development, and *Kythereia* may owe nothing to Cyprus and Kythera, although there is a remote possibility that they might have contributed to the establishment of the cult on these two islands. That someone as lovely as Aphrodite is born from the result of the grim act of castration is no stranger than the birth of light (Day) from darkness (Night). After all, grim sacrifices are usually performed precisely in order to bring about very positive results. The myth may point to Aphrodite's origin as a goddess of fertility and generation, a role that she, especially when attended by Eros, fits so well. Originally, she too may have been earth-born, but the connection of her name with *aphrós* and the idea that she was carried by the sea to the two islands, where she was conspicuously worshiped, may have given rise to the myth that has her born in the sea. Both Homer and the poet of the exquisite *Homeric Hymn to Aphrodite* (5) deliberately suppress this horrific version of Aphrodite's birth. To Homer, Aphrodite is *Dios thygatêr,* "Zeus's daughter," and her mother is Dione (*Iliad* 5.370–71).

211–32. Moros, Ker, and Death are synonymous and basically mean death, although, originally, perhaps death of three different kinds. On Sleep and Death, see 756–66 and *Orphic Hymns* 85 and 87. Dream is already personified in the *Iliad* (2, 6, 8, 16, and so forth). For the brood or race of Dreams, see *Odyssey* 24.12, in which we are told that the realm of dreams lies beyond the stream of Okeanos and the gates of the Sun (see *Orphic Hymn* 86). Momos is "carping" personified, a literary figure with no cultic significance; likewise, Oizys, "Distress," "Woe." The Hesperides, who guard the golden apples in a mythical island in the farthest western extremity of the world, are prominently connected with the twelfth labor of Herakles. It should be remembered that they are daughters of Night and sisters of Death and that in the Herakles myth they probably symbolize the hero's encounter with, and conquest of, the ultimate challenge man faces, death. The names *Klotho, Lachesis,* and *Atropos* belong to the Fates, who in 901–4 are given as daughters of Zeus and Themis. Although the Keres are usually distinguished from the Moirai, "Fates," since *kêr* means "death," it is possible that in 217 "the Keres and Moirai" is Hesiod's way of saying "the Fates of Death," the allotment of death being the primary function of the Moirai. Their names, Spinner, Alloter, and Irreversible, suggest a metaphor that comes from the idea of the thread of life that has to be spun and then irreversibly cut at the moment of a man's death. Originally, the Moirai were most likely birth-spirits that visited newborn children to grant them various gifts, including lifespan. This is, at least, how they have survived in modern Greek folk belief.

It is interesting that Nemesis, "Retribution," is a child of Night and a sister of Strife. Unlike many of her siblings in the loathsome brood of Night, Nemesis was worshiped rather widely in Greek cult. Her origin has not been determined yet. It is obvious from the hideous progeny that Hesiod ascribes to Eris (Strife) and from his elaboration on the theme of Strife in the *Works and Days* that he was already preoccupied with the nature of strife but had not yet fully developed that view of it that made it into a mixture of a curse and a blessing. Oath (Horkos) is the personification of the curse that a man lays upon himself when he calls upon the gods to punish him, if what he avers as true proves to be false.

233–64. It is the progeny of the three sons of Pontos that occupies Hesiod for more than a hundred lines of his poem: 233–336. The first son, Nereus, was imagined as a wise "Old Man of the Sea" (cf. *Iliad* 1.358). He is, it should be remembered, grandfather of Achilleus through his daughter, Thetis (for Nereus, cf. *Orphic Hymn* 23). Thaumas is obscure. Phorkys is occasionally identified with his father, and his name may be an attribute of Nereus. Of the fifty daughters of Nereus, Amphitrite, the temperamental wife of Poseidon, and Thetis, the mother of Achilleus, are the only figures of importance. Although, collectively, the Nereids were important figures of folk religion, the rest of the Nereids probably owe their names more to Hesiod's, or some other poet's, fertile imagination than to any real role in popular cult. Slightly changed to *Neráides,* their name is applied by modern Greeks to all fairies of woodland, spring, and mountain. Shepherds, if seduced by their charms, wander off bereft of their minds, voices, and even of their manhood. In modern Greek belief, they have lost all connection with the sea, and they are more like the Nymphs of Greek antiquity— and in the beauty of their voices and their skill in dancing, even a bit like the Muses. But the *Neráides* are as beautiful as they are fickle and treacherous. Their extremely strong survival in the Greek countryside offers good proof that the Nereids and the Nymphs held a correspondingly strong position in religious belief and cult practice among the country folk of ancient Greece. Yet, Hesiod's ambitious onomastic elaboration is probably a demonstration of poetic skill and of metrical ingenuity.

There is another very important old man of the sea, Proteus, who is the subject of a fascinating tale in the fourth book of the *Odyssey* (351–586). Hesiod must have known about Proteus, but he omits any reference to him. Proteus may have come to Greece from the shores of the Baltic Sea and the Greek colonies of the northern littoral of the Black Sea. Baltic amber reached the Hellenic world through such arduous trade routes, and trade often comes with new ideas. Proteus's outlandish connection with his flocks of seals and his even more bizarre transformation from lion to serpent, to leopard, to great boar did not fit into Hesiod's theology. Incidentally, Proteus's name may not be Greek, and Nereus is most likely the Hellenized version of the name of an Illyrian divinity (cf. Albanian *njer,* "man"). Hesiod tells us that Nereus had fifty daughters (250). Yet, he lists fifty-two names. However, two of the names, both mentioned at the beginning of his catalogue in line 243, are repeated again. Proto of line 243 appears again in line 248. Amphitrite, also of line 243, shows up again in line 252. The ancient manuscripts support both names in line 243, as well as in lines 248 and 252, where the repetitions occur. Some scholars have proposed emendations, which eliminate what seems to be a glaring inconsistency. I am inclined to think that there is no inconsistency. The poet refers his audience twice to the beginning line of his catalogue. Proto, the "First One," appears first on the list. Amphitrite, who shares space with her in line 243, is at least as well known as Thetis (244). The repetition, I believe, is purposeful. The singer reminded and teased his audience. A couple of significant repetitions could be very effective. "Here is Proto again. She is at the head of my list. Close to her in the same list is Amphitrite. Let's go! I have more names for you!" Modern performers of music and song repeat for effect. To deny this artifice to ancient singers, especially such as belong to the oral tradition, is tantamount to denying them the essentials of their craft. We may have, in the present case, a rare instance of the preservation of oral performance features that writing eventually eliminated.

Such catalogues may indeed go back to lists of names by which a divinity is addressed. Their purpose is to invoke, indeed, to provoke, the divinity to come to the aid of someone who prays to it. More examples can be found in certain other religions, e.g., the ninety-nine names of Allah in the Koran. The most instructive analogue to come from the Greek world consists of the many names by which Panagia is addressed, five hundred or so. Also, the many names by which the bear is addressed in the culture of the Sami offer an instructive analogue. They number about five hundred (see Pentikäinen, *Golden King of the Forest*).

265–69. For Elektra, cf. 349. Iris is goddess of the rainbow and hardly distinguishable from it. In Homer, she is the swift messenger of the gods. The Harpies were probably in origin wind spirits. They were imagined as winged female beings of monstrous appearance with the ability to snatch and sweep one away (cf. *Odyssey* 20.77). With their birdlike bodies and women's faces in art, they resemble the Sirens.

270–86. Hesiod mentions only two of the Graiai; the third one, Deino, is not included in this passage. Despite the euphemistic epithet *fair-cheeked,* the Graiai were the personification of hideous old age and its accompanying ills. Of the three Gorgons, Medousa is the only one who deserves attention. In typical fashion, we are probably dealing with one Gorgon figure expanded into a trio by poetic elaboration. The insignificance of Sthenno and Euryale is indeed telling in this connection. Medousa's eyes were so fierce that they could petrify people. Her face was round and practically halved by a row of ugly teeth. This hideous visage was encircled by hissing snakes instead of hair. Perseus, son of Zeus and Danae, killed Medousa with the help of Athena. For a full account of this complex legend, see Apollodoros 2.34ff. Pegasos was tamed by Bellerophon and helped him in his battle against Chimaira (325), the Amazons, and the Solymoi. The famous spring Hippokrene was created by Pegasos with a kick of his hoof.

289–94. Hesiod returns to this story in 979–83. The detail that Herakles crossed the ocean in

Theogony

the golden cup of the Sun is not given here. For a much more detailed version of what constitutes the tenth labor of Herakles, see Apollodoros 2.106–12.

295–336. According to Apollodoros 2.4, Echidna (Snake) was a daughter of Tartaros and Gaia, and she was slain by the hundred-eyed Argos Panoptes. It is true that 295 begins in such a way that one might think that Chrysaor and Kallirhoe are her parents, but Phorkys and Keto are more likely candidates for parents of this hideous creature who proceeded to give birth to a series of monsters and scourges: Orthos, Kerberos, Hydra, Chimaira, Sphinx, and the Nemean Lion. For her mate Typhoeus, see 820–35. Kerberos is more fully described in 769–74. In art, this monstrous hound usually has three heads (so, too, in Apollodoros 2.122). As his twelfth labor, Herakles overpowered Kerberos, fetched him before King Eurystheus, and then returned him to Hades. The slaying of the Nemean Lion and the Lernaean Hydra constitutes the first two labors imposed by King Eurystheus on Herakles (see Apollodoros 2.74–80). Hesiod describes Chimaira as three-headed. According to *Iliad* 6.181, her front part was a lion, her rear a dragon, and her middle a goat. Paradoxically, little is said about the Sphinx, whose place in Greek art and mythology is prominent. She is definitely of Egyptian origin, and she is usually portrayed with a woman's head and a lion's body. Sent to Thebes by Hera, she became a local menace, devouring any man who failed to solve her riddle about the three ages of man. She killed herself after Oedipus solved the riddle. The later enigmatic figure whom the tragic poets call "the wise virgin" is a far cry from the dreadful daughter of Echidna.

337–70. The idea that the rivers of the earth are the sons of Okeanos, the stream that encircles the earth, is natural within a system that considers Okeanos the primary water element. This belief is found in the *Iliad*, where Homer explains that all springs and all wells come from Okeanos (21.195–97). In the *Odyssey*, the stream of Okeanos is a deep-flowing river that can be crossed by ship (10.508; 11.3; 14.1). Its circular, cosmic dimension is not clearly underscored anywhere.

Like Homer (*Iliad* 18), Hesiod conceptualizes Okeanos as "the stream surrounding the earth." As a personified entity, Okeanos, a child of Gaia and Ouranos, was firstborn among the Titans (127–36). The mighty stream flows back on itself (777). In many significant ways, Okeanos is like the rivers familiar to most people. It does have fords (291–92), sources (282), and water that flows in streams (695, 841). Okeanos is the sacred stream (*Works and Days* 566) which, like other streams and rivers, falls "into the briny sea" (791). In his list of rivers born of Okeanos and Tethys (337–45), Hesiod names Acheloios. The land between Dodona and Acheloios served as a cradle of the proto-Hellenic religious and national identity (Aristotle *Meteorológica* I, XVI, 352; Plato *Phaedo* 112d, 113a–c). It is quite likely that the greatest river of Greece, such a dominant presence in the Greek northwest, served as the real-life model for the concept of a mighty river surrounding the entire circular earth.

It is interesting that *Orphic Hymn* 22 identifies Tethys, the mother of the rivers, with the sea. The list of the rivers is not entirely haphazard or unsystematic, but it is selective (cf. 367–70) and it does leave out several important rivers. Conspicuous is the omission of Acheron, the river which, according to standard Homeric, indeed Hellenic, belief was crossed by the souls of the dead on their journey to the underworld (*Odyssey* 10.504–20; 11.13–22, 636–40; 12.11–14; *Iliad* 23.69–74). Hesiod makes no reference in his poems to the Homeric belief that after death there was such a thing as the human soul that journeyed to the underworld to remain there forever. Having determined to exclude this belief as inconsistent with his own much stricter and reformist ideology, he omitted Acheron from his list of rivers, thereby deterring popular belief from what he may have considered a useless thought. Etymologically, both Acheloios and Acheron may share a common root meaning "water," the root most easily seen in *aqua,* the Latin word for water, and in its many derivatives in various languages that originated with Latin. The catalogue of the Okeanids has many features in common with that of the

Nereids. Most of the Okeanids are obscure and unimportant, and one does wonder about Hesiod's motive in being so thorough, even though he himself could claim that he is very selective, having—mercifully I should say—chosen to name less than fifty and not all three thousand! Some of the names recur in the list of Okeanids, who, as Persephone's companions, picked flowers with her on a beautiful meadow before the earth gaped and her ravisher appeared (*Homeric Hymn to Demeter* 2.1–9).

We should note that Hesiod, who knew of Europe and Asia as lands, most likely as continents, represents them here as Okeanids, daughters of Okeanos and Tethys. The Asian meadow of *Iliad* 2.461 is the earliest indirect mention of Asia. Europe in the sense "continental land" appears for the first time in the *Homeric Hymn to Apollon* 251, 291.

371–74. In *Homeric Hymn to Helios* (31), Helios (Sun) is the son of Hyperion and Euryphaessa. In *Homeric Hymns* 2.62–63, 4.68–69, and 28.12–16, he is portrayed as a celestial charioteer, but this image occurs nowhere in the *Iliad* or the *Odyssey*. The identification with Apollon is later. Rhodes was the only place with a strong sun cult. In general, the place of the sun in Greek religion is quite insignificant. Selene (Moon) was not worshiped either except insofar as she was identified with Artemis or Hekate. The Moon figured prominently in Greek poetry, sorcery, and time reckoning. According to the poet of *Homeric Hymn* 32, Zeus was once her lover. *Orphic Hymn* 9 contains an almost comprehensive list of her various aspects. Eos (Dawn) is the lovely goddess whom Homer describes with such beautiful epithets as "rosy-fingered," "saffron-cloaked," and so forth. Many of her lovers came to an unhappy end (so Orion in *Odyssey* 5.121–24; cf. also Apollodoros 1.27). The tragic story of another one of her lovers, Tithonos, is recounted in the *Homeric Hymn to Aphrodite* 5.218–38. Although she is a figure of myth and not of cult, recent scholarship has made it certain that in origin she is an old Indo-European goddess.

375–82. All three sons of Kreios are insignificant. Lines 99–100 of the *Homeric Hymn to Hermes* (4)

make Pallas, rather than Hyperion, father of the Moon. Perses is Hekate's father (409–11). Eos (Dawn) is mother of the winds because in Greece winds frequently rise at dawn. Zephyros is the west wind, Boreas the north wind, and Notos the south wind (cf. *Orphic Hymns* 80, 81, 82). That Dawn is mother of the dawn star is logical; not equally logical, however, is the idea that she is mother of all the other stars, which much more convincingly in *Orphic Hymn* 7 are called "children of dark Night."

383–403. This is an etiological myth that explains why Kratos (Power) and Bia (Force) belong only to Zeus and why all the gods swear by Styx. Zelos (Rivalry) is a mere Hesiodic personification. Nike may have started only as an abstraction, but she eventually became the well-defined and revered goddess of victory, to whom many important shrines were dedicated and who captured the imagination of Greek artists, especially after the Persian wars. The Hellenistic Nike of Samothrace, which now stands in the Louvre, is only one of the superb examples of statues of Nike. Zelos never acquired any importance, but Kratos and Bia were important enough to play a significant role in the opening scene of Aeschylus's *Prometheus Bound,* and Pausanias in 2.4.7 reports that on the way up to the Akrokorinth there was a sanctuary to Ananke (Necessity) and Bia, to which local tradition forbade entry.

404–8. Leto is far better known than her rather obscure parents, Phoibe and Koios. She is chiefly known as mother of Apollon and Artemis. Hesiod and Homer do not give the details of how she gave birth to these two important gods. The fullest and best-known account of how Leto gave birth to Apollon is given in the major *Homeric Hymn to Apollon.*

409–52. Hekate is not mentioned in Homer or elsewhere in the *Theogony,* but here she is credited with wide-ranging powers, and Hesiod lavishes on her so much praise that the piece is usually referred to as a hymn to Hekate. It should be noted here that an error contained in the first two editions of the *Oxford Classical Dictionary* made Hekate the daughter of Koios and

Phoibe. This error has passed into several handbooks of Greek mythology and even into several translations. The Hesiodic text is clear on the matter. Hekate is the daughter of Perses and Asteria. Scholars usually trace her origin to Asia Minor, and, given the origin of Hesiod's family, they are inclined to attribute his obvious devotion to her to ancestral connections with the territory in which the goddess was strongly worshiped. Her absence from the Homeric pantheon is proof either of late arrival or of connections that were too chthonic for Homer's taste. In the later tradition, she is strongly connected with magic and superstition, and is more like a malevolent and dangerous demon with ghoulish and funereal associations (cf. *Orphic Hymn* 1). She is frequently associated with Artemis and even with Selene. In her lunar aspect, she presides over certain aspects of women's lives. However, her origin is most likely chthonic. The epithet *kourotróphos,* "nurturer of youths," which she shares with Artemis, and her role in the breeding and increasing of livestock do point to a chthonic deity with powers over generation and growth. Her rather teratomorphic statues with three faces or even three bodies may in a way preserve her originally extensive powers, which encompassed land, sea, and sky, and this trinitarian nature is also mirrored in her triple identity as Hekate, Artemis, and Selene. I tend to think that Hekate's connection with magic and with unappetizing sacrificial practices was old and familiar to Hesiod. As is obvious from all of his surviving poetry, Hesiod was fervidly devoted to new ideas that promoted the combination of justice and collaborative social values necessary for the emergence and prosperity of the *polis,* the civilized and law-abiding city. Religious practices and beliefs that undermined rational social values must have been most unwelcome to him. Lines 409–52 remake an old goddess whose worship was rooted in primitive, regressive, and potentially harmful practices into a benign and powerful goddess who posed no threat to the new social order. The transformation of

the repulsive and vindictive Furies by Aeschylus in the *Eumenides* into benign powers of fertility and givers of blessings from Attica presents us with a fine analogue.

453–58. At this point, Hesiod, after a long interval, resumes his narrative on the succession myth. After the lavish praise he has heaped on Hekate, the haste with which he bypasses such divinities as Hestia, Demeter, Hera, Hades, and Poseidon comes as a surprise. The reason for this haste is too obvious. Hesiod's purpose is the recounting of Zeus's birth and coming to power. Besides, a series of digressions, similar to the so-called "Hymn to Hekate," roughly in the middle of the *Theogony,* would definitely rob the poem of whatever unity it now possesses. Of the five gods mentioned above, Hestia (this spelling is more common than Histia) is the least important in Greek mythology, though not in Greek private and even public worship. Originally, she must have been completely identified with the hearth and the fire that burned in it, but she was gradually personified and invoked as an anthropomorphic goddess both on familial and civic religious occasions, since public buildings also contained a hearth on which the well-being of the city depended. Her Roman counterpart, Vesta, was also a virgin goddess worshiped by virgin priestesses. Her virginal nature is stressed in the *Homeric Hymn to Aphrodite* (5), and, in line 30 of this hymn, as well as in line 2 of *Orphic Hymn* 84, she is said to "dwell in the house center," the concept obviously originating in the plan of the Homeric *megaron,* which had its hearth in the center. She was the first and the last deity to whom libations were poured at public festivals. *Zeus Ephestios,* "Zeus of the Hearth," was invoked together with her (for the beginnings of such a concept, cf. *Odyssey* 14.158–59). There are two *Homeric Hymns* (24 and 19) and one *Orphic Hymn* (84) devoted to her.

459–501. Zeus's parents are the Titans Kronos and Rheia. As has already been said, Kronos is the least violent of his brethren and the one who is spared confinement in the nether gloom. For Rheia, see notes on 133–38. It is agreed among

HESIOD

most scholars that the Hesiodic account is the result of religious syncretism and the blending of an account of Near Eastern origin with one of Minoan origin. The Near Eastern account contains the element of the swallowing of the stone and is best paralleled in the Hurrian-Hittite myth about Kumarbi, the god who, forewarned by the sky-god Anu, swallows a stone in order to prevent the birth of a child destined to overthrow him. Interestingly enough, this child is the result of fecundation caused by Anu's genitals, which Kumarbi bit off and swallowed at the end of a battle with Anu. The Minoan god with whom the Hellenic Zeus was identified was doubtless a chthonic god of generation and fertility, the divine son and consort of the great Cretan earth-goddess, whose presence is so abundantly evident in Cretan art of the Minoan period. Archaeological finds in a number of mountain caves in Crete point to the worship of a "cave-Zeus" from Minoan times on down to Hellenistic and Roman times. The story of Kumarbi and the kindred nature of the Semitic Adonis and the Egyptian Osiris seem to indicate that the Hesiodic account represents a triple fusion of Near Eastern, Creto-Minoan, and Hellenic elements. Such colorful details connected with the birth of Zeus as the role of the she-goat or nymph Amalthea and of the shield-clashing Kouretes, who danced round the infant Zeus to muffle his cries, must belong to the Cretan tradition, and their omission by Hesiod is worth some speculation on our part. In the first episode of the succession myth, Ouranos hides each child in the womb of Gaia and prevents it from coming out into the light. Then Gaia conspires with her children and has Kronos cut off his father's genitals. In the second episode of the myth, the children are swallowed by Kronos and kept in his belly. Gaia, through her daughter Rheia, is again instrumental in the deception and suppression of Kronos, the new celestial overlord, although Hesiod tells us that Ouranos was equally instrumental in contriving the plot. This second conspiracy, too, has all the makings of female

scheming. A second sky-god is required by Mother Earth's double—her daughter Rheia—to make room for a third sky-god, who will defeat the Titan generation once and for all to rule as king and father of gods and men. The relative unimportance of Ouranos and Kronos most likely indicates that they both represent figures from the pre-Hellenic pantheon, probably docile consorts of the Mediterranean earth mother, who were sacrificed by their wife and mother in favor of the supreme new sky-god. The second succession myth is, in some ways, an elaboration of the same theme, the struggle of the new gods against the old ones. But the old gods had to be born before they could be overpowered; hence, the need for the second variant. Lyktos (477, 481) is listed in *Iliad* 2.647 (cf. also 17.611) as one of the seven most important Cretan towns. There are three Minoan sacred caves in the proximity of Lyktos: Psychro, Arkalochori, and one in the foothills of Lasithi. Perhaps Arkalochori, the closest one to Lyktos (only one to one and a half hours on foot), is the cave of line 483. In later Minoan times, the cave at the summit of Mt. Ida became the most important of the various Cretan cult caves and the one referred to by classical sources as the cave of Zeus. No other primary literary source mentions Mt. Aigaion (484). There are some arguments in favor of identifying Mt. Aigaion with modern Mt. Lasithi. The stone of lines 497–500 was an object of veneration in historic times. In his tenth book, Pausanias reports that, as one walked upward from the grave of Neoptolemos, one came to a stone of modest size upon which the Delphians poured oil daily and which they covered with unspun wool during festivals. This stone, he says, was believed by some to be the one swallowed and disgorged by Kronos (10.24.5). Cf. also the Latin oath *per Jovem lapidem* ("by Jove the stone") and Jacob's stone at Bethel (Genesis 28).

507–615. Here Hesiod is interested in the Prometheus legend and makes only desultory mention of the other sons of Iapetos. Atlas, who figures in the Herakles myth, is Calypso's father and a giant guarding the pillars of heaven (*Odyssey* 1.51–54). Here (518–20) he supports the sky and lives near the Hesperides. In the myth that connects him with Herakles, Atlas offers to go and fetch their fabulous apples, if Herakles will support the sky in the meantime. Menoitios is an obscure figure. Epimetheus (Afterthought) becomes proverbial for his foolishness. The guilt of Prometheus is clear, but the other three brothers seem to have been punished simply for their descent from the violent Titan Iapetos.

The punishment of Prometheus (521–31) creates certain problems. Its place in this part of the narrative at first appears rather odd. Prometheus is not guilty of anything yet, but neither are Epimetheus, Menoitios, and Atlas. Hesiod speaks of the punishment of Prometheus while he is still on the subject of the punishment of all the sons of Iapetos. There is also a seeming inconsistency between lines 526–31 and lines 614–16. In lines 526–31, we are told that Herakles slew the eagle and "freed [Prometheus] from his wretched plight." Because in later versions of the myth Herakles does not merely slay the eagle but also frees Prometheus from his bonds, some scholars have taken lines 526–28 to mean that Herakles also freed Prometheus. However, a careful reading of the lines, a comparison with lines 614–16, and an examination of the early version of the myth make such an assumption impossible. The plight from which Prometheus is freed is the eagle that preys on his liver. Thus, according to the older version of the myth, Zeus mitigates the punishment considerably but does not remove it altogether. As certain similar myths from the Caucasus area show, the myth may have originally been invented to explain some natural phenomena. In the Caucasus myths, earthquakes are caused by the struggle and anguish of a giant who has been tied to a pillar or in a mountain cave, presumably by a god. Be that as it may, elaboration and accretions have made the Greek Prometheus myth a symbolic story whose universal appeal is adequate proof that it is the product of a profound need of the human mind to come to terms with some unanswerable questions about the human condition.

The story of Prometheus as told by Hesiod both in the *Theogony* and in the *Works and Days* (47–106) is clearly etiological. Its purpose is to explain Greek sacrificial practice, which for all its avowed piety did not give the gods the choice parts of the animal; the presence of fire among men; and finally, the character of woman, who, at best a mixed blessing, is a curse that man is doomed to contend with.

Despite the grandiose character of Homeric feasts, the people of the Greek countryside must have eaten no more meat in ancient times than they did until very recently. Meat was eaten only on major religious holidays, and the fiercely pastoral and archetypally Greek nomadic tribe of the Sarakatsani still refer to the animals they slaughter on religious holidays as *kourbánia* (from Arabic *kurban*, "sacrificial victim") and still consume meat almost exclusively on major religious holidays. In pastoral societies, the animal is too important to be slaughtered, too useful as a source of food to be burned or allowed to rot away. The unfair division of portions, with the inedible parts given to the gods and the edible flesh to men, may have originated at a time when the bones wrapped with skin and paunch were given to the gods in the hope that the gods would replenish the flock by resurrecting the animal. Yet one gives the best to those he honors and not the worst, and the inequity was strongly felt by the Greeks, who not infrequently considered themselves hosts of the gods at the religious feasts held in their honor. This sentiment has survived in modern-day Greece, as one may gather from the following folk song, of which I give only the first few lines:

As we sit at this table, at this dining board,
we give to the angel and treat Christ to
wine
and sweetly greet the All-Holy Virgin. . . .

I venture to suggest that the sense of guilt and embarrassment engendered by the unfairness of the division of the sacrificial victim may be responsible for the attribution of the unflattering prototype to Prometheus as a way of self-exoneration. In other words, it is not a good thing, but Prometheus established a precedent and therefore he is to be blamed and not the mortals who follow it.

The theft of fire belongs to a motif that is both primordial and widespread. That fire should have come from the sky must have appeared as a self-evident reality to primitive man, who observed lightning and many luminous, firelike elements in the sky, not the least of which is the blazing sun. The inference that fire was originally hidden from man will be easily understood by anyone who does not have ready access to the means of making it. The withholding of fire, an element so necessary to man, is an act of punishment for what is treated almost like some sort of original sin committed by Prometheus. The analogies between the figures of Prometheus and Christ have tempted the minds of many scholars and will always challenge the imagination of man. Whatever the difference, one thing is certain: both figures belong to an archetypal motif and both are of profound significance for the human psyche.

In the *Theogony*, it is the original woman herself who is sent to men as punishment for the action of Prometheus in their behalf (he stole the fire from Zeus). In the *Works and Days* (60–105), Pandora, who is not mentioned by name in the *Theogony*, is not the evil but the bearer of it. The attitude toward women in the *Works and Days*, despite certain harsh indictments of women, is best summed up by the epigrammatic

> Nothing is better for man than a good wife,
> and no horror matches a bad one . . .
>> (702–3)

and this sentiment is definitely the result of afterthought and reconsideration. As in the case of Eris (Strife), which is one in the *Theogony* but twofold, good and bad, in the *Works and Days*, so too in the case of the woman Hesiod's thought seems to advance from simplicity to complexity. Yet, the basic problem remains, and what under-lies the creation of the Hebrew Eve, the Hellenic Pandora, and the Icelandic Hallgerthr in the *Njálssaga* may be something subtler and far more complex than male prejudice. It may, in the final analysis, be the antithetic relationship, which is a precondition for symbiotic attraction, the negation that is a precondition of affirmation. See also notes on *Works and Days* 60–105.

617–721. *The Titanomachy:* As is easily gathered not only from Hurrian, Babylonian, and Norse myths, but also from the myths of many other peoples, war between two hostile groups of gods is one of the most widespread mythological motifs. In some versions, gods do not fight against other gods but against monstrous giants that must be subdued. A case in point is the Babylonian myth about the god Marduk. Of course, this element is not absent from Hesiod, whose account of the battle of Zeus against Typhoeus certainly corresponds to this variation of the motif. In the Titanomachy, Zeus enlists the aid of the rather teratomorphic Hundred-Handers in the battle against the Titans. Haunting parallels exist between the Titanomachy, especially if it is taken in conjunction with the Typhoeus episode, and the *Völuspá*, the first poem of the *Poetic* or *Elder Edda*, as well as the magnificent prose elaboration of the theme of this poem in the *Snorra Edda* by Snorri Sturluson. The subject of the poem is the myth of *Ragnarök*, or "Doom of the Gods," and it deals not with the battle of younger gods against older gods but with the destruction of the world and of the gods by the monsters that are unleashed on them on the day of their doom. The gods are survived by their sons, who live to see the eerie calm and the renewal of life that follow the deluge and conflagration. The theme of rebirth is very clear from the visionary lines of the sixty-third stanza:

> on unsown land the ears will grow,
> woe will turn to weal, and Baldur will
>> come again.

The *Völuspá* is a prophetic poem, and the *Ragnarök* is set in the distant future and not in the past. Therefore, it is true that the concept of the *Ragnarök* is more like the equally terrifying concept of the Armageddon than like the Titanomachy. This doomsday element in the Norse myth should not mislead us into mistaking its heathen elements as mere appendages to an imitation of Judaeo-Christian eschatology or linking them with the equally heathen elements in the Titanomachy.

The *Orphic Hymn to the Titans* (37) begins with the words:

> Titans, glorious children of Ouranos and Gaia,
> forebears of our fathers, who dwell down below
> in Tartarean homes, in the earth's bowels.

Indeed, it was Orphic belief that man was created from the ashes of the Titans whom Zeus burned with his thunderbolt for having torn to pieces and devoured his son Dionysos. The same belief, even more comprehensively, is mirrored in the *Homeric Hymn to Apollon* 3.334–36:

> Hear me now, Earth and broad Sky above,
> and you Titans from whom gods and men are descended
> and who dwell beneath the earth round great Tartaros.

It is Hera praying after having struck the ground with the palm of her hand. The angry goddess is not appealing to Zeus, the new sky-god, but to the old powers, his chthonic adversaries who were suppressed by him, and the broad sky of line 334 is obviously the old Ouranos. The Titans are in all likelihood the older earth-born gods who lost in the battle against Zeus and his brothers. We have here a literary record, obviously fashioned from surviving myths, of the inevitable conflict between the Indo-European sky-god and the old chthonic order of pre-Hellenic gods, which was subdued and assimilated by him.

The language of the poem, especially after line 676, is grand and bold, as befits the subject. The thunder-god spreads such conflagration on the battlefield that forests are consumed by fire as the sea heaves and seethes with unbearable heat. This is the battle to end all battles, a conflict that assumes elemental and cosmic proportions. In later art and literature, the theme gave birth to masterpieces that match the majesty of the Hesiodic account. Understandably, in later times the Titanomachy and the Gigantomachy became hardly distinguishable.

721–819. *The Realm of the Underworld:* The description of the underworld does begin with line 721, but, technically at least, this line concludes the preceding section. There is a temptation to look upon this section as a digression, especially because of the suspect character of certain of its lines on the ground that they constitute repetitions or inconsistencies (cf. 734–38 with 815–19, for example). Even though repetitions and inconsistencies are not altogether out of character in epic poetry, the prudent and well-argued rejection of lines 734–39 and 740–45 by M. L. West should be given serious consideration. The section appears as a digression because such a long excursus on the underworld comes as a disproportionately large and anticlimactic capstone to the magnificent Titanomachy. The Titanomachy is characterized by frenetic action and blazing conflagration. The underworld is a stagnant and murky wasteland. Although there is something to be said about the effect of the inevitable contrast, the excursus describing the underworld is appealing not for the contrast it introduces but because in both theogonic and cosmogonic terms the underworld is for Hesiod a necessary element of his three-tiered universe.

One enters the underworld by crossing the gates of marble and a threshold of bronze (811). The location of this gate is not specified. Then comes the gaping chasm (Chaos), which is sort of an infernal gullet leading to Tartaros. This chasm is surrounded by three layers of darkness, beyond which and above Tartaros lie the roots of earth and sea. The Titans and Typhoeus occupy the gloomy and dank Tartaros, but the dwellings of Hades and Styx, of Atlas and of the complementary pairs Night-Day and Sleep-Death, are vaguely placed somewhere in the dark underworld but not specifically within the confines of Tartaros, obviously

HESIOD

because "hell proper" had to be reserved for the crushed enemies of Zeus. The tripartite division of the universe is essentially shared by Homer despite *Iliad* 8.13–16, in which we are given four regions: Sky, Earth, Hades, and Tartaros, which lies as far below Hades as the Sky lies above the earth. Such a concept constitutes a violation of the tripartite and symmetrical universe, and it is entirely possible that it is due to an extension of the lower part of the universe by means of epic exaggeration. Whatever the nature of this elaboration, no postulation of a Homeric universe as opposed to a Hesiodic one is necessary. The details are unimportant and any attempt to construct a logical map of the underworld would be as foolish as trying to systematize and render concrete our own notions about the afterlife or the precise location of paradise and hell in Christian eschatology. Tartaros has survived in modern Greece in the neuter plural form *Tártara* and is vaguely imagined as the darkest place of the underworld, which is still referred to as Hades. The concept of the division of the world into upper (*apáno kósmos*) and lower (*káto kósmos*) is still a very strong and unquestioned belief in the Greek countryside. The modern Hades is the dark subterranean world to which one goes after death, and the geographic and "demographic" details that Hesiod gives have not survived. The division is abundantly evident in these lines from a folk song:

> There are three good things in this world,
>   the upper world:
> youth, and *levendiá*, and the beautiful girl.
>   (*levendiá*, "manly excellence, *aretê*")

Yet, the same people, whose belief in the existence of the upper world and netherworld is very deep, claim no knowledge of the netherworld and cheerfully shrug off the question by replying, "Who has come back to tell?" Once I put a group of old Greeks in the Epirotan village of Megalochari to what I thought was the acid test by suggesting that at least Jesus and Lazarus had come back, to which remark one of them replied that these are tall tales in which not even the priests themselves believe. Yet, the

belief that Hades is a dark realm of terror and suffering is universally shared:

> Tell us, Lazarus, what you saw in Hades?
> I saw fears and terrors, I saw torments and
>   pains.

These are the words of the song little Greek children chant as they go from house to house in Greek villages on Lazarus Saturday. Curiosity about what awaited one in the lower world gave rise to the motif of *Katábasis,* the descent to Hades, and such heroes as Odysseus, Herakles, Theseus, and Aeneas went through what is the ultimate rite of passage. Tragedy and comedy seized on the motif, but the attempt resulted in varying exercises in serious or comic hellish teratology and never in the illumination of a theme that is best left to apocalyptic vision rather than to scientific inquiry.

It is worth noting that in Hesiod's underworld there is no space for the souls of the dead. Hesiod's deliberate omission of any reference to this belief is of a piece with his rejection of the heroic world of Homer as well as of many very traditional and very old ideas which, he must have felt, conflicted with his own more progressive and reformist ideology. Along similar lines of thought, Hesiod suppressed any reference to the heroic code of honor, which must have been very much alive practically in the entire Hellenic world of his own day.

721–25. In *Iliad* 1.591–92, we are told that Hephaistos took one day to fall from the sky to the island of Lemnos. There is probably no numerical significance in the number 9. As a multiple of the universally important number 3, nine is a natural choice. The Muses are nine, Demeter wanders over the earth for nine days and nine nights, and modern Greeks take *kóllyba,* wheaten offerings to the dead, to church on the ninth day after a man's death (cf. also line 801, in which a god who has sworn a false oath by Styx becomes an outcast for nine years). Originally the number may have been an important calendar subdivision. Here the idea must be that if such a heavy object as an anvil takes nine

Theogony

days and nights to reach Tartaros, the place must indeed lie far below the earth.

726–39. The line "roots of the earth and of the barren sea" (728) must be more than a metaphor; probably underlying it is the belief in a world tree, a widespread motif best exemplified in the Western world through the Norse Yggdrasil, the mighty ash tree whose trunk is the center of the world. An eagle is perched on its topmost branch, and a great serpent lies at its third root. Belief in such a cosmic tree existed in Egyptian and Babylonian mythology as well, and the Christian *arbor vitae* or *arbor crucis* may represent a rarefied evolution of it. Nereus in *Orphic Hymn* 23 is addressed as possessor or guardian of the roots of the sea, but in the Kallimachean fragment 623 it is Poseidon who is addressed as "holder of the roots." In line 736, "the sources and the limits" seems, despite the wording, to return to the concept of roots (cf. 807–9).

740–45. Note the unexplained discrepancy between 740–43 and 722–25. The discrepancy has forced scholars to doubt the authenticity of these lines, and it is true that they seem much like an interpolation.

746–57. The idea in these lines seems to be that the house of Night is also the house of Day, and alternately both Night and Day have to descend into darkness. This alternation is also described in *Orphic Hymn* 3.10–11:

> you force light into the netherworld, and again
> you flee into Hades.

In *Iliad* 14.259, Night is called "tamer of the gods." Being the daughter of Chaos, she is of primeval origin. In the *Rhapsodic Theogony,* she is the daughter of Phanes, the creator, and assumes a power of supremacy that continues unchallenged through the reigns of Ouranos, Kronos, and Zeus.

759–66. On Death and Sleep, see notes on lines 211–12.

769–74. On Kerberos, see notes on 311.

775–806. There is a waterfall of awesome beauty at Nonacris in Arcadia; in ancient times it was called Styx. Since ancient times, many travelers have been impressed by its rugged beauty and some inevitably made the connection between Hesiod's Styx and the Arcadian one. It is possible that the Arcadian Styx influenced the notions about the mythical Styx, but the concept of a Styx, such as the one Hesiod describes here, must antedate familiarity with the Arcadian Styx; in origin, the myth must be independent of the Arcadian waterfall.

The details of the myth that concern divine perjury and consequent grave illness are not easy to explain. The water of the Styx is immortal (805–6) and so are gods. Therefore, when a god pours a libation of this water and then swears a false oath, he is severely punished by coming as close to death as an immortal can, because he has sworn by "immortality" itself. In other words, he is almost denied his immortality for swearing falsely by it and thereby dishonoring it. It seems to be the power of the water that makes the gods sick, for the water of the Styx is the water of life, and therefore the oath would be tantamount to swearing upon one's life.

The immortal water of the Styx has no doubt survived in the modern Greek belief in the *athánato neró* ("immortal water"), which plays a part in the eschatology of folk religion as the wondrous water that can procure immortality. It is guarded by a dragon or by Lamia, the grotesque woman of monstrous size, who brings the water out of a rock by striking it with a hammer. The beginning of a very traditional wedding song that I learned from my father goes as follows:

> Down by the laurel-river,
> where the many laurels and golden rose bushes grow,
> to the right and left stand best man and father-in-law,
> and they hew the marble to bring out the immortal water.

It is possible that the river Styx was part of an older, pre-Olympian cosmology, one in which it was the source of water and hence life in the upper world. We must not forget that the new, victorious Olympian dynasty cast the old-world order and its powers into the under-world. The Titans are a case in point. The oath that has to be taken by gods suspected of lying may thinly mask an ordeal whose ritualistic details antedate the establishment of the Olympian order.

Lines 720–819 of the *Theogony* offer us the most complete and most systematic description of the underworld in all of archaic Greek litera-ture. Readers of Homer will recall how a man's soul (*psyche*), which is a material entity—though sometimes a mere image of the person—leaves the body and journeys to the underworld to remain there forever. The underworld Hesiod presents to us in the *Theogony* is vast. Yet, the poet has no space for souls anywhere in it. The omission is not accidental. Hesiod accounts neither for the creation of man nor for what might follow after death. The Homeric concept of the soul did not fit Hesiod's highly formal-ized and materially organized concept of the world (*kosmos*).

820–80. *The Defeat of Typhoeus:* Scholars who chal-lenge the authenticity of this piece of the *Theog-ony* have, on the whole, come up with a variety of not very convincing arguments, including the condemnation of the episode on the ground that it is a doublet of the Titanomachy. The na-ture and scale of the battle are such in both cases that stylistic similarities are inevitable. One may argue that once the Titans have been defeated, Zeus should remain unchallenged. Such a view would make the Typhoeus episode a somewhat jejune repetition of the same theme. Repetitions do exist in epic poetry, but this is not one of them, because Typhoeus is not the double of a Titan, but the primordial serpent, which must be defeated before evil and anarchy can be brought into subordination.

Near Eastern analogues such as the Hurrian Ullikummi and the progeny of Tiâmat in the *Enûma Eliš,* have been adduced more or less as proof of Near Eastern connections. Although such connections are possible, the presumed analogues are by no means clear enough to be convincing. The motif is widespread, so wide-spread that even the biblical serpent and the

dragon slain by St. George surely have some connection with Typhoeus. Even in the Greek tradition, there are important variants of the birth and fate of Typhoeus. In what must be the most important of them in the *Homeric Hymn to Apollon* 3.305–55, we are told that in anger at the birth of Athena, who stood in such con-trast to her own lame son, Hephaistos, Hera prayed to Earth, Sky, and the Titans for another child. Without having mated with Zeus, when the due time passed she gave birth to Typhoeus, a creature that was more like a hideous mon-ster. Hera did not keep the child, but she gave it to the serpent Pytho to rear. There is no mention here of a battle against Zeus, since the poet of the hymn was more anxious, and for good reason, to tell of what happened to Pytho. One very important element of this story is that Typhoeus is not a child of Zeus and that his birth is the work of those gods who had to be put aside or subordinated for Zeus to come to power.

A more convincing counterpart for Ty-phoeus is to be sought in Norse mythology. The great serpent or World Serpent of Norse mythology lies at the root of the World Tree, Yggdrasil. Scores of snakes gnaw at the Ygg-drasil, and its chief adversary is an eagle perched on the topmost branch of the tree. The serpent's father is the mischievous god Loki, who also fathered the wolf Fenrir and Hel, the ruler of the land of the dead. Thor encountered the serpent on a fishing trip dur-ing which he sank an ox head as bait into the sea. The serpent was caught by this bait, but his fishing companion, the giant Hymir, an-gered because the bait was the head of his big-gest ox, cut the line just as Thor raised his hammer to kill the serpent. In the final en-counter between gods and monsters, Thor slays the serpent, but he himself succumbs to its venom. Thor may not be, as Snorri main-tains, a grandson of Priam, but his hammer—the fabulous and dreaded *Mjöllnir,* which is an analogue of Zeus's thunderbolt—and his general character very much bespeak the Norse Zeus. It will also be remembered that the serpent's adversary, the eagle, is in the Greek tradition the symbol of Zeus's power. The Norse tradition offers us many more analogues than any other one. Thor, much like Zeus, slays the serpent in a terrible battle, and this is the kernel of the myth. His own death as well as the death of the other gods in the apocalyptic *Ragnarök* is an element that, if original, either represents an extension of a death and rebirth cycle, or, if not original, is to be attributed to Christian influence. This latter possibility is the less likely one.

With the defeat of Typhoeus, Zeus rises supreme, and his power is not to be challenged again. The last of Gaia's children, the ultimate hope of the monstrous chthonic order, is banished forever into the gloom of Tartaros. Even if his progeny, the furious and destructive winds, suggest that in origin Typhoeus was a wind spirit, this is of little account for Hesiod, who sees him as the last enemy of the Olympian gods.

Readers with a special interest in menacing monsters that threaten humanity and even world order may wish to familiarize themselves with the several versions of St. George and the Dragon, as well as with portions of the medieval Greek epic romance *Digenes Akritas*, which seems to date back to the eighth century. Chapters 12 and 13 and lines 20.1–3 of John's Revelation are hauntingly relevant to the nightmares of humankind.

885. For the apportionment of power among the Olympians, see *Iliad* 15.187–93.

886–900. In these lines, we have a repetition of the Kronos motif. By swallowing Metis (Resourcefulness, Wisdom), Zeus assimilates her and at the same time prevents the birth of a son, who would surpass and succeed him. This son is never born, and when the daughter is born she is born from his own head (924). Thus, Zeus makes sure that Metis is only his, that she will mate with no one else. Tritogeneia (895) is another name by which Athena was invoked. The origin of the word is unknown, but Hesiod surely takes it to mean "Born for Three," that is, for her mother Metis, her mighty brother, and herself. Although the motif itself is something

that Hesiod inherited, the particular form that he gives it here is shaped by folk-etymological concepts, such as influenced his account of the birth of Aphrodite. Since, by implication, none of the other wives of Zeus is like Metis, the danger of begetting a son more resourceful than himself is permanently eliminated.

In the not too distant past, some prominent scholars supported the view that Athena's origin goes back to the so-called snake-goddesses of the pre-Hellenic Minoan civilization. However, it seems far more reasonable to connect both the name *Tritogeneia* and the main attributes of Athena with the tripartite division of Indo-European societies into priests, warriors, and shepherds/workers. It is worth mentioning here that, once the Christian faith ousted the ancient gods from the Hellenic world, the Virgin Mary took several of Athena's functions and was and is frequently hailed as invincible *strategos,* leader of armies, protectress of cities, bringer of victory, unwed maiden. Clearly, these warlike ideas and titles were simply transferred to the Virgin Mary and put in the service of Byzantine political and military ideology.

901–11. Themis is a Titaness and a daughter of Gaia and Ouranos (135). Her name means "established custom" and is derived from the word *tithêmi,* "to set down," "to establish." She is doubtless an earth-goddess akin to Gaia (see Aeschylus's *Prometheus Bound* 209–25), and her name may have been conflated with that of one of the numerous indigenous goddesses the Indo-European sky-god married. Yet, it is more probable that Hesiod dwelt more on the meaning "established custom, law" and that this was his way of saying that Zeus now proceeded to establish his rule, to lay down the law as it were, and to beget offspring for a pantheon of his own, free from the upheavals that threatened the new order. In *Orphic Hymn* 79, Themis is a manic prophetess, a sort of primeval Pythia who taught Apollon the art of giving laws. In Aeschylus's *Eumenides* 1–7, Gaia is the first prophetess at Delphi, and Themis is her daughter who succeeds her. The revered position of Themis as a prophetess is also evident from Pindar's *Isthmian Ode* 8.34ff.

The names of the Seasons reveal the character of this new order, which will be marked by lawfulness, justice, and peace. In it, the Fates will ensure cyclical and regular inevitability. The Graces, too, are born of a goddess who stands for law and order—Eurynome means "she of the Wide Law"—and their names, Splendor, Joy, and Festivity, clearly suggest the blessings that lawful peace guarantees.

912–29. Lines 915–17 do not fit well into this passage, which is an account of the birth of the major Olympian divinities. The birth of Eileithyia (923) also comes as a surprise. Eileithyia is the goddess of childbirth and very much a secondary figure. In popular cult, she was sometimes confused with Artemis (see *Orphic Hymn* 2). The birth of Athena from the head of Zeus belongs to an old primitive belief that holds the head as the seat of procreative power. Etiologically, it accounts for her nature, since, despite her warlike character, she is after all the goddess of wisdom. Zeus can afford to allow such a birth to take place. Athena is mighty and wise, but she is a daughter and as such no threat in Zeus's patriarchal household.

930–33. Amphitrite is one of the Nereids (243). Triton seems to be a pre-Hellenic marine god whose importance gradually declined. Eventually, Tritons became decorative mermen portrayed with Nereids riding on their backs (*Orphic Hymn* 24).

935–36. We encounter this pair in several places in the *Iliad* (4.440, 11.37, 15.119; cf. also the *Shield* 195–200).

937. Harmonia is the daughter of Ares and Aphrodite. When Harmonia married Kadmos, she was given the celebrated necklace by Hephaistos, the necklace that figures prominently in the Theban saga.

938–39. For the birth of Hermes, see *Homeric Hymn* 4.1–16. The name *Maia* probably means "mother," "nurse."

940–42. Semele, deceived by Zeus's jealous wife Hera, asked her divine lover to appear in his full splendor. When he did so, she was consumed by the fire of his thunderbolt (Euripides *Bacchae* 6–9; Ovid *Metamorphoses* 3.259–341). The god of line 942 is Dionysos.

943–44. Alkmene was visited by Zeus while her husband, Amphitryon, was away on an expedition to punish the Taphians and the Teleboans for having slain Alkmene's brothers (see *Shield* 1–56).

947–49. Dionysos found Ariadne on the island of Naxos, where Theseus had left her. She had given Theseus the legendary thread that helped him find his way out of the labyrinth after having slain the Minotaur.

950–55. Since deification of Herakles belongs to the late stage of Greek mythopoesis (cf. *Iliad* 18.117–19), it is certain that these lines represent a later accretion to the Hesiodic *Theogony*.

956–62. The same genealogy for Kirke and Aietes is given in *Odyssey* 10.137–39. Idyia is one of the Okeanids in 352. Medeia became Jason's wife and in Euripides's powerful play named for her played a very important role, chiefly as a potent witch.

969–74. Demeter's union with Iasion is also related in *Odyssey* 5.125–28, in which we are told that Zeus smote Iasion with his thunderbolt. Both the Homeric and the Hesiodic passages contain a precious reference to the primitive practice of ritualistic copulation on a plowed field, a practice of sympathetic magic intended to ensure the fecundation and fertility of the earth. Such ritualistic copulation has been recorded by scholars of modern Greek folklore in Thrace and Macedonia. The child of Demeter's union with Iasion is naturally Ploutos, "Wealth." The resemblance of the name *Ploutos* to *Plouton,* one of the names by which Hades is known, cannot be accidental. Plouton is lord of the dead, but as Persephone's husband he has serious claims to the powers of fertility.

976. Agaue becomes the mother of the ill-fated King Pentheus. He is struck with madness for failing to receive Dionysos at Thebes and is eventually torn to pieces by his frenzied mother and her sisters (Euripides *Bacchae* 1043–152).

979–83. See notes on 287–94.

984–92. For Eos and her lovers, see notes on 371–74. Memnon is king of the Ethiopians and comes to Troy as an ally of his uncle, Priam. Emathion was slain by Herakles in his search for the golden apples. Apollodoros makes

Kephalos son of Hermes and Herse and, as here, lover of Eos but, unlike here, father of Tithonos and grandfather of Phaethon (Apollodoros 3.181). Phaethon is usually said to be son of Helios, not of Eos.

993–1002. These are highlights of the saga of the Argonauts, which is the subject of the long epic *Argonautika* by Apollonios Rhodios. It was King Pelias who dispatched Jason and his companions on the *Argo* to fetch him the golden fleece. Medios is tacitly understood here as being the eponymous hero of the Medes. Cheiron, the wise old centaur who was so well versed in medicine (*Iliad* 4.219), was also the teacher of Jason and Achilleus.

1005–20. Aiakos is father of Peleus and grandfather of Achilleus. In *Iliad* 21.188–89, Achilleus boasts only of the patrilineal side of his ancestry, which, through his father Peleus and his grandfather Aiakos, takes his line back to Zeus. His mother, Thetis, is one of the many daughters of Nereus. Both names seem to be of Illyrian origin. For Nereus, see notes on 233–64. Thetis, and perhaps also Tethys, wife of Okeanos, are names of Illyrian origin (of Albanian *tete*, "maternal aunt"). The details on such important loan words and the creation by the Illyrians of a rudimentary maritime theology are hidden in the murk of prehistory. Phokos is the eponymous ancestor of the Phokians. The love affair between Aphrodite and Anchises is the subject of the lovely *Homeric Hymn* 5. Aineias is mentioned by name in line 198 of the hymn, and the poet dwells on his birth in lines 255–90. The seduction of Odysseus by Kirke is related in the tenth book of the *Odyssey* (especially lines 325–47). There is no mention in the *Odyssey* of the three sons of Odysseus and Kirke. In Vergil's *Aeneid,* Latinus is appropriately enough king of Latium. Since there is a connection between Latium and Latinos, the question is with what place or tribe is Agrios to be linked.

The adventures of Telegonos were related in the lost *Telegonia* of Eugammon of Kyrene. It is clear from lines 1015–16 that the author places the Etruscans (Tyrsenians) somewhere off the coast of northwestern Greece. He is altogether ignorant of the existence of the Italian peninsula. The reader should not be misled by the phrase "sacred islands" into mistaking these islands for the Isles of the Blest.

For another use of the same phrase, cf. *Iliad* 2.625–26 and remember that, among other places, Ilios (city of Troy) is called "sacred." For the love affair between Odysseus and Kalypso, see *Odyssey* 1.45ff. and 5.1ff. In the *Odyssey,* Nausithoos is the first king of the Phaeacians and a son of Poseidon and Periboia (7.55–68). The poet here cannot possibly intend this Nausithoos to be connected with the Phaeacians. In terms of the *Odyssey,* such a connection would be inexcusable.

1021–22. The poem really ends with line 1020, and lines 1021–22 (almost identical with 965–66) in all likelihood were to mark the end of the *Theogony* and the beginning of the *Catalogue.* A careful reading of the poem shows that after the Typhoeus episode, which ends with line 880, it is difficult to tell where the original Hesiodic *Theogony* ended. The rambling character of the lines that follow and their extremely loose connection with the main body of the poem make it quite certain that we are dealing with interpolations and accretions. It is obvious, of course, that Hesiod could hardly have ended his ambitious creation with an excursus on the relatively unimportant progeny of Typhoeus (869–80), and it is equally obvious that nothing of what we now have between lines 869–1022 can be patched together to serve as the end of the *Theogony.* But if the poem is truncated, it is not truncated by much, and this ought to be the source of some consolation to us.

The *Works and Days*

The *Works and Days* is a fairly long didactic poem composed in dactylic hexameter, the meter of the Homeric epics. However, its subject matter is such that to call it an epic is to apply to it a misnomer that may force upon the poem wholly inappropriate standards for gauging its merits. It should also be said that putting into verse material that hardly lends itself to poetry was dictated by the absence of an alternative. Greek prose had not been developed yet, and, besides, verse could be committed to memory much more easily. Therefore, it would be wrong to charge Hesiod with ineptitude even if long stretches of the *Works and Days* fail to reward the reader with that quintessential elation that is expected of good poetry.

When contemplating a literary composition of the antiquity of the *Works and Days,* one is confronted with the baffling problem of sources. The only thing that can be said with some certainty is that what Hesiod himself did not invent must have come to him from other oral poets and from the traditional wisdom lore of his native Boeotia. With the exception of the myth of the five ages, analogues from Near Eastern literature are at best instructive and furnish no secure evidence for direct borrowing. Even where similarities exist, they are by no means proof of borrowing. I find striking similarities between the *Hávamál*, a poem of the Poetic Edda, and portions of the *Works and Days.* Yet, the poet or poets of the *Hávamál* owe nothing to Hesiod. In this case, however, a cautious attribution of similarities to inherited Indo-European elements is, at least prima facie, justified.

Other didactic poems, such as the *Great Works,* the *Precepts of Cheiron,* and the *Astronomy,* were attributed to Hesiod. We know too little about these works to decide whether they were Hesiodic. Chances are that they were no more Hesiodic than the Homeric Hymns are Homeric. We can be sure that, much like Homer, as a composer of didactic poems Hesiod stands at the apex and not at the beginning of the development of this genre. Of those who followed after him, Phocylides and, to a greater extent, Theognis deserve mention, but they were concerned only with morals and not with practical matters. The combination of practical and moral aspects of human life on a rather ambitious, if not comprehensive, scale makes the *Works and Days* a sort of prototype without a successful rival in Greek literature.

We know very little about conditions in eighth- and seventh-century BC Boeotia. It seems that Hesiod's compatriots at this time were mostly farmers ruled by a wealthy class of landed nobility, the so-called kings. Trade was practiced on a modest scale, but craftsmen, such as the potter or the blacksmith, probably did not do more than supply local needs. I think we can safely assume that class struggle and social injustice of the kind that later led to the Solonian reforms in Attica were no strangers to Hesiod. Yet Hesiod is in no sense a political revolutionary. He is not against "kings" but against kings who "devour" gifts.

With his *Theogony* Hesiod set out to instruct his fellow Greeks on how the world and the gods came to be and on how Zeus established the supremacy of his rule. Although this constitutes a departure from the main concern of the singer of heroic epic, men's glorious deeds, the theme of the *Theogony* is so grand and the clashes that it portrays so kindred in language and spirit to the Homeric epic that one has the feeling that Hesiod deliberately keeps close to that elevated tenor that is so characteristic of heroic epic. But in the *Works and Days*, the break with the values of the heroic epic is complete. This is a manual of instruction in verse, which addresses itself principally to the tiller of the soil.

Hesiod had an indolent and wayward brother, Perses, who, after the division of the patrimony, tried to take more than his fair share by suborning the local kings, who had juridical power over the matter. Hesiod does not give us details about the dispute and its outcome because they are not relevant to his purpose. We also have no such thing in the poem as a character drawing of Perses. He remains a shadowy figure. Many scholars have dismissed him as a mere literary convention. Nothing in the poem forces this assumption on us. Yet, it is one thing to say that Perses did not exist and quite another to maintain that he did not become part of a literary device. We can easily believe in the existence of a greedy Perses and in the reality of a quarrel between the two brothers without having to believe that the *Works and Days* was written solely for the benefit of Perses. Even if Hesiod once wrote admonitory verses to his brother, the poem as we have it is addressed not only to the Boeotian farmer but to all men who care to improve their lot through righteousness and industry. Hesiod's name as well as his brother's name may be fictional. The purpose of assuming fictional names is not to seek and find anonymity but, rather, to build a special reputation. Hesiod was the son of an immigrant from Asia Minor. He does not mention his mother anywhere. It is quite possible that she married Hesiod's father because she was not such a desirable bride among her own local community. It was then through marriage that Hesiod's father acquired land in Askre. It does not seem that Hesiod is married. Everything about his brother, Perses, points to the life of a bachelor in search of opportunities for good times. Nothing is said about the possibility of an extended family.

For Hesiod, the wretchedness of the human predicament is the result of the gradual deterioration of moral values. This is illustrated by the myth of the five ages. The contrast between the men of the age of gold and the men of the iron age is startling. We are not told why the men of the golden age perished, but violence was what destroyed all the other successive races. The iron age, Hesiod's own, is the worst of all and it, too, will come to an end. It is an age of injustice and shameless violation of all moral standards. It is also an age of want and harsh toil. But the presence of suffering among men is not altogether of their own making. Men have been punished by Zeus for the deviousness of Prometheus, who cheated Zeus at a famous sacrifice, and also stole fire from the Sky and gave it to man. The punishment was twofold: the means to livelihood were "hidden," and woman was created as the bearer of all the evils that she eventually unleashed on man. Hesiod does not try to place this punishment chronologically within his scheme of five ages, but it seems that it took place after the golden age. In attempting to explain the origin of man's plight and moral decadence, Hesiod set before himself a difficult problem to which he did not give an entirely satisfactory explanation. As has already been mentioned, we are not told why the golden race came to an end. Once violence and injustice became part of human life, deterioration followed its inevitable course. But for all his lack of belief in the basic goodness of man, Hesiod cannot bring himself to accept that the evils that beset man existed from the very beginning:

> Earlier, human tribes lived on this earth
> without suffering and toilsome hardship
> and without painful illnesses that bring death to men—
>
> (91–93)

Hesiod accepts the new and inferior lot of man as the reality with which man must contend. There is no hint at a possibility of return to a condition free of suffering and toil. If Hesiod thought that man could in no way improve himself and his lot, the message of the *Works and Days* would be pointless. He must then consider improvement possible but certainly subject to the limits imposed by the two punitive actions of Zeus. This is perhaps what lies behind the allegory that has Hope imprisoned within Pandora's jar.

The first virtue Perses, and therefore every man, must be taught is justice. In his long sermon on the subject (213–85), Hesiod presents justice as a sine qua non for peace and prosperity and looks upon it as a moral force of a higher

Works and Days

order. This is why justice personified is the daughter of Zeus and why wrong-doers bring the wrath of Zeus upon themselves. By making justice into a personified abstraction of divine origin, Hesiod elevated it above the body of established customs that have the force of law. Here then we have for the first time an attempt to distinguish between concrete manifestations of justice and justice itself. Hesiod is not concerned with the effects of disobedience to justice only on the individual but also on the city; that is, on civilized society. Justice is, above all, a civic virtue and the shibboleth by which a civilized man is distinguished from a savage or a wild beast:

> This is the law Zeus laid down for men,
> but fish and wild beasts and winged birds
> know not of justice and so eat one another.
>
> (276–78)

The second cardinal virtue is work. Before coming to the practical aspects of farm work, Hesiod embarks on a second sermon, this time on the value of honest labor. This section of the poem (298–382) is replete with proverbial wisdom and ethical maxims that are aimed at teaching prudent and decent conduct with regard to both management of resources and conduct toward relatives, friends, neighbors, and people in general. The poet begins and ends the section with an impassioned exhortation for work. If the unjust are faced with the anger of Zeus, the indolent have an equally dread prospect, hunger. But a man must avoid hunger not through deception and robbery but through the sweat of his own brow: "not stolen wealth, god-given is much better" (320). Poverty is neither glorified nor considered conducive to moral improvement. A man must strive to attain wealth, "because glory and excellence follow riches" (313).

After Hesiod has preached on the moral and practical value of work, he comes to the main body of the poem, the long section (383–617) on the proper way for the performance of major agricultural tasks. A farmer must know when to plow, to sow, to prune and hoe his vines, to reap, and to thresh. He also must know how to make a plow and a wagon, and how to choose his team of oxen. The advice he gives is sketchy and not adequate for someone who has no skill and no experience. He tells the farmer what sort of lumber to choose for each part of the plow, but not how to fit the pieces together. If one wants to make a wagon, he may profit from the information Hesiod gives, but he certainly cannot make the wagon if he does not already know how to make one. There is far more emphasis on doing things at the right time, chiefly through the observation of the rising and setting of certain stars and the return of migratory birds. Even this section—the most technical in the poem—is interspersed with moral exhortations. Hesiod cannot have

HESIOD

been unaware of the dryness of the subject matter, for it is here that, more than anywhere else, he cleverly deploys quaint turns of expression, playfully enigmatic names for animals, and other whimsical stylistic devices to counterbalance the inherently prosaic nature of his topic. It is also here that he deploys, almost like tactical weapons, what he, too, must have considered the two most forceful passages of the poem: the long description of the grimness of winter and the delightful lines on how to find refreshment in the scorching summer heat.

Lines 618–93 constitute a lengthy excursus on sailing. Again, Hesiod tells us much about the right time for sailing and very little about sailing itself. He talks about the size of the cargo and the perils of the sea, and he knows of the significance of the Etesian winds, but he is all too self-conscious about his meager knowledge of ships and the sea:

> This is all I know about well-riveted ships
> but even so I can speak the mind of aegis-bearing Zeus,
> for the Muses taught me to sing and never weary.
>
> (660–62)

But if Hesiod knows so little about navigation, why does he venture into the subject at all? He may have wished to give some useful information to farmers who became sea traders for a brief part of the year. He may have also wished to pay tribute to his father by recording for the benefit of others some rudiments on sailing he had learned from him. Be that as it may, the most remarkable feature of this portion of the poem is the precious autobiographical information: how and why his father came to Askre and how he himself crossed over to Chalkis to become the victor at a poetic contest. If all else had perished and only these autobiographical lines had survived, we would have enough material to declare Hesiod the first known exponent of the surge of individualism in the Greek world.

Thus far Hesiod has dwelt on the subject of the right time of the year for the undertaking of various types of work. What of the right days of the month? He now comes to that, but not before he devotes lines 695–759 to more practical, moral, and religious matters. This section is as coherent as the diversity of the subject matter allows. It is a mixture of savoir vivre and savoir faire given with an eye not to gentility but to survival in a world where poverty and injustice, on the one hand, and the displeasure of numinous powers and gods, on the other, threaten man's existence. In this part of the poem, even when Hesiod is dealing with arcane religious prescripts, we are not altogether at a loss for explanations that make some sort of sense. However, in the final section of the poem (765–828), which is devoted to a catalogue of days favorable or unfavorable for certain tasks and events, it seems that reason and religious sentiment yield to pure superstition. In the notes to this section of the poem, I have suggested that there is some evidence that originally there may have been a more or less obvious connection between religious beliefs and taboos associated with a particular day. Indeed, lines 771 and 802–3 offer some evidence to that effect. But all that has been said about how untypically "irrational" for Hesiod the conclusion of the *Works and Days* is fails to take into account that such inconsistency as he is charged with is common even in our days. One of the tasks of a didactic poet in Hesiod's days was to record for posterity not simply what he believed in but also the accumulated wisdom of his race.

The *Works and Days* is the first work in Greek literature that offers us a glimpse into the life of the common people, and especially of the farmers. Admittedly, it depicts conditions as they were in Boeotia of the late eighth century, but we can be fairly sure that the situation was not very different in other parts of mainland Greece. Life was hard—a perennial struggle with the earth for survival—and it left little room for the pursuit of anything that was less than useful or practical. The small farmer had to protect himself against the whim of the elements and the greed of privileged aristocracy. More interestingly, the poem gives us a wealth of information on the religious, social, and moral beliefs of the common man. Since the poet sets out to teach not only his brother but humanity as well justice and propriety, there is much the reader learns about the inception of certain fundamental concepts of justice, both legal and ethical.

It is obvious that the *Works and Days* can be rather easily divided into sections. It is also obvious that by its very nature it must have invited interpolation. Yet, I feel that there is an underlying unity to the poem, a unity Hesiod secures not only by his well-placed references to his brother, Perses, but much more by his all-pervasive fervor to instruct humanity on justice and work. Close scrutiny of the poem shows that Hesiod moves with calculated leisure and that his digressions never lead him too far from his goal.

Whether we want it or not, the shadow of Homer is cast over Hesiod. There is such magic attached to the Homeric epics that poetry written in the same language and meter cannot escape comparison. But the difference between the *Works and Days* and the Homeric epics is such that comparison is hardly appropriate. Homer's subject is man in his pride. In the *Works and Days*, Hesiod proposes to make the life of the humble farmer his theme. Thus, quite naturally, Homeric splendor and grandness give way to the stark realities of the workaday experience of the Boeotian peasant. Therefore, we cannot expect the *Works and Days* to be even like the *Theogony*, much less like the Homeric epics. Where Hesiod gives his fancy free rein, as in the description of winter and summer, he becomes a poet of great power. The rest of the time, he instructs in the only medium he knows, verse. The *Works and Days* may not be a great poem, but it is an invaluable document and a moving testimony to the moral ardor of a great teacher and civilizer.

Although in his account of generations Hesiod includes the heroes, he says nothing about heroic poetry. He also says nothing about Homer. This is in keeping with a tradition to which we are not privy. The scale of religious activities recommended by Hesiod is moderate. People are told to eat modest portions of choice meat. Nowhere do we have mention of a hecatomb. There is nothing in Hesiod like the festive activities we find in Book 4 of the *Odyssey*. Conspicuously absent from the *Works and Days* is also the celebration of athletic games. Perhaps Hesiod wants to emphasize the difference between aristocracy and the common people. This may go hand in hand with his aversion to the "gift-devouring" kings. Hesiod mentions his participation in the funeral games in honor of Amphidamas in Chalkis; however, we do not know whether these games included athletic contests.

Hesiod recommends a sensible life of thrift. Resources must be well managed. If a man does not know what he should do, he should ask for advice. He should also be careful about what he says. Hesiod connects religious activity with observation of certain types of ritual. He does not recommend investing anyone with any kind of metaphysical power. Of course, this is true of the relationship of man and god in the Homeric epics. This attitude is far more pronounced in the *Works and Days*. Hesiod's approach to a sensible life is founded on common sense, on a calculated sociology. It lends itself to instruction by example:

> What should a man do to cope with summer heat?
> What should a man do to survive the severity of the Boeotian winter?
> When should a man marry? Whom should he marry?
> How many children should a man have?
> Which one of his children should he choose to live with when old age
>   comes to him?

The above questions are calculated to teach a man to take sensible action when it is necessary. The answer is not always obvious. It is not obvious that a man should choose to live with his youngest son. Yet, it is the youngest son who has the authority to protect his father's patriarchal standing within the family. In turn, the father is in a position to bequeath his share of the property to his youngest son.

On the whole, Hesiod gives advice to farmers who cultivate the land to exact a living from the grain it gives. We do not know much about the lives of wealthy people. What was the system of giving names to members of a family, and when was this done? Everything in the *Works and Days* is small-scale. There are no big flocks of sheep and goats. Boeotia means "ox country." Euboea, the large island across the straits of Euripos, also means "land good for oxen." These names go back to a time when wealth was counted in oxen. During the Dark Ages, which followed the eleventh century BC, economic realities changed and both places suffered great economic losses. Boeotia had an economy which was similar to that of the villages of modern Greece. Until the arrival of the tractor, ploughing in modern-day Askre was done by oxen. However, times have changed. Ploughs and looms have disappeared. Flocks of sheep and goats are small. Harvesting grapes and making wine have survived because there is a market for good wine.

WORKS AND DAYS

Muses of Pieria, your songs bring glory.
Come! Let us sing the praises of your father,
great Zeus, through whose will men
are exalted by the speech of others or remain unknown.
5   With ease he grants power, with ease he crushes the mighty,
and with ease he lowers the noble and raises the lowly.
Yes, Zeus who thunders from his lofty dwelling
with ease straightens the crooked and shrivels the insolent.
Hear and see, O Zeus! Let your decrees be straight and fair!
10   I will speak to Perses the naked truth:
there was never one kind of Strife. Indeed on this earth
two kinds exist. The one is praised by her friends,
the other found blameworthy. These two are not of one mind.
The one—so harsh—fosters evil war and the fray of battle.
15   No man loves this oppressive Strife, but compulsion
and divine will grant her a share of honor.
The other one is black Night's elder daughter;
the son of Kronos, who dwells on ethereal heights,
planted her in the roots of the earth and among men.
20   She is much better, she stirs even the shiftless on to work.
A man will long for work when he sees a man of wealth
who rushes with zeal to plow and plant
and husband his homestead. One neighbor envies another
who hastens to his riches. This Strife is good for mortals.
25   Potters eye one another's success and craftsmen, too;
the beggar's envy is a beggar, the singer's a singer.
Perses, treasure this thought deep down in your heart,
and do not let malicious Strife curb your zeal for work
so you can see and hear the brawls of the marketplace.

65

30   Not much can be spared for gatherings and brawls
      by the man in whose house the season's plentiful harvest,
      Demeter's grain, fruit of the earth, has not been stored.
      Have plenty of this and then incite brawls and strife
      over another man's possessions. Lose no time! Seize
35   your only chance to let straight justice
      —Zeus's fairest—settle this quarrel.
      Our inheritance was divided, but there is so much
      you grabbed and carried away as a fat bribe
      for gift-devouring kings, fools who want to be judges
40   in this trial; they know neither how the half is greater
      than the whole, nor how asphodel and mallow nurture.
      The gods keep livelihood hidden from men.
      Otherwise, a day's labor could bring a man enough
      to last a whole year with no more work.
45   Then you could hang your oar over the smoke of your fireplace
      without a thought for the work of oxen and hardy mules.
      But Zeus was angered in his heart and hid the means to life
      because Prometheus with his crooked schemes had cheated him.
      This is why Zeus devised sorrows and troubles for men.
50   He hid fire, but Prometheus, noble son of Iapetos,
      stole it back for man's sake from Zeus, whose counsels are many.
      In the hollow of a fennel stalk he slipped it away,
      unnoticed by Zeus, who delights in thunder.
      So the cloud-gatherer in anger said to him:
55   "Son of Iapetos, craftiest of all,
      it pleases you to trick my wits and steal the fire
      which will be a curse to you and to the generations that follow.
      The price for the stolen fire will be a gift of evil
      to charm the hearts of all men as they hug their own doom."
60   This said, the father of gods and men roared with laughter.
      Then he ordered widely acclaimed Hephaistos to mix earth with water
      in all haste and place in them human voice
      and strength. His orders were to make a face
      such as goddesses have and the shape of a lovely maiden;
65   Athena was to teach her skills and intricate weaving,
      and golden Aphrodite should pour grace over her head,
      and stinging desire and limb-gnawing passion.
      Then he ordered Hermes the pathbreaker and slayer of Argos
      to put in her the mind of a bitch and the habits of a thief.

70   So he spoke, and they obeyed lord Zeus, son of Kronos.
Without delay the renowned lame god fashioned from earth,
through Zeus's will, the likeness of a shy maiden,
and Athena, the gray-eyed goddess, clothed her and decked her out.
Then the divine Graces and queenly Persuasion
75   gave her golden necklaces to wear, and the lovely-haired Seasons
stood round her and crowned her with spring flowers.
Pallas Athena adorned her body with every kind of jewel,
and the slayer of Argos—Hermes the guide—through the will
of Zeus whose thunder roars placed in her breast
80   lies, coaxing words, and the habits of a thief.
The gods' herald then gave her voice and called this woman
Pandora because all the gods who dwell on Olympos
gave her as a gift—a scourge for toiling men.
Now when the Father finished his grand and wily scheme
85   he sent the glorious slayer of Argos and swift messenger
to bring the gift of the gods to Epimetheus,
who did not heed Prometheus's warning never to accept
a gift from Olympian Zeus, but send it back,
for fear that some evil might befall mortals.
90   First he accepted it and then saw the evil in it.
Earlier, human tribes lived on this earth
without suffering and toilsome hardship
and without painful illnesses that bring death to men—
a wretched life ages men before their time—
95   but the woman with her hands removed the great lid of the jar
and scattered its contents, bringing grief and cares to men.
Only Hope stayed under the rim of the jar
and did not fly away from her secure stronghold,
for in compliance with the wishes of cloud-gathering Zeus
100   Pandora put the lid on the jar before hope could come out.
The rest wander among men as numberless sorrows,
since earth and sea teem with miseries.
Some diseases come upon men during the day, and some
roam about in silence and bring pains to men
105   because Zeus the counselor took speech away from them.
So there is no way to escape the designs of Zeus.
I will give you the pith of another story—if you wish—
with consummate skill. Treasure this thought in your heart:
men and gods have a common descent.

110   When Kronos was king of the sky
       the immortals created a golden race of mortal men.
       They lived like gods, carefree in their hearts,
       shielded from pain and misery. Helpless old age
115   did not exist, and with limbs of unsagging vigor
       they enjoyed the delights of feasts, out of evil's reach.
       A sleeplike death subdued them, and every good thing was theirs;
       the barley-giving earth asked for no toil to bring forth
       a rich and plentiful harvest. They knew no constraint
120   and lived in peace and abundance as lords of their lands,
       rich in flocks and dear to the blessed gods.
       But the earth covered this race,
       and they became godlike spirits that haunt it,
       benign protectors of mortals that drive harm away
125   and keep a watchful eye over lawsuits and wicked deeds,
       swathed in misty veils as they wander over the earth.
       They are givers of wealth by kingly prerogative.
       The gods of Olympos made a second race—
       an inferior one—this time of silver,
130   unlike the golden one in thought or looks.
       For a hundred years they were nurtured by their prudent mothers
       as playful children—each a big baby in his house—
       but when they grew up and reached adolescence
       they lived only for a short while, plagued by the pains
135   of foolishness. They could not refrain from reckless violence
       against one another and did not want to worship the gods
       and on holy altars perform sacrifices for them,
       as custom differing from place to place dictates.
       In time Zeus, son of Kronos, was angered and buried them
140   because they denied the blessed Olympians their due honors.
       The earth covered this race, too;
       they dwell under the ground and are called blessed mortals—
       they are second but, still, greatly honored.
       Zeus the father made a third race of mortals,
145   this time of bronze, not at all like the silver one.
       Fashioned from ash trees, they were dreadful and mighty
       and bent on the harsh deeds of war and violence;
       they ate no bread and their hearts were tough as steel.
       No one could come near them, for their strength was great

150 and mighty arms grew from the shoulders of their sturdy bodies.
Bronze were their weapons, bronze their homes,
and bronze was what they worked—there was no black iron then.
With their hands they worked one another's destruction
and they reached the dank home of cold Hades

155 nameless. Black death claimed them for all their fierceness,
and they left the bright sunlight behind them.
But when the earth covered this race, too,
Zeus, son of Kronos, made upon the nourishing land
yet another race—the fourth one—better and more just.

160 They were the divine race of heroes, who are called
demigods; they preceded us on this boundless earth.
Evil war and dreadful battle wiped them all out,
some fighting over the flocks of Oedipus
at seven-gated Thebes, in the land of Kadmos,

165 others over the great gulf of the sea in ships
that sailed to Troy for the sake of lovely-haired Helen;
there death threw his dark mantle over them.
Yet others of them father Zeus, son of Kronos, settled at earth's ends,
apart from men, and gave them shelter and food.

170 They live there with hearts unburdened by cares
in the islands of the blessed, near stormy Okeanos,
these blissful heroes for whom three times a year
the barley-giving land brings forth full grain sweet as honey.
I wish I were not counted among the fifth race of men,

175 but rather had died before, or been born after it.
This is the race of iron. Neither day nor night
will give them rest as they waste away with toil
and pain. Growing cares will be given them by the gods,
and their lot will be a blend of good and bad.

180 Zeus will destroy this race of mortals
when children are born gray at the temples.
Children will not resemble their fathers,
and there will be no affection between guest and host
and no love between friends or brothers as in the past.

185 Sons and daughters will be quick to offend their aging parents
and rebuke them and speak to them with rudeness
and cruelty, not knowing about divine retribution;
they will not even repay their parents for their keep—
these law-breakers—and they will sack one another's city.

190　The man who keeps his oath, or is just and good,
　　　will not be favored, but evildoers and scoundrels
　　　will be honored, for might will make right and shame will vanish.
　　　Base men will harm their betters with words
　　　that are crooked and then swear they are fair.
195　All toiling humanity will be blighted by envy,
　　　grim and strident envy that takes its joy in the ruin of others.
　　　Then Shame and Retribution will cover their fair bodies
　　　with white cloaks and, leaving men behind,
　　　will go to Olympos from the broad-pathed earth
200　to be among the race of the immortals, while grief and pain
　　　will linger among men, whom harm will find defenseless.
　　　Though kings are wise, I will tell them a fable:
　　　this is what a hawk said to a nightingale with a many-hued neck
　　　that he snatched with his claws and carried high up in the clouds.
205　As his hooked talons skewered her she raised a pitiful cry,
　　　and he spoke to her these lordly words:
　　　"Lady, why all the screaming? You are your better's captive;
　　　you have to follow me, though you are a great singer.
　　　I can have you for dinner, or let you go, if I wish,
210　for only fools oppose their betters in strength
　　　to suffer the pain of defeat topped with shame."
　　　So spoke the hawk, that fast, long-winged bird.
　　　Perses, obey justice and restrain reckless wrongdoing,
　　　for such wrongdoing harms the poor, and even the noble
215　find it an unwelcome burden that weighs them down
　　　and brings them ruin. The road to fair dealings
　　　is the better one. Justice is the winner in the race
　　　against insolent crime. Only fools need suffer to learn.
　　　The Oath Demon follows the trail of crooked decrees;
220　Justice howls when she is dragged about by bribe-devouring men
　　　whose verdicts are crooked when they sit in judgment.
　　　Weeping and clothed in mist, she follows through the cities
　　　and dwellings of men, and visits ruin on those
　　　who twist her straight ways and drive her out.
225　Those who give straight verdicts and follow justice,
　　　both when fellow citizens and strangers are on trial,
　　　live in a city that blossoms, a city that prospers.
　　　Then youth-nurturing peace comes over the land, and Zeus
　　　who sees far away does not decree for them the pains of war.

　　　　　　　　　　　　　　　　　　　　　　　H E S I O D

230   Men who honor justice know neither hunger nor ruin,
       but amid feasts enjoy the yield of their labors.
       For them the earth brings forth a rich harvest; and for them
       the top of an oak teems with acorns and the middle with bees.
       Fleecy sheep are weighed down with wool,
235   and women bear children who resemble their fathers.
       There is an abundance of blessings and the grainland
       grants such harvests that no one has to sail on the sea.
       Far-seeing Zeus, son of Kronos, is the judge
       of wanton wrongdoers who plot deeds of harshness.
240   Many times one man's wickedness ruins a whole city,
       if such a man breaks the law and turns his mind to recklessness.
       Then the son of Kronos sends a great bane from the sky,
       hunger and plague, and the people waste away.
       Women bear no children, and families dwindle
245   through the counsels of Zeus the Olympian,
       the son of Kronos, who punishes wrong by wiping out
       large armies, walls, and ships at sea.
       Kings, give this verdict no little thought,
       for the immortals are ever present among men,
250   and they see those who with crooked verdicts
       spurn divine retribution and grind down one another's life.
       Upon this earth that nurtures many Zeus can levy
       thirty thousand deathless guardians of mortal men,
       who keep a watchful eye over verdicts and cruel acts
255   as they rove the whole earth, clothed in mist.
       Justice is a maiden and a daughter of Zeus;
       the gods of Olympos respect her noble title,
       and whenever men mistreat her through false charges
       she rushes to sit at the feet of Zeus Kronion
260   and she denounces the designs of wrongdoers,
       so that the people pay for the reckless deeds and evil plans
       of kings whose slanted words twist her straight path.
       Keep her commands, O gift-devouring kings, and let
       verdicts be straight; yes, lay your crooked ways aside!
265   He that wrongs another man wrongs, above all, himself,
       and evil schemes bring more harm on those who plot them.
       The eye of Zeus sees all and perceives all;
       it sees all this, too, if it wishes, and knows exactly
       what sort of justice the walls of this city contain.

270 As matters stand, may neither I nor my son
     be just men in this world, because it is a bad thing
     to be just if wrongdoers win court decisions.
     I do not believe yet that Zeus's wisdom will allow this.
     Perses, put all this deep down in your mind,
275 obey the voice of justice and always refrain from violence.
     This is the law Zeus laid down for men,
     but fish, wild beasts, and winged birds
     know not of justice and so eat one another.
     Justice, the best thing there is, he gave to men;
280 Zeus who sees far away grants good fortune
     to the man who knows justice and also proclaims it.
     If a witness knowingly swears a false oath
     and lies, and so in his incurable folly tramples on justice,
     his offspring will sink and slowly vanish,
285 while the seed of him whose oath is true will prosper.
     I will speak to you, Perses, you great fool, for your own good;
     you can choose to have evil, and heaps of it, too,
     for its house lies near and the path to it is smooth.
     But the immortals decreed that man must sweat
290 to attain virtue; the road to it is steep and long
     and rough at first, but even so the journey
     gets easy once you set foot on the peak.
     Best is the man who thinks for himself
     and sees how things will turn out at the end.
295 Noble is the man who listens to good advice.
     Useless is the man who has no brains of his own
     and, worse yet, pays no heed to good counsel.
     But you, well-born Perses, never forget my command:
     Work! Work, and then Hunger will not be your companion,
300 while fair-wreathed and sublime Demeter
     will favor you and fill your barn with her blessings.
     Hunger is the idling man's companion.
     Both gods and mortals resent the lazy man,
     a man no more ambitious than the stingless drones
305 that feed on the bees' labor in wasteful sloth.
     Let there be order and measure in your own work
     until your barns are filled with the season's harvest.
     Riches and flocks of sheep go to those who work.
     If you work, you will be dearer to immortals

310 and mortals; both loathe the indolent.
No shame in work but plenty of it in sloth.
If your work brings you wealth, you will be envied by the slothful,
because glory and excellence follow riches.
Whatever your lot, nothing will be as good as work,
if, as I urge you, you turn your foolish mind
315 away from the possessions of your fellow men
to labor in the service of what is your own.
Shame of the useless kind attends the poor,
and shame can both harm and profit men;
shame brings poverty while boldness leads to riches—
320 not stolen wealth, god-given is much better.
If a man by might of hand seizes great wealth,
or robs with clever words—and such things do happen
when men's minds are seduced by greed for profit
and regard for man loses the race to shamelessness—
325 then easily the gods stain a man's name and obscure
his house. Yes, such fortunes do not last long.
It is equally bad to mistreat suppliants and strangers,
or to sleep with your brother's wife,
flouting decency in the secrecy of her bedroom,
330 or through foolishness to wrong someone's orphaned children,
or to fling cruel words at aging parents
as they stand before the threshold of old age.
Such acts of injustice anger Zeus himself,
who deals with them harshly upon their completion.
335 But do restrain your foolish mind from such deeds.
In proportion to your means offer the gods sacrifices
that are pure and unblemished, and burn choice thighs for them.
At other times seek their favor with burnings and libations
when you go to sleep and when the holy light looms on the horizon,
340 so that you win their favor for your affairs,
not having to sell your land, but buying more from others.
Invite your friends to dinner, exclude your enemies,
and remember that neighbors come first.
If misfortune strikes your house, neighbors will come
345 in their bedclothes; kinsmen will dress up.
Bad neighbors are pests, good ones a great blessing.
A good neighbor is a boon to him who has one.
If your neighbor is honest, your ox is safe.
Neighbors should measure with fairness. Give back

73   Works and Days

350 no less than you take, and even more if you can,
    that you may find enough when you are in need again.
    Ruin trails dishonest profit; keep away from it.
    Love those who love you, and help those who help you.
    Give to those who give to you, never to those who do not.
355 Gifts go to givers, the stingy go away empty-handed.
    Giving is good, robbing is bad—it courts death.
    The man who gives from the heart, even if his gift is great,
    takes pleasure in it and is rewarded with inner delight.
    Even a small thing grabbed by the shameless man
360 may chill his heart like a coat of hoar frost.
    If you pile one little thing on top of another,
    and do this often, you will soon have a heap.
    The man who adds to what he has fends off hunger that glazes the eyes.
    One does not worry about what lies stored in his home.
365 Home is safer; the outdoors may come with harm.
    To take from what one has is good, but grief comes
    with longing for what one lacks. Do think of all this.
    Drink all you want when your jar is full or almost empty;
    sparing is good at midpoint and useless when the bottom shows.
370 Wages promised to friends should always be paid,
    and even with your brother smile and get a witness,
    for blind faith is as dangerous as excessive trust.
    Do not be deceived by a woman who wags her tail
    as she chatters sweetly with a greedy eye on your possessions.
375 You trust a thief when you trust a woman.
    Wealth will increase inside your house,
    if you beget an only son to nurture it,
    and may you die old leaving another son behind.
    Zeus can grant his bounty just as easily to many;
380 more children mean more cares, but more income too.
    If your heart is set on becoming wealthy,
    do as I say and put more work on top of work.
    Start reaping when the Pleiades rise, daughters of Atlas,
    and begin to plow when they set.
385 For forty days and forty nights they lie hidden,
    but as the year moves on in its cycle
    they can be seen again when you first sharpen your iron.
    Nature has laid down this law for all whether they live on the plain,
    or dwell by the sea, or whether far from the stormy deep

390   they farm a rich piece of land in the hollow woodlands.
        Strip down when you sow, and strip down again when you plow
        or reap, if you want to bring home for storage
        each of Demeter's gifts in the right season.
        This way each thing will grow in season, and need will not
395   compel you to knock on doors in vain as a beggar.
        This is how you came to me but I have given enough
        and shall give no more. Work, foolish Perses!
        The gods have decreed work for men!
        Your heart will be sad when you will drag your wife and children along
400   to beg support from neighbors deaf to your pleas.
        You will be successful once or twice but, if you annoy them further,
        you will be wasting your many words;
        your clever words will not succeed. But I urge you
        to find ways to pay your debts and escape hunger.
405   First build a house and get an ox for the plow, and a woman
        for a price—no formal wedding—to follow your oxen,
        and keep everything in readiness at home,
        because it will break your heart to ask and not receive,
        while the time passes and you suffer a loss.
410   Do not postpone for tomorrow or the day after tomorrow;
        barns are not filled by those who postpone
        and waste time in aimlessness. Work prospers with care;
        he who postpones wrestles with ruin.
        When the sun's fierce swelter abates
415   with the coming of Zeus's rains in autumn,
        a man's body feels much lighter
        because the Dog Star, now night's lover
        much longer, stands only a brief part of the day
        over the heads of men, death's fattened victims;
420   then wood cut with the ax from deciduous trees
        that stop sprouting is too tough to be eaten by worms.
        Remember! That is the right time for lumbering.
        Cut a three-foot log for your mortar and a three-cubit pestle.
        A seven-foot axle makes for a perfect fit,
425   and an eight-foot piece will give you a mallet as well.
        For ten-palm wagons cut fellies no longer than three spans;
        for this you need many curved pieces. Bring a plow beam home,
        and try to look for one of holm oak in some hill or flatland;
        it is the sturdiest kind for your oxen when they plow

430 after a craftsman fastens it to the share
and drives pegs through it to attach it to the pole.
Make sure to keep two plows at home,
one of a single stock, the other of pieces fitted together.
This is best, for if you break the one, you yoke the oxen to the other.
435 Poles of elm or laurel are the most immune to worms.
Make your share of oak and your beam of holm oak.
Own a pair of nine-year-old oxen in their prime,
their strength endures and they are best for work.
They will not kick and butt over the furrow
440 and so break the plow and leave the work undone.
A forty-year-old farmhand should follow your oxen—
he needs a loaf of bread that breaks into four and then into eight—
he will tend to his labor and drive a straight furrow;
too old to look about for companions, he will keep his mind
445 on the job. Younger men than he cannot scatter
the seed better and avoid waste.
Younger men are too eager to join their companions.
When the crane flies high above in the clouds
each year, pay heed to her cry.
450 This signal that winter's rains are about to come
knifes the heart of the man who has no oxen.
Then you must feed well the curved-horned oxen you keep in your barn.
You can easily say "Give me a pair of oxen and a wagon"
and just as easily hear "Sorry, my oxen have work to do."
455 Fanciful men build wagons only in their minds;
fools do not go even so far; yet, a hundred pieces of wood
for making a wagon must be at home in ready supply.
As soon as time for plowing comes
you and your farmhands must rush to the task
460 the season dictates and plow both wet and dry land;
early risers harvest fields laden with grain.
Plow in the spring. Fallow land plowed in the summer will produce.
Sow fallow land when the soil is still loose;
such land will spare you curses and the clamor of hungry children.
465 Pray to Zeus of the earth and holy Demeter
to make Demeter's holy grain ripen to fullness.
Pray when you start plowing just as your hand grasps
the handle and the whip comes down hard
on the backs of your oxen as they tug at the strap pins;

HESIOD

470 and let a young farmhand follow you with a mattock
to make the birds toil hard for the seed he hides.
For mortals order is best, disorder is worst.
This way grain-heavy ears will bend over the ground,
if the lord of Olympos himself grants success in the end,
475 and you will wipe your pots clean of cobwebs.
Yes, joy will be yours when you draw on your stored supplies,
and, well-stocked, reach spring as it blossoms white,
not casting begging glances at others—others will need you.
If you plow the good earth at the winter solstice
480 you will reap tiny handfuls, squatting in the dust
to cross-bind them with little thrill in your heart;
few will admire what you bring home in a basket.
Aegis-bearing Zeus has a design for each occasion,
and mortals find this hard to comprehend.
485 But here is some consolation for the man who plows late;
when the cuckoo's song is first heard among the oak leaves
to the delight of mortals throughout the wide earth,
then may Zeus send rain three days later,
just enough to fill an ox's hoofprint.
490 This way the late plower will be a match for him who plows early.
Treasure all this in your heart and always mark
the coming of spring with its white blossoms and of rain in season.
Walk past the smithy and its crowded lounge
in winter when cold keeps men away from work
495 —even then an industrious man can increase his fortune—
so that in the grip of an evil winter's needy impasse
you are not forced to rub your swollen feet with a scrawny hand.
The lazy man trusts in empty hope and is left
without means; so his mind is turned to wrongdoing.
500 It is the wrong kind of hope that courts the poor,
who do not have enough and yet gossip in idleness.
Before midsummer has passed tell your farmhands:
"Build barns! It will not be summer forever."
In the month of Lenaion the days are bad;
505 they skin oxen alive. Beware of this month and its frosts
that grip the earth when the gusty north wind
stirs the broad sea and blows through Thrace
—that nurturer of horses—as land and forest bellow.
Up in the mountain woodlands it blows against

510 many high-crested oaks and sturdy firs
and fells them to the rich earth as the vast forest groans.
Wild beasts shiver then and curl their tails under their bellies—
chilly wind pierces the shag that coats the breasts
even of animals whose skin is covered with deep fur;
515 it will go through the hide of an ox
and through a goat's long hair, but fleecy sheep
are safe from the blast of the north wind.
It sends an old man scurrying for protection,
but does not blow through to a maiden's soft skin,
520 for she stays indoors with her dear mother,
still unaware of golden Aphrodite's deeds;
she bathes her tender skin well and rubs it down
to sleekness with oil and then lies down, hidden away in her bedroom.
So it is in the winter when Mr. Boneless chews his foot
525 in his gloomy haunts, where his fireless house lies;
the sun does not show him the way to the feeding grounds
but circles over those who dwell in the lands
of black men and is slow to shine on all the Greeks.
Then horned and hornless lodgers of the forest,
530 teeth chattering wretchedly, flee throughout the woodlands,
their hearts bursting with only one nagging drive:
they long to find shelter in windproof lairs
inside some hollow rock. Then mortals have three legs;
their backs are bent and their heads sweep the ground—
535 they are walking tripods fleeing the white snow.
At that time you must clothe your body well
with a fringed tunic and a soft cloak over it.
Weave cloth in which there is much weft for little warp
and wear it, so that your hair does not stand on end
540 and bristle all over your body.
From the skin of a slaughtered ox make sandals
lined with felt and bind them snugly about your feet.
When the cold season comes stitch together skins
of firstling kids with an ox sinew and wrap your back
545 with them to keep the rain off; and on your head
wear a tight-fitting cap to keep your ears dry.
Mornings are cold when the north wind blows
and damp fog descends from the starry sky
and hovers like a chilly veil over men's wheat patches.

550 This is a mist drawn up from ever-flowing rivers
and then raised by stormy winds high above the earth;
sometimes it comes as evening rain and often as wind
when Thracian gusts whip thick clouds to frenzy.
Run faster than this wind; finish work and head home,
555 wary of a dark cloud that swoops down from the sky to envelop you
and soak your body and clothes until you are dripping wet.
Take precautions. This is a wintry and stormy month,
cruel for men and cruel for sheep.
Give oxen half rations and men more than their usual share
560 because the kindly nights are now too long.
Heed this advice until the end of the year,
when nights and days are no longer unequal
and until the earth, mother of all, gives her many fruits.
When—Zeus willing—counting from the winter solstice
565 sixty days have passed, then the star Arcturus
leaves the sacred stream of Okeanos
and first rises brilliant at eventide,
then the swallow, shrill-voiced daughter of Pandion,
flies up into the light when the new spring begins;
570 it is best to prune your vines before her arrival.
When the house-carrier from the ground climbs on plants,
fleeing the Pleiades, then no longer hoe your vines
but sharpen your sickles and wake up the farmhands.
Do not dawdle on shady benches and do not sleep past dawn,
575 when it is time to reap and the sun shrivels the skin.
At that time rise before the crack of dawn
and bring your crop home to secure abundance.
The dawn claims the third portion of a day's work,
the dawn gives a headstart for journeys and jobs,
580 the dawn's arrival sends many men on their way
and puts the yoke on the necks of many oxen.
When the thistle blooms and the chirping cicada
sits on trees and pours down shrill song
from frenziedly quivering wings in the toilsome summer,
585 then goats are fatter than ever and wine is at its best;
women's lust knows no bounds and men are all dried up,
because the Dog Star parches their heads and knees
and the heat sears their skin. Then, ah then,
I wish you a shady ledge and your choice wine,

590   bread baked in the dusk and mid-August's goat milk,
meat from a free-roving heifer that has never calved,
and meat from firstling kids. Drink sparkling wine,
sitting in the shade with your appetite sated,
and face Zephyr's breeze as it blows from mountain peaks.
595   Pour three measures of water fetched from a clear spring,
one that flows unchecked, and a fourth one of wine.
As soon as mighty Orion rises above the horizon
exhort your farmhands to thresh Demeter's holy grain
in a windy, well-rounded threshing floor.
600   Measure it first and then store it in bins.
When your grain is tightly stored inside the house
then hire an unmarried worker and look for a female servant
with no children—nursing women are a burden.
Keep a dog with sharp teeth and feed it well,
605   wary of the day-sleepers who might rob you.
Bring in a lasting supply of hay and fodder
for your oxen and mules. Once this is done let your farmhands
rest their weary knees and unyoke the oxen.
When Orion and the Dog Star rise to the middle of the sky
610   and rosy-fingered Dawn looks upon Arcturus,
then, Perses, gather your grapes and bring them home
and leave them in the sun for ten days and nights,
in the shade for five, and on the sixth day
draw the gift of joyous Dionysos into your vats.
615   When the Pleiades, the Hyades, and mighty Orion set,
remember the time has come to plow again—
and may the earth nurse for you a full year's supply.
And if longing seizes you for sailing the stormy seas,
when the Pleiades flee mighty Orion
620   and plunge into the misty deep
and all the gusty winds are raging,
then do not keep your ship on the wine-dark sea
but, as I bid you, remember to work the land.
Haul your ship onto land and secure it to the ground
625   with stones on all sides to stay the blast of rain and wind,
and pull out the plug to avoid rotting caused by rain water.
Store up the tackle compactly inside your house
and neatly fold the sails, the wings of a seafaring ship.
Hang your rudder above the fireplace

630   and wait until the time to sail comes again.
Then drag your swift ship to sea and load on it
a tight cargo—one that will send you home with profit.
This is how our father, Perses, you precious fool,
sailed on ships, pressed by the need for a better life.
635   He once left Aeolian Kyme and on his black ship
came to this place, after a long bout with the sea,
and he was not fleeing great riches and comforts
but grim poverty that Zeus gives to men.
He built his house near Helikon in the worthless village
640   of Askre, a place bad in winter, worse in the summer, never good.
But, Perses, do remember that each kind of work has its season
and, above all, navigation.
Praise a small ship, but load your cargo on a big one.
The bigger the cargo the greater the profit heaped on profit,
645   if the winds keep nasty gales in check.
Whenever you want to turn your foolish mind to trade
to escape your debts and the hunger that plagues you,
I will teach you the rules that govern the sea,
though I am no expert on navigation and ships,
650   since I never sailed the open seas on a boat,
except when I went to Euboea from Aulis, where once
the Achaeans weathered a grim storm and then with a great host
from holy Greece sailed over to Troy, land of fair women.
There I crossed over to Chalkis for the prizes
655   in honor of wise Amphidamas, the many prizes proclaimed in advance
by his magnanimous sons. I claim that there
I was the victor in a song contest and won an eared tripod,
which I dedicated to the Helikonian Muses,
where they first taught me mastery of flowing song.
660   This is all I know about well-riveted ships,
but even so I can speak the mind of aegis-bearing Zeus,
for the Muses taught me to sing and never weary.
For fifty days, past the summer solstice
and past the end of summer's toilsome part,
665   men can sail with safety, for then a ship
will not be shattered, and the sea will not wipe out the crew,
unless this is the will of Poseidon who shakes the earth,
or Zeus, king of the gods, wants you destroyed;
both have power over good fortune as well as misfortune.

                        Works and Days

670 Then the winds have clear directions and the sea is safe.
Then, free of care, trust the winds
and draw your swift ship to sea and load it full.
But rush home as soon as you can;
come back before the new wine and the fall rains,
675 well ahead of winter and the violent gales of the south wind.
This wind trails the great fall rains sent by Zeus
and makes the sea stormy and too rough for sailing.
The second season for sailing comes in the spring:
when a man sees on the topmost shoot of a fig tree
680 leaves as large as a crow's footprint,
then he may sail across the sea.
This is the time for spring sailing. I myself do not have
one good word for it—it does not fill my heart with glee.
The whim of chance rules it, and disaster is hard to escape
685 but men take it up because their minds are foolish.
Man is witless, and his soul is in his purse.
The death of those who die among the waves is harsh,
and I ask you not to let my advice go unheeded.
Do not load all your goods on hollow ships;
690 your cargo should be less than what you leave behind.
The disaster you chance upon at sea is dreadful,
and dreadful the outcome if you overload your wagon
and thus break the axle and see your load destroyed.
Observe due limit and timeliness in all your actions.
695 The right time to bring a wife to your home
is when you are only a few years younger than thirty,
or just a few years older. This is the time for marriage.
Five years past puberty make a woman a suitable bride.
Marry a virgin so you can teach her right from wrong.
700 Choose from among the girls who live near you and check
every detail, so that your bride will not be the neighborhood joke.
Nothing is better for man than a good wife,
and no horror matches a bad one, a glutton
who reclines to eat and needs no fire to roast
705 even a stalwart man and age him before his time.
Heed the vengeance of the blessed immortals
and do not make a friend your brother's equal.
If you do so, do not be the first to do wrong
and to lie for the sake of lying.

710   If a friend is first to displease you by word or deed,
      remember to pay him back doubly in kind.
      If he offers his friendship and wants to make amends,
      be gracious. Only scoundrels change their friends.
      Your face should mirror what is on your mind.
715   Do not be called a host of too many or of none,
      and neither befriend the lowly nor quarrel with the noble.
      Do not allow yourself to mock baneful poverty
      that wears men's hearts away; it, too, comes from the gods.
      A man owns no better treasure than a prudent tongue;
720   there is no small delight in it, if it moves with grace.
      Bad words flung at others bounce back with double strength.
      Let your manners be gentle at feasts attended by many.
      When all share the cost, the expense is little and the joy great.
      Never pour a libation to Zeus after dawn,
725   or to the other immortals, if you have not washed your hands.
      They will not hear your prayers but will spit them back at you.
      Do not piss as you stand facing the sun,
      but do it after the sun sets and before it rises,
      and even then do not be naked, for nights belong to the gods.
730   Do not piss either off or on the road while you walk.
      The devout and wise man squats for this act,
      or does it against the sturdy wall of some yard.
      Even in your house do not sit by the hearth
      with your genitals exposed and bespattered with semen.
735   Sire your children when you return from a feast of the gods,
      not when you return from an ill-omened burial. Never piss into springs.
      Never cross the fair waters of ever-flowing rivers
      before you wash your hands with lovely and limpid water
      and pray as you look upon the stream before you cross.
740   If a man crosses a river with unwashed hands and impure heart,
      the gods bear a grudge and bring pains upon him later.
      At a joyous feast for the gods never with gleaming iron
      cut off the dry from the green of your five-branch.
      Let those who drink never place the serving cup
745   over the mixing bowl; bad luck comes with this, too.
      And on the house you build carve a luck-bringing sign
      so that no crows will perch on it and caw.
      When you eat and bathe do not use vessels
      unhallowed by sacrifice; otherwise you may be harmed.

750 It is not good for boys twelve days or twelve years old
   to sit on that which is motionless,
   for such an act unmans even a man in his prime.
   A man should not sleek his body with a woman's bath water,
   for in time even this is cruelly punished.
755 If a man chances on victims burning in sacrifice,
   let him not mock the unknown and thus anger some god.
   Never piss where rivers pour into the sea
   or into springs, but always avoid this.
   It is just as bad to relieve yourself in such places.
760 Do as I say, and remember how destructive gossip is;
   it is easy to get a bad reputation
   but hard to live with it and harder to shed it.
   What is said of you does not vanish,
   if many say it; rumor is a kind of god.
765 Zeus sends the days; observe them in due measure
   and explain to your farmhands that the thirtieth is best
   for overseeing work and giving men their rations.
   Here are the days that come from Zeus the counselor,
   if people judge their true nature and live by it:
770 the chief sacred days are the first, the fourth, and the seventh;
   Leto bore Apollon of the golden sword on the seventh.
   The eighth and the ninth of the waxing month
   are outstanding days for men to engage in work.
   The eleventh and the twelfth are both good days
775 for shearing sheep and reaping a fine harvest.
   The twelfth is much better than the eleventh;
   spiders hover in the air and spin their yarn
   at this day's fullness, and the wise one piles up his harvest.
   On this day let a woman set up her loom and weave.
780 Do not start your sowing on the thirteenth day
   of the waxing month; this day is best for nurturing plants.
   The sixth day of midmonth does not favor plants
   but is good for the birth of boys; it does not favor
   either the birth or the marriage of girls.
785 The sixth day of the month's first part is not proper
   for the birth of girls, but gelding of kids and lambs
   hurts less then, and pens built for your flocks will be better.
   It favors the birth of boys who are sharp-tongued
   and who lie and coax and are fond of secret whispers.

790   On the eighth of the month geld your boar and bellowing bull
and on the twelfth do the same to your hardy mules.
Men born in the fullness of the great twentieth day
are wise, and their minds are never slack.
The tenth is good for the birth of a boy and the fourth
795   of midmonth for the birth of a girl. On this day stroke your sheep,
your shambling curved-horned oxen, your sharp-toothed dog,
and your hardy mules. And keep in your mind
the ills of the fourth day when the month waxes and wanes;
guard against this day, it can break your heart.
800   Bring a wife to your home on the fourth of the month,
but first watch for the bird signs best for this venture.
Be on your guard on all fifth days; they are harsh and dread.
They say that on the fifth the Furies assisted
at the birth of Oath, whom Strife bore as a scourge to perjurers.
805   On the seventh of midmonth look about with care
and then pour down Demeter's holy grain on a threshing floor
that is well-rounded. On this day the lumberman should cut
beams for the house and tight-fitting timbers for ships.
On the fourth day start building your trim boats.
810   The ninth of midmonth is better toward evening,
and the least harm for men is found in the first ninth;
this is a good day for men and women both to plant offspring
and to be born themselves. Yes, this day is never all bad.
Few know that the twenty-seventh is the best day
815   for opening a cask or placing the yoke on the necks
of oxen, mules, and fleet-footed horses,
and for dragging to the wine-dark sea a ship
of many row locks. Few men call this day by its true name.
Open wine jars on the fifth. The fourth of midmonth is holiest.
820   Again, few men know that after the twentieth of the month
the fourth is best at dawn and not as good toward evening.
The people of this earth profit greatly from these days.
The other days are meaningless, untouched by fortune.
Men have days they favor, but few really know.
825   The same day can be a mother now, a stepmother later.
Happy and blessed is the man who knows all this
and does his work without offending the immortals,
ever watching birds of omen, ever shunning transgression.

Notes

1–10. Lines 1–10 constitute the proem, which usually contains the invocation of a divinity and the main theme of the song that is to follow. In the *Iliad* and the *Odyssey*, this is achieved swiftly in the first line of the proem. Hesiod very cleverly includes the Muses by asking them to "hymn" Zeus, their father, and then goes on to appeal to him as the highest authority from which straight justice comes. This is a very deft stroke. As an *aoidos*, a singer, he cannot and does not want to bypass the source of his inspiration and memory, but he needs the aid of the supreme judge to help him in a case in which human justice is subject to bribery and corruption. In the *Theogony*, Hesiod invokes the Muses of Helikon, but here he calls upon the Muses of Pieria, a mountain far to the north of his native Boeotia. This may have offended local patriotism and even led to excision of the whole proem. Indeed, Pausanias reports that the Boeotians of Helikon showed him a lead sheet that contained the *Works and Days* without lines 1–10 (9.31). Even the great Alexandrian scholar Aristarchos considered these lines a later accretion to the text, but neither language nor content sustains this suspicion, which has not been entirely laid to rest. The proem seems both genuine and essential to a large portion of the poem.

If we consider Homer as the norm for epic poetry, the invocation of the Muses rather than of one Muse or "Goddess" is an innovation. It is entirely possible that the Muse or Goddess of the Homeric poems is none other than Mnemosyne (Memory), mother of the Muses, whose assistance is urgently needed by both oral poet and reciter. Interestingly enough, in the *Homeric Hymn to Hermes* 4.429–30, the god sings to his lyre and first pays tribute to Mnemosyne. For the Muses in general, see notes on *Theogony* 53–115. Perses of line 10 is Hesiod's unfair brother.

11–26. In these lines, we are told that there are two different kinds of Strife, good and bad. The good Strife is noble and fair emulation; the bad one is malicious and invidious contention.

So then the Eris, which Hesiod's brother is promoting, is really self-serving conflict. Hesiod says to Perses that good Eris does not promote conflict; in fact, it actually stirs even the shiftless men to work. It should be remembered that both good and bad Strife were born of Dark Night. That the good Strife is planted in the roots of the earth may imply a belief that she plays a role in the growth of all living things, a growth that seems governed by principles of regularity and benevolence. That Night should give birth to a benevolent Strife is not so strange. In the Bible, God creates light out of darkness, and in *Theogony* 123–24 Night is the mother of Ether and Day. Hesiod is careful to tell us that "No man loves this oppressive Strife, but compulsion / and divine will grant her a share of honor" (15–16). Necessity or compulsion is connected with Night elsewhere. In *Iliad* 14.259, Night is called "tamer of the gods." In a sense, the bad Strife is a necessary evil born of the same mother who has given birth to luminous forces. It is more than likely that Empedocles was influenced by *Theogony* 116–22, which makes

Eros (Love) one of the first elements of creation and by Hesiod's division of Strife into good and bad. It will be remembered that Empedocles taught that Love and Strife are the primary creative forces in the never-ending cosmic cycle. In Empedocles, Love unites and Strife separates (see Kirk and Raven, 326–32; Jaeger, 12–16).

It should be pointed out that Hesiod tells us in the *Theogony* that Night gave birth to Love and Strife (224–25). His division of Strife in the *Works and Days* represents either a correction of earlier doctrine that made Philotes (Love) a child of a mother who otherwise bore noxious offspring, or an elaboration of the concept of Strife, or perhaps both. Of course, Philotes of *Theogony* 224 should not be confused with Eros of *Theogony* 120, even though we inadequately translate both as "Love."

27–41. Hesiod exhorts his brother to work rather than spend his time listening to brawls and bringing an unfair lawsuit against him. The corrupt "kings" of line 39 are probably no more than local nobles with political as well as juridical authority. The barons/kings do not know how the half of something can be greater than all of it. They do not know how much nurture there is in mallow and asphodel. In other words, once more they are greedy. The proverbs of lines 40–41 reinforce each other and mean essentially the same thing: virtuous poverty is better than corrupt wealth. (Cf. Psalm 37:16 with the first proverb. For the plants mentioned in the second one, see Horace *Odes* 1.31.16; Theophrastos *Hist. Plant.* 7.12.1; Pliny *N.H.* 21.108).

42–57. Hesiod starts to probe the problem of the necessity to make a living through hard toil and the problem of the presence of the many evils that make man's life difficult. It goes without saying that in Hesiod's account of the "fall" or degeneration of man, which preoccupies him up to line 201, analogies from the Bible and in general from myths that attempt to explain the wretched lot of mankind ought to be considered for both similarity and difference. Men forfeited their once carefree existence because the Titan Prometheus cheated Zeus by not giving him his rightful portion of meat at the banquet of Mekone (for a full account of the story, see *Theogony* 535–616). The angered god hid men's livelihood inside the earth and took fire away. Prometheus did nothing about the hidden livelihood, but he stole the fire back (for the account of this celebrated theft, see *Theogony* 535–70). Iapetos, father of Prometheus, was a Titan and a child of Sky and Earth (*Theogony* 132–36). Prometheus was the offspring of the union of Iapetos with Klymene, incestuous child of the Titans Okeanos and Tethys (cf. *Theogony* 506–16). The question is: Why should men be punished for the fraudulent act of a Titan? The account according to which Prometheus as master craftsman created man from clay (Paus. 10.4.3) does offer an explanation, but of course we do not know how old this tradition is. According to the *Homeric Hymn to Apollon* 3.334–36, men and even gods are descended from the Titans. Orphic belief had it that man was created from the ashes of the Titans whom Zeus burned with his thunderbolt for having torn to pieces and devoured his son Dionysos (cf. *Orphic Hymn* 37.4). It should be remembered that the Titans, who were very old gods, stood in opposition to the reign of Zeus and his progeny. It seems then that Zeus punished men for a very fundamental and perhaps derivative relationship to the Titans and especially to Prometheus, who eventually championed their cause. Prometheus himself was punished for cheating Zeus of his sacrificial portion (*Theogony* 535ff. and especially lines 613–16; Aeschylus, however, in *Prometheus Bound* 7–11, gives the theft of fire as the main reason for his punishment).

60–105. Zeus has already taken two punitive actions against man. He has hidden livelihood inside the earth and taken fire away. The effects of the second action are canceled by Prometheus, who steals the fire back. It is in place of this canceled punitive action that Zeus decides to visit a fresh suffering upon men by creating an irresistibly charming but basically wicked woman who unleashes evil on mankind. In the account of the same event in *Theogony* 570–616, it is woman herself, not a jar filled with evils, who constitutes the bane sent by Zeus. Here, however, the woman is named Pandora, and the evils she unleashes are greater than those peculiar to her nature and do not originate with her. Zeus ordered Hephaistos to take earth and give it strength and speech, and a beautiful feminine form. He also ordered Athena to teach her skills and Aphrodite to teach her feminine charm. Then he ordered Hermes to place inside her a shameless mind and a thievish nature (line 67). The gods gave Pandora her well-known pithos and dispatched her to Epimetheus. Epimetheus did not know what was in store for him, so he accepted the gift. Hesiod says there was a time in the past when men lived a carefree life, without labor and illness. Pandora lifted the lid of the jar and thousands of illnesses flew away. They bring harm to men, for they move in silence. Zeus took away their voice. It is fairly certain that Pandora, "The Giver of All," was originally an earth-goddess, whose name Hesiod borrowed and, using folk etymology, interpreted as "she to whom all (the gods) gave a gift." For Pandora as earth-goddess, see Farnell, *The Cults of the Greek States,* Oxford, 1886–1909, 1:290; A. H. Smith, "The Making of Pandora," *JHS* 11 (1890): 278–83; also, J. E. Harrison, "Delphika," *JHS* 19 (1899): 205; and J. E. Harrison, "Pandora's Box," *JHS* 20 (1900): 99. As such, Pandora would be another of the myriad names under which mother earth has been worshiped. If Hesiod knew this connection, he certainly did not dwell on it but merely borrowed the name and, as it were, twisted its meaning. Yet, even the borrowing of the name from such an ancient goddess might be significant. Hesiod might indeed wish to connect woman more with the earth. Both the manner of her creation and her baneful dowry are more chthonic than celestial. The more fundamental problem, however, is: Why does woman have to be the instrument that brings suffering to man? Here, I am afraid, one has to appeal to more than Hesiod's obvious misogyny in order to account for a pattern that is truly archetypal. Some scholars understand lines 82–83 (81–82 in the Oxford Classical Text)

to mean "all the gods who dwell on Olympos gave her a gift—a scourge for toiling men." I am inclined to take this interpretation as less probable. Hope (97–99) was left inside the jar because this was the wish of Zeus. The question is: Why is Hope singled out and kept within the jar? People try to improve their lot because they have hope. Could Hesiod mean that it is hopeless to hope, that man cannot improve his lot? I think this is highly unlikely, unless one understands the withholding of Hope as signifying man's inability to transcend his limits, to escape from the human predicament. Hesiod's moral sermons to his brother imply that, if he becomes a just man and if he works, he can improve his lot. Hesiod is also certainly aware that there is no human effort that does not involve hope. Now if Hope is entirely bad, she should have been released together with all the other ills that plague man. On the other hand, if Hope is entirely good, she should have no place in Pandora's jar. Perhaps she is treated differently because she can be both good and bad. Lines 500–501, "It is the wrong kind of hope that courts the poor / who do not have enough and yet gossip in idleness," seem to indicate that in Hesiod's mind Hope, much like Eris (Strife), could be good in one set of circumstances and bad in another. In this sense, Hope could not be unleashed with all the evils, because she can be bad but she can also be good. In this connection, it is interesting to point out that the evils are not specified, whereas Hope is. If Hesiod faced a logical dilemma, he solved it in a manner that shows that he was probably inclined to consider Hope more of a positive than a negative factor in human affairs.

106–201. *The Myth of the Five Ages:* The idea that humankind is gradually degenerating and headed for destruction is both extremely old and extremely modern. This idea is so common to many cultures and so old that we can be absolutely sure that it did not originate with Hesiod. Hesiod himself says, "I will give you the pith of another story" (107), thereby meaning the main points of a myth that is not his personal creation.

Homer has nothing like the myth of the five successive ages. This does not mean that the myth was unknown to him. It simply means that since his theme was the glory of extraordinary men, the heroes, there was little reason for him to dwell on the theme of degeneration. In the *Works and Days,* it is the common man, the toiling farmer, who is the poet's concern. His lot is so wretched that there is good reason to account for it and to describe it as the lowest point on a descending scale. The closest we come to a mild version of the theme of degeneration in Homer is when in the first book of the *Iliad* (244–84) Nestor takes it upon himself to mediate between Achilleus and Agamemnon. He tells them that in his youth he was honored by the company of legendary heroes of great stature and physical strength. These men, says Nestor, were such that "no man of this generation could fight against them" (271–72). The clear implication is that those men of old were far superior to heroes such as Achilleus and Agamemnon. There is no elaboration in Nestor's speech and no attempt to provide some sort of genealogical pyramid. Such hints at the existence in olden days of a race of heroic giants are found elsewhere in Homer (*Iliad* 5.636–46; *Odyssey* 8.223–33 and 11.308–20).

To readers of the Bible, the theme is familiar from the statue of which Nebuchadnezzar dreams (Daniel 2:31–35). The feet of this statue are of iron and clay, the legs of iron, the thighs and the belly of brass. The upper part is made of nobler metals: the breast and arms of silver, and the head of gold. Daniel explains to Nebuchadnezzar that the golden head represents his kingdom, which is to be succeeded by four inferior kingdoms. Among the Sumerians and the Babylonians, as one can see from their king lists, there was a belief that men, kings at any rate, once could live for several thousand years and that these incredible lifespans became progressively shortened as evil increased in this world. In Indian literature, there is a more fully developed theory of four major world ages. There is no metal symbolism, but these ages are named after the four throws of the die. As

time goes on, evil and disease proliferate and lifespans decrease to the point that men beget children at ten and age with the arrival of the sixteenth year. A more striking parallel to the Hesiodic myth is to be found in the Zoroastrian belief that Zoroastrianism is to last for four successive ages corresponding to the four branches—one of gold, one of silver, one of steel, and one of iron alloy—of the tree revealed to Zoroaster by Ahura Mazdáh in a vision.

The oriental sources that speak of four ages associated with the symbolism of noble and inferior metals are later than Hesiod. This might lead us to believe that it is some early Hellenic myth that is the progenitor of the oriental models. Yet, the more standard Hellenic belief was in a mythic age of heroes. This belief is somewhat modified and introduced by Hesiod into what seems to be a more formalistic and structured concept. It is then probable that we are dealing with an importation from the East. The specific point of origin cannot be fixed with any certainty, but the trend of gradual deterioration and the absence of a similar doctrine in the Homeric corpus argue for oriental provenance.

Whatever vestigial beliefs in the concept of deterioration exist in modern Greece are more like the general Homeric idea and have no connection with the Hesiodic account. This, too, is an argument, albeit not a strong one, for looking upon Hesiod's scheme as a literary importation that never took roots in folk belief. For Homer, the heroes were much stronger than his own contemporaries (cf. *Iliad* 5.302–4; 12.447–49, and so forth). In many parts of modern Greece, people still believe in the existence of a race of Hellenes, men of gigantic size and superhuman strength. They point to massive ruins as their work and attribute to them feats that require extraordinary power. At other times, they speak of the *palioí,* "the men of old," who were much stronger, healthier, and handsomer than themselves.

109. This line seems misplaced here, and its position in the poem cannot be justified by the argument that it really means that once men lived like gods.

109–26. Hesiod does not mean that the gods used gold to fashion men, but rather that his first race had the positive properties that are associated with gold. Gold is precious, pure, incorruptible. Gold does not become oxidized; that is, it does not age with time, but it can be destroyed by other means. So, too, these men were left unchanged by the passage of time but they were doomed to die. The golden masks in the National Archaeological Museum of Athens, Greece, are very important. They testify to a desire for immortality. The facial features of the dead person must be preserved, so that he can be recognized in the underworld.

The statement that the golden race lived when Kronos was king of the sky (112) probably means no more than that these mythic men lived in the beginning of time. They lived in a veritable utopia, free of care and not cursed with the blight of old age. It will be remembered that in the *Theogony* Hesiod made Old Age a child of Night (223–25). In the same passage (211–25), Hesiod tells us that Death and Sleep are brothers and also children of Night. The men of the golden age are not immortal, but they are subdued by the kindlier of the two brothers. They do not experience the agony of death because first they fall into a deep coma. The idea that the golden race enjoyed the fruits of the earth without toil is consistent with the idea expressed in lines 40–47. According to these lines, livelihood was hidden from men by Zeus as a punishment for the treachery of Prometheus. The men of the age of gold die only to the extent that their bodies decompose inside the earth. They are not destroyed altogether, since they live on as benevolent guardian spirits that can grant wealth (note the frequent end of many Orphic hymns: "Grant me wealth and peace"). The hero cults of the ancient Greeks also mirror a similar idea and so does the so-called demonification of Oedipus in the *Oedipus Coloneus* of Sophocles. This belief has doubtless survived in the modern Greek veneration of the saints as potential benefactors.

128–43. Much as silver is inferior to gold, so too the silver race is inferior to the golden race. The people who belong to it stay with their mother for a hundred years and when they reach puberty, they become violent and they do not want to honor the immortal gods. Finally, the earth covers this race. The men of the golden generation are *epichthonioi* while the men of the silver generation are *hypochthonioi*. This is all the comparison seems to indicate. Except for the long childhood lived in the bliss of ignorance, there is nothing conferred on the men of the silver age that could be looked upon as a blessing. Once they come of age, they foolishly refuse to worship the gods and offer them the proper sacrifices. They also perpetrate acts of violence against one another. The transition from the age of gold to the age of silver is quite abrupt in terms of the qualities of the two races. This creates a problem that is somewhat mitigated by the fact that their crime against the gods is one of omission and not of commission. Lines 142–43 add to the problem because, although Zeus destroyed them, Hesiod tells us that they are called "blessed mortals" and are honored. It will not do, I think, to try to remove the difficulty by weakening the meaning of "blessed" to mean no more than our "of blessed memory" or than the modern Greek *makarites*, "blessed," which has become a byword for dead. Nor will it do to construe the phrase "they are . . . honored" as meaning honored in the way all the dead are generally honored. By calling them men of the silver age, Hesiod may have implied no more than that they were a trifle better than the more violent men of the bronze age, but the difficulty remains and it should perhaps be attributed to Hesiod's inability at this point to draw a sharper distinction between all the inferior races and the truly outstanding race of the age of gold.

144–56. Here Hesiod faces a dilemma. His scheme is one of gradual deterioration. The third age is bound to be worse than the preceding one, which is bad enough. Yet, he is keenly aware of the heroic age. This age—quite correctly—is the age that precedes the iron age, and historically, especially in light of the Homeric epics, he could have characterized the age of the heroes as the age of bronze. This violates the progression

91

from good to bad to worse. So he links the inferior metal with an inferior race and then inserts the race of the heroes in a way that interrupts the pattern of degeneration.

The men of the bronze age are fashioned from ash trees. The word for ash tree is *meliê* and in Homer it also means "spear," since its hard wood was used for making spear shafts. This is doubtless a race of violent warriors. These are men of the spear (cf. the "bronze-tongued ash" of *Iliad* 22.225). Their violence and mighty bodies make them somewhat resemble the Giants, who, according to the *Theogony*, were born of the Earth before the Meliai, the Ash Tree Nymphs. The implication of the phrase "they ate no bread" (148) is that in their savage state they were strangers to the civilized art of agriculture, much like the cannibalistic Kyklopes and Laistrygones of the *Odyssey*. The men of the third generation destroyed one another and went down to Hades nameless. Iron was not discovered yet. Bronze is produced by mixing copper with tin. This metal did not exist in Greece. It was brought from England by Greek and Phoenician merchants.

157–73. Hesiod is aware of the Theban and Trojan sagas. He knows that the heroes of these sagas were the semidivine men who belonged to the age preceding the iron age. The epics about these bronze-geared warriors were also known to him. Therefore, it is all the more remarkable that he did not link the age of heroes with its proper metal, bronze. Such a linkage would accord well both with tradition and with reality. On the other hand, Hesiod does not tell us anything about their weapons. He only tells us that they destroyed one another in war. Here Hesiod deliberately suppresses what must have been common knowledge in his day, but he does so by omission. This way, he could adhere to his symbolism and at the same time does not leave himself completely defenseless against criticism. He could agree that he only said that bronze was the metal of the age of the men of bronze, who used it for everything, and that he did not say that the race of heroes did not use

it. It is obvious that Hesiod could not omit the age of heroes, probably the only age with which his listeners contrasted their own. Chronologically, he introduced it at the right point, just before the iron age. Still, the resulting awkwardness forced him to resort to cleverness. These are the blessed heroes to whom the earth gives blossoming fruit three times a year. Elsewhere, I suggested that this significant detail is Orphic in origin. I also pointed out that it was incorporated into the Greek funeral service by Ioannis Damaskinos. The Isles of the Blest to which some heroes go are obviously identical with the Elysian Field that is described in *Odyssey* 4.561–69. It is a place that knows neither rain nor snow but only Zephyr's gentle breezes. There, favored heroes live in bliss and dine with the gods when the latter choose to visit them. It should be noted that the more standard Greek belief was that heroes went to Hades and that Menelaos went to the Elysian Field because he was Helen's husband and hence a son-in-law to Zeus.

174–201. The age of iron is Hesiod's own age, and it is so terrible that Hesiod wishes he were not part of it. Hesiod does not consider himself as living at the apex of the iron age, when evil and misery reach their calamitous peak. Part of what he says about it is in the form of a prophecy of doom. There will be signs of imminent destruction when children are born gray at the temples. Further portents of doom will be a total breakdown of those virtues that hold family and society together: conjugal fidelity, guest-host ties, filial piety, respect for law, and regard for honor and shame. The lowest point of deterioration will be reached when Shame and Retribution (Aidos and Nemesis) seek refuge among the gods. *Aidos* is the shame one feels when contemplating an improper or wicked act, or the strong sense of embarrassment that follows such an act. *Nemesis* is the retribution that comes from public censure (cf. *Iliad* 3.156–60; 13.121–24). The meaning is that when people do not feel constrained by either of these, society will break down and Zeus will put an end to it. If Hesiod places himself at some point before the end, he also seems to hint that the end is near. Lines 193–94

> Base men will harm their betters with words that are crooked and then swear they are fair

describe the very predicament in which he finds himself vis-à-vis his crooked and mendacious brother, who has lost the feeling of love that brother felt for brother in the good old days. As all good readers of the Hebrew prophets will surely remember, this sentiment is part of the stock-in-trade of all prophets of doom, but Hesiod here could exploit a motif that was bound to appeal to his listeners and at the same time serve as fair warning to his brother, whose behavior not only wrongs Hesiod but portends the destruction of the whole society. Although there is a hint in line 175 that somehow life will not be as bad after the fifth generation, there is no prophecy that Zeus will make a better race to take the place of this one. To offer strong hope at this point would be uncharacteristic of a poet who consigned Hope inside the jar in which Pandora carried the evils that plague mankind.

202–12. The fable of the hawk and the nightingale creates certain difficulties. The genre is best known to most readers through Aesop, and parallels can be found in Hebrew, Sumerian, and other Eastern literatures. The genre was so well developed in the East that many scholars consider the Greek fable derivative, but this need not be so. After all, there is hardly a people living close to the soil without animal tales illustrating ethical principles and human foibles. Anyone familiar with the use of fables in literature is bound to be puzzled by this one. It is addressed to the kings and to Hesiod's brother, Perses. The kings, of course, are the local powerful nobles who have sided with Perses in the dispute over the patrimony. Both they and Perses are greedy. Perses robs his brother and bribes the kings with gifts in order to secure their support. We are dealing with an allegory in which the rapacious hawk stands for the kings and for Perses. Hesiod the poet is the captive nightingale whose protestations are dismissed as useless and ineffectual because the captor is stronger. What is missing in the fable is the punishment of the hawk's hubris. The moral, too, is given by the offender and amounts to the proverbial might makes right. Hesiod's admonition to Perses is "obey justice and restrain reckless wrongdoing." There is a chance that the fable ended with the punishment of the hawk and that Hesiod left the end out because it was too well known. From the lines that follow the fable, it is obvious that Hesiod feels that the hawk is an ignorant fool. This is clear from the epigrammatic "only fools need suffer to learn" (218).

213–85. In these lines, Hesiod embarks on a sermon on the theme of justice and the evils that follow its violation. In part of this sermon, he personifies the concept and refers to Justice, daughter of Zeus. In the *Theogony*, Hesiod has given Justice a very high place. She is Zeus's daughter by Themis (Established Custom) and a sister of Peace and Good Law (Eirene and Eunomia). Thus, Justice (Dike) is an important force in the civilized order that is concomitant with the rule of Zeus. She and her two sisters "watch over the works of mortal men" (*Theogony* 903). Crooked verdicts and perjury violate Justice inasmuch as "The Oath Demon follows the trail of crooked decrees" (219). The Oath Demon "more than any other brings pains to mortals / who of their own accord swear false oaths" (*Theogony* 231–32). The perjurer and the wrongdoer harm not only themselves. They are public menaces because their misdeeds can destroy whole cities. Actions against Justice can bring about infertility of crops and of women, thus causing death through famine and dwindling of population through sterility. Indeed, Zeus is so angered by offenses against his beloved daughter that he visits havoc on whole armies and fleets. An act of injustice is thus made to be like a crack in the very foundation of civilized society with serious consequences. Zeus's eye sees everything, and he has no less than thirty thousand guardians of his order on earth, who constitute a sort of invisible police force that watches out for violations. The rule of justice is so essential to civilization that nothing else distinguishes with equal sharpness the societies of man from the savage beasts that devour one another. One of the worst forms of injustice is perjury, and Zeus not only punishes the perjurer himself but his descendants as well. The lies of which Perses is guilty will be avenged not only on the community of Askre but also specifically on the progeny of Perses and thereby on Hesiod's next of kin.

This is a very impassioned appeal to Perses to mend his ways before it is too late. The present situation in which the noble suffer injustices is so bad that Hesiod finds it impossible to be a just man surrounded by people who violate Zeus's most fundamental law for man. Hesiod wants to be a just man, and he is sure that Zeus will make this possible for him by not allowing injustice to triumph. His sense of responsibility and his concern are not only personal but civic as well. The evil perpetrated on him must be rectified before it spreads to the rest of his community, since "many times one man's wickedness ruins a whole city" (240).

216–18. The imagery in these lines is compound. First we have the idea of two roads, one leading to fair dealings and the other leading to unfair ones. Then we have the idea of a race between Justice and its enemy, Injustice or, more accurately, Hubris. The meaning is clear: Hubris always seems to have a head start but at the end Justice is always the winner.

219. Horkos, the Oath Demon, is grandson of Night and son of Strife (Eris); he is born after Lawlessness and Ruin, and his siblings constitute an evil brood that plagues humanity (*Theogony* 226–32). Horkos himself is not evil inasmuch as he pursues those who swear false oaths. Originally, the Oath Demon may have been a personification of the imprecation whereby a man called death upon himself, should he swear a false oath. The Roman god of the underworld, Orcus, may have evolved from this concept and he may owe his name to the Greek Oath Demon. Later on (lines 802–4), Hesiod cautions,

> Be on your guard all fifth days; they are harsh and dread.
> They say that on the fifth the Furies assisted at the birth of Oath, whom Strife bore as a plague to perjurers.

The presence of the Furies at the birth of Oath clearly shows that he is connected with punishment and specifically with revenge.

220–29. Justice is portrayed as an innocent maiden overcome by cruel and unjust men. In gatherings she sits next to her father, Zeus. Animals know not what Dike is. Zeus gave it to humans. The man who honors his oath shall leave a noble offspring while the man who violates his oath will be inherited by an inferior generation. Under mistreatment Justice becomes a vengeful spirit that brings ruin on those who are bent on driving her out of the city. She is essentially a benevolent and beneficent spirit that brings prosperity and peace to the cities of just men. Here Hesiod is working very much along lines that he establishes in the *Theogony* when he gives the genealogy of Justice (Dike) and makes her the sister of Peace and Lawfulness (literally, Good Law) in line 902.

230–31. It should be remembered that Thalia (Festivity) is one of the three Graces—the other two are Splendor (Aglaia) and Joy (Euphrosyne)—and a daughter of Wide Law (Eurynome). These lines are then a continuation of the same theme. In other words, Justice finds herself surrounded here by states of prosperity and happiness that correspond to the divinities with which Hesiod surrounds her when he gives her genealogy in the *Theogony* (901–11).

233–34. Scholars have connected the image of the acorn-laden oak with the practice of eating the acorns. It should be noted that the men to whom Hesiod alludes here are men who live in a civilized settlement and who are not strangers to agriculture. It is more probable that what Hesiod means is that the cultivated land gives them a plentiful harvest for themselves, and the uncultivated forest a rich yield for their animals. An oak whose middle teems with bees is also a blessing. The bees do not swarm on the acorn-laden branches but on the middle of the oak. By "middle of the oak," Hesiod means a hollow in the middle or even the top of the trunk, thereby counting the leafy part of the tree as the upper half.

234–35. This is a picture of abundance, in which hallowed custom is respected. This city in which children resemble their fathers is unlike the city that Hesiod has prophesied for the last stage in the deterioration of his own age, the age of iron (182). Hesiod's Askre must have been not so very different from today's Greek village, in which deviation from the "family look" is guaranteed to bring the unfortunate mother's reputation into suspicion and to give cause for wild speculation. Ordinarily, to tell a Greek boy that he is the "spitting image" of his father is to pay him a cherished compliment. Mention of resemblance to the mother is not received with equal enthusiasm.

236–37. Sailing on the sea was considered a peril which one took only under the constraint of dire need.

240–43. The sentiment is common in Greek thought. Thus, in the *Iliad*, for the offense Agamemnon has committed against Chryses, Apollon brings pestilence upon the entire Achaean host. The whole land of Thebes is struck by a blight because of the presence among the people of Oedipus, a parricide who has married his own mother.

252–55. The idea of invisible divine watchers is found both in the *Avesta* and in the *Vedas*, and must be of Indo-European origin. In *Odyssey* 17.485–87, we are told that the gods wander through the cities of men in the likeness of strangers in order to spy on violations of law and order.

259. In *Orphic Hymn* 62, we are told that Justice (Dike)

> Sits upon the sacred throne of Lord Zeus
> looking down on the lives of the many
>   human
> races and crushing the unjust with just
>   retribution.

For this idea, cf. also *Oedipus Coloneus* 1382; and Kern, *Orphicorum Fragmenta* 23.

267. In the *Iliad*, Agamemnon prays thus: "Father Zeus, ruling from Ida, most glorious and greatest / and you all-hearing and all-seeing Sun" (3.276–77). Also, in *Odyssey* 11.109 and 12.323, we are told that the sun sees all and hears all. Omniscience cast in similar terms is attributed to certain gods in Indian and Iranian literature. We are doubtless dealing with a common Indo-European tradition for which the Greek lines quoted above preserve some valuable evidence. It is the sun that courses the heavens and sees, and therefore knows, all, and it is a rather small step to transport this attribute of the sun to the ruling sky-god. Yet, as we know from the *Iliad*, Zeus is not, strictly speaking, omniscient.

275–78. What these lines say amounts to a seminal concept of natural law. It is unnatural for men to contravene Justice through brute force and natural for beasts to devour one another. What is natural in human society coincides with the order imposed by Zeus. The idea seems to be that, since Justice and for that matter Good Law (Eunomia) come from Zeus, such "laws" as govern proper conduct also come from Zeus.

286–319. In the preceding sections of the poem, Hesiod admonishes his brother to be just and law-abiding. Here he proceeds to counsel him to be industrious as well. Perses has a choice. He can choose either the evil or the virtuous path. He can also choose sloth over work, but he must not. In both cases, he must make a positive choice. The evil path is easy. It seems to be thought of as a road that leads downhill, but the virtuous path is long and rough like an arduous climb. Hesiod is conscious that his moral sermon may fall on deaf ears. Perses may wish to think for himself. Hesiod does not deny him this right but tells him that, whereas it is best when a man thinks for himself, it is also noble to listen to good advice. The idle man is like a drone and therefore a potential thief of the labor of others. Hunger is his companion because riches go to those who work. The industrious man is envied only by the indolent, who are also indigent, but he is loved by both gods and men. The work that Hesiod has in mind is manual work, and Perses, bearing in mind the examples of the idle men who belong to the nobility and who probably set the pace in the latest fashion, may prefer to avoid honest labor and to attach the wrong kind of shame to it. The right kind of shame is a positive force, much like the right kind of strife, but in any case, shame cannot be associated with industry. The moral imperative is unequivocal: "No shame in work but plenty of it in sloth" (311).

320–26. Of course, this is addressed to all, but it is interesting that Hesiod begins the long section of moral imperatives with advice that is especially pertinent to his brother, Perses.

327. Zeus was protector of both suppliants and strangers (cf. *Odyssey* 9.270). He that harms a stranger commits an act similar to harming a suppliant. In Homer, however, the position of a stranger is weaker, and strangers occasionally take certain steps that are necessary to identify them as suppliants. Thus, once in the palace of Alkinoos, Odysseus sits on the floor near the hearth (*Odyssey* 7.153–54).

328–29. Adultery with a brother's wife was, and still is, a hideous crime in Greece. It is one of the commonest causes of fratricide. For the harsh lot that might await an orphan, cf. Andromache's fears about the future of Astyanax in *Iliad* 22.490–501. Then, he who through foolishness wrongs orphaned children or insults with harsh words his aging father will at the end be punished by Zeus.

336–41:

> In proportion to your means offer the gods sacrifices
> that are pure and unblemished, and burn choice thighs for them.
> At other times seek their favor with burnings and libations
> when you go to sleep and when the holy light looms on the horizon,
> so that you win their favor for your affairs,
> not having to sell your land, but buying more from others.

In Hesiod's suggestions we find no evidence for huge sacrifices such as we find in Homer. This goes hand in hand with a shift in the economy from heroic wealth to the modest ways of the eighth and seventh centuries BC.

342–54:

> Invite your friends to dinner, exclude your enemies,
> and remember that neighbors come first.
> If misfortune strikes your house, neighbors will come
> in their bedclothes; kinsmen will dress up.
> Bad neighbors are pests, good ones a great blessing.
> A good neighbor is a boon to him who has one.
> If your neighbor is honest, your ox is safe.
> Neighbors should measure with fairness. Give back
> no less than you take, and even more if you can,
> that you may find enough when you are in need again.
> Ruin trails dishonest profit; keep away from it.
> Love those who love you, and help those who help you.
> Give to those who give to you, never to those who do not.

Hesiod suggests that reciprocity is best.

353. A modern Greek analogue commends, "Be good to those who are good and bad to those who are bad."

354–58. Cf. *Hávamál* 48: "He who gives gladly leads a good life and is seldom plagued by sorrow." Cf. also *Hávamál* 39, 42, 52.

Giving is good in the sense that it promotes positive social relations. Not giving is bad because it does the opposite. Here Hesiod emphasizes the superior value of giving. Giving to others cultivates good will. Taking from other people's property creates ill will. There is no trace of Christian ideas in these lines or, for that matter, in all of Hesiod.

359–60. This is a further elaboration of line 320: "—not stolen wealth, god-given is much better." In the lines that follow 320, Hesiod dwells on the punishment that the gods inflict on a man who robs another man's wealth. Here the emphasis is on the psychological effects that stealing has on the thief. The sense of guilt chills the man's heart and settles on it like "a coat of hoar frost."

368–69. Hesiod's concern is not with the quality of the wine that the jar contains but clearly with thrift. When the jar is full, one may drink all one wants because there will still be enough left for him to drink again. Likewise, when the bottom shows, one does not have to exercise any restraint because it is too late. This should not be taken to mean that Hesiod thinks that lack of restraint is a virtue at any point. Rather, he is saying that there can be a departure from thrifty habits only when there is abundance and that thrift is useless when one has exhausted his supplies.

370–73. These lines are most likely a result of interpolation. The strongest argument for interpolation stems not from the idea that they represent a break in the train of thought in this passage—after all, many lines here and elsewhere in Hesiod are digressive—but rather from the fact that they are not found in the oldest manuscripts.

373–75. These lines imply that certain thievish women would enter a man's house and then proceed to use their feminine charms in order to divert his attention and steal something valuable. Some scholars have assumed that the woman Hesiod has in mind was one who wagged her tail, as it were, in order to seduce a man of substance into matrimony, but this may be reading too much into the text. Distrust of women is characteristic of all patriarchal societies, and in those parts of Greece where traditional Greek values are still strong the caveat "never trust a woman" is passed on from father to son as a piece of hallowed wisdom. In the strictly pastoral sections of the country, the explanation given for the supposed wickedness of women is that "they are like goats; they have the devil in them!" Along similar lines, cf. *Hávamál* 84:

> No man should trust the words of a
> maiden, nor what
> a woman says, because on whirling wheel
> their hearts
> were made and fickleness was placed in
> them.

376–80. These lines are problematic if, as the weight of ancient tradition dictates, in line 378 we read "and may you die old leaving another son behind" rather than "and may he die old leaving another son behind," which may have its roots in ancient emendation. If we go along with the latter reading, the sense is simple and straightforward: each man is advised to beget an only son and leave him behind as his sole heir. This would be quite sensible, since it would involve no division of patrimony and would prevent the sort of strife that arose between Hesiod and his own brother. With the former and more traditional reading, we are left with what, at least to us, appears to be a contradiction. Indeed, lines 377 and 378 do seem to stand in contradiction, but this contradiction is mitigated considerably by the afterthought of lines 379–80, which express the idea that Zeus may provide for more sons than one and that more children mean more working hands and, therefore, more income. This only mitigates the contradiction; it does not remove it. That daughters are not mentioned at all comes as little surprise to anyone familiar with attitudes among the rural folk of modern Greece. If pressed, a peasant will admit that a daughter is a child too (*paidí*), but it is still not uncommon to hear a man say that he has, for example, *"tria paidiá kai éna korítsi,"* that is, "three children (sons!) and one girl!" In rural modern Greece, even when a man is poor, ordinarily having an only son or just two sons is almost never preferable to having many sons. By contrast, having an only daughter is considered ideal, since it means having to give away only one dowry, which rarely consists of land even if there is only one son in the family.

Hesiod may have compressed within these lines more than we are able to extract from them. He does not advise a man to have many sons most likely because he is addressing farmers, and many sons would entail the division of the father's land into lots that could not support them. The phrase "may you die old leaving another son behind" shows that his wish is made with the parent's welfare in mind. If a man marries when he is thirty and begets a son, this son may in turn marry when the father is approaching sixty and then have a family of his own to look after. By this time, a late-born son, perhaps one born when the father is forty or even fifty, will grow into manhood just about when a man who lives into ripe old age begins to be plagued by the infirmities of old age. Thus, if we paraphrase Hesiod, he seems to be saying: "As far as property is concerned, one son is ideal, but if you live to be old—and I hope you do so—may you leave a second, late-born son behind." It is interesting that in rural modern Greece, parents usually move in with the family of the youngest son and frequently refer to him affectionately as their *psimádi*, their "late-born" or "youngling." It is with the idea of care for the parents in their old age and the raising of memorial cairns that the poet of *Hávamál* counsels,

> It is better to have a son, even one born late,
> after the father's death. Seldom do cairns
>   stand
> by the roadside except such as kinsman
>   raises over
> kinsman. (72)

With line 380, the moralizing part of the poem, so replete with maxims of popular wisdom, is essentially over. Lines 381 to 617 constitute a distinct unit on the farmer's year, filled with agricultural advice.

383–87. It is not clear at all why the seven Pleiades are identified with the seven daughters of Atlas, whose names are Alkyone, Gelaino, Elektra, Maia, Merope, Sterope, and Taygete. The rising Hesiod has in mind is the "heliacal" rising. The Pleiades, in other words, rise over the horizon before sunrise and thereby become visible. The heliacal rising of the Pleiades in Askre for the year 700 BC fell on May 11, a somewhat early date for reaping. When Hesiod says "for forty days and forty nights they lie hidden" (385), he means the forty days that precede their heliacal rising. During this period, the Pleiades rise after sunrise and set before sunset, and are, there-

fore, invisible. Now, the Greeks and the Romans considered their heliacal rising as the beginning of the summer. As the summer goes on, they rise earlier and earlier until there comes a time when they are seen setting before sunrise. The time of their setting, hence plowing time, in Hesiod's day was close to the end of October. With the coming of the winter, the Pleiades rise earlier and set earlier. Thus, by the beginning of April, they rise so early that they set before night. Then comes the period of forty days when "they lie hidden," and the cycle repeats itself. Line 387 refers to the late October date when they are visible as they set and when the farmer sharpens his plowshare. Fall plowing in the area of Askre nowadays begins with the first part of September and ends usually somewhat before the end of October. Sowing usually takes place in November.

The Pleiades have a secure place on the physical as well as on the poetic firmament of Greece. Their antiquity and importance from earliest times is guaranteed by their prominent position at the center of the Shield of Achilleus (*Iliad* 18.486). In modern Greek folk song, they are referred to collectively by the word *poulia* (fem. sing.) and, because of the greater visibility of one of the seven stars of the cluster, they have come to be felt as one star. In folk song, they are frequently found in the company of the dawn star. Not long from now, even in Greece, the Pleiades will be known only to astronomers. In my own village (Astrochori, Arta, Epirus), the last man who predicted the weather from the way the Pleiades set on December 4 has been dead for many years. The old songs that mention the Pleiades so very affectionately are known only by a couple of men well into their nineties, and none of the younger people know the rare lines "Poulia leads six stars / it is a chorus of seven maidens"—the boring weather report dispenses with the need for memory and observation.

388–93. No religious or ritualistic significance is necessarily implied in the advice to sow, to plow, and to reap stripped down. Hesiod most likely means that the farmer should perform these tasks as unencumbered as possible by clothing. Modern Greek farmers frequently strip down to their waist in order to perform these very same tasks.

405–9. The priorities for the farmer are a house, a woman, and a plowing ox (this is the order in the Greek text of line 405). Since work on the land is men's work (441–47, 459, 470, 502, and so forth) and we have no specific mention of slave women in the rest of the poem, line 406 has caused much discussion. The line may well be interpolated. Also, on the other hand, it may be a reference to the "bride-prize" a man should pay the woman's family. However this may be, the woman of line 406 is to follow the oxen, presumably scattering the seed. In those parts of modern Greece where plowing is not done by tractor, it is not uncommon to see the plowman followed by his wife scattering the seed. This task is traditionally women's work.

407. Hesiod advises farmers to store their things in a tight-fitting way and emphasizes saving space. Houses were very small, and agricultural tools were usually stored inside the house, thus limiting the available space.

415–19. The heliacal rising of the Dog Star in Hesiod's day took place on July 19. From this date on, the star was in the sky all day with the sun, but by the third week of September the Dog Star rose four hours earlier and thus was "night's consort much longer." The ancients believed that the Dog Star brought heat, diseases, and sunstroke. The belief clearly arose because its long presence in the sky coincided with July and August, the two hottest months in the Mediterranean. Indeed, "July's heat and August's sunscorching" is an almost proverbial expression in Greek. The first rains, *protovróchia,* arrive in Greece about the middle of September.

420–22. This is sound advice. Woodcutting is best done in the fall or even in the winter, when the sap is less active. Hesiod may be suggesting early fall because this way the wood will be allowed to lie and dry up for a longer period.

423. The Hesiodic foot is roughly twelve inches long. The log for the mortar should be a thick one that would stand three feet high so that it could be used by a man in a standing position. The cubit was one-and-one-half feet, and this measure makes the pestle four-and-one-half feet long. The suggested length for the pestle seems a bit short. This may indicate that the average man was then shorter or, most likely, that the grinding or, more accurately, the crushing of corn by means of pestle and mortar was ordinarily a task given to women.

424–25. The seven-foot axle is meant to be used for a cart. If we assume that the entire seven-foot axle was between the two wheels, we have an unusually broad cart. Evidence from classical times suggests that the distance between the two wheels was closer to five feet. It is entirely possible that in the more primitive Hesiodic cart the axle projected roughly by one foot at each end. The one-foot piece left for a mallet, if a man should cut an eight-foot piece, being too short for the handle, must be intended for the head of the mallet. On the other hand, since wood cut for an axle piece would not be very thick, the extra foot might be used for the handle of a short mallet.

426–27. It is not easy to decide exactly what sort of wagon Hesiod has in mind here. Is the wagon four-wheeled or two-wheeled? Does the measure of ten palms refer to the height of the wagon, to its breadth, or to the length of the vehicle from front to back? When Hesiod uses the word that I translate as "felly," does he mean a whole wheel, a sort of block wheel, or a quarter-felly? Then there is the question whether the wheel had spokes. The ancient scholiasts took the felly to be a quarter-felly and the measure of ten palms to refer to the diameter of the wheel. A three-span felly would be roughly twenty-four inches long, and this would give us a ninety-six-inch circumference for the wheel. A ten-palm diameter would be forty fingers long and therefore roughly again thirty-one to thirty-two inches long. If we assume the presence of spokes formed by two crossed sticks, we may well imagine the two sticks crossing at rectangular angles and dividing the wheel into four equal fellies of twenty-four inches in length. The two crossed sticks would be equal in length, and each would be equal to a diameter of thirty-two inches. Now, the ratio of circumference to diameter, $96:32 = 3$, is inexact, but we should remember that measures given in spans and palms cannot be expected to produce constant measures and perfect ratios. This solution is based on the assumption that wagons were classified by the diameter of the wheel. Such an assumption cannot be proved, but it is not unreasonable. That by felly here Hesiod means a quarter-felly and not the whole felly is an even safer assumption. A wheel whose entire felly was approximately twenty-four inches, if one goes by the imperfect ratio of three for the ratio of the circumference to diameter, would have a diameter of eight inches, and this would make for a minuscule wheel, indeed one that would be small even for a wheelbarrow.

427–36. Hesiod is referring to two types of plows in this passage. The more primitive type is the single-stock plow, in which beam and share are of one piece. The main pieces of the more advanced type of plow in which the various pieces are fitted together by wooden pegs are: (1) the long handle (curved at the upper end) fitted into the back part of the share; (2) the share itself to which the iron share referred to by Hesiod in line 387 is attached; (3) the beam that is fastened roughly into the middle of the wooden share (the word used for this piece, *gyes*, suggests that at some appropriate point it curved toward the yoke); (4) the pole, which at one end was fastened by pegs (431) to the beam at the one end and by one peg to the middle of the yoke; (5) the yoke, which sits on the necks of the oxen and is kept from slipping away by a pair of (6) *zeuglai* for each ox. These are curved wooden pieces that are driven through the yoke and form a sort of collar round the neck of the animal. At the lower end, they are fastened together by thongs. Hesiod does not mention the *zeuglai*. He recommends oak for the share and holm oak (M.Gr. *pournári*) for the beam, which has to bear the stress of constant traction. Unlike the beam, the pole is straight, and traction alone will not break it. Hesiod recommends elm or laurel for this piece. Both trees yield wood less tough than oak and were probably in readier supply than oak. Farmers from the village of Panagia (recently renamed Askre), which lies very close to ancient Askre, told me that wooden plows were used in the area until 1935 or so. They agreed that oak was best for the share and holm oak for the beam. The pole, they said, could be made of laurel, of elm, or even of plane tree.

437–40. I have been told by Greek farmers that, although they start using oxen for plowing usually when the animals are three years old, a nine-year-old ox is more mature and disciplined, and still in the peak of its strength. However, the recommended age here may also be dictated by the tendency of epic convention to give formulaic ages.

441–47. Hesiod's recommendation that the farmhand who follows the oxen should be forty years old should be taken somewhat more literally than his recommendation that the team of oxen should be nine years old. He tells the farmer to choose a mature man and not a scatterbrained youth. Is the task of this man to plow or to scatter the seed? Line 443 seems to suggest that he is a plowman; lines 445–46 clearly imply that he scatters the seed. This is a contradiction. Plowing takes a great deal of experience, and it is not likely that a poor farmer will entrust his precious plow and his oxen to a hired hand. The difficulty remains, if we read the Greek of 443 to mean "drive a straight furrow," but in my opinion the forty-year-old man in question is one whose task is to scatter the seed. Cf. lines 467–68, in which the farmer himself clearly is the plowman.

448–49. It is clear from the lines that follow that Hesiod advises the farmer to take the flight of cranes on their southward migration as another sign for plowing. The other more dependable sign, the setting of the Pleiades, was mentioned in line 384. Cranes no longer come to the area of Askre, because the lake Kopais does not exist anymore. It was drained many years ago.

456. The number 100 need not be taken literally. It is Hesiod's way of saying "many."

462–64. I was told in modern-day Askre that fallow land should be plowed first in the spring between the middle of April and the end of May, and then again in July or August. The second plowing is called *dibólisma* and may be followed by sowing after the first fall rains.

465–66. I translate "Zeus Chthonios" as "Zeus of the earth" and take this god to be Zeus and not Hades or Plouton, who is called "Chthonic Zeus" in *Orphic Hymn* 18 (line 3). Although it is Hades who is more frequently associated with Demeter, it is clear from line 474 that Hesiod means Zeus. For this epithet applied to Zeus, see *Oedipus Coloneus* 1606.

467. Prayer to the god on whom all depends is natural and necessary at the beginning of such an · important task. Modern Greek plowmen frequently cross themselves as they begin plowing and then, if the plow hits a stone or the oxen are unruly, proceed to shower scores of saints with blasphemies. The idea, if there is any idea at all in this contradictory behavior, seems to be that it is as natural to ask heaven for help as it is to curse it and hold its powers responsible for adversities.

479–90. Hesiod advises against plowing late at the time of the winter solstice. Although the winter solstice is fixed with precision, by "plowing at winter solstice" Hesiod means plowing that is done late in December rather than at the recommended time in October. Hesiod says that late plowing is bad, but early and gentle spring rains have such a beneficial effect that the harvest of the late plower can be as good as that of the farmer who plows at the right time.

The meaning of line 481 is not entirely clear. A poor crop may consist of short-stalked wheat or barley, but cross-binding the sheaves will not remedy the situation. There is some merit to the suggestion that Hesiod's recommendation is intended to deceive the eyes of malevolent neighbors. A cross-bound sheaf may be made to look somewhat longer and fuller at both ends. Boeotian farmers in the area of Askre told me that they cross-bind sheaves at all times because this makes for a tighter and securer sheaf and for one that is better balanced and therefore easier to carry.

The song of the cuckoo heralds the advent of spring, and for this reason this bird is greatly loved by the Greeks and figures prominently in their folk songs. The expression "We will not hear the cuckoo this year" is equivalent to "We will not survive the winter this year." In folk songs, the expression "the cuckoo will not sing this year" means that the year will be a year of sorrow and mourning.

493–94. It was the warmth of the smithy that made it a favorite place for idle men to gather.

497. This is Hesiod's way of saying, "lest you come close to death because of starvation." The hand is scrawny because of weight loss. Prolonged hunger causes swelling of the lower extremities.

504. The month of Lenaion roughly coincides with part of January and part of February for us and is therefore in the very heart of the winter. The name is not Boeotian but was used in Ionian states other than Athens. The Athenians called the same month Gamelion.

524–25. These lines constitute a kenning. "Mr. Boneless" is most likely the octopus. The ancient belief that the octopus occasionally ate his "foot"—one of his tentacles, that is—seems based on freakish biological fact—a rare one to be sure—rather than on pure fancy. Such riddle names for animals and people are used by Hesiod playfully, very much as in riddles or folk tales: thus "house-carrier" for the snail (571), "five-branch" for the hand (743), "the wise one" for the ant (778), and so forth. In Epirus, there is a kind of spider that is called "the sunless one." The Cypriots call the viper "the deaf one." As this example indicates, such names are frequently applied to dangerous creatures as a sort of code name that is calculated to leave them unaware that they have been mentioned. Lurking behind this practice is the naive fear that mention of such a creature by its true name will bring about its appearance. However, when Hesiod uses such words as *boneless* and *house-carrier*, it is clear that he does so for artistic effect.

527–28. The Greeks believed that in winter the sun spent much of its time over Africa (cf. also *Odyssey* 1.22–25).

Works and Days

533–35. The walking tripod of these lines is a hunched-over man who walks with the aid of a stick.

538. The cloth Hesiod suggests here for winter wear is a heavy "weft-backed" cloth in which the weft is double and the warp is single. Interestingly enough, a woven cloth called *dimito(n)* by Greek weavers is produced by doubling the warp and is considered more durable and more resistant to cold. The emphasis is on keeping warm. Until recently shepherds wore capes made of goat hair. Such capes are heavy and protect against rain and snow. The Boeotian farmer needs very warm clothes to survive the winter. Judging by the clothes recommended by Hesiod to battle the fury of the Boeotian winter, the high skills of a Boeotian woman were absolutely necessary. The loom itself must have been made by skilled carpenters. In Greece it survived down to fifty years ago. Hesiod's instructions about the kind of clothes a man should wear during the winter preserve astonishing information.

541–42. Such sandals, sometimes also made of pig, horse, or cow skin, were worn by Greek mountaineers in northern Greece as late as 1945. They are called *sgaronia* and are not like ordinary sandals since they cover the whole foot snugly. It must be some such footwear that Hesiod is suggesting and not the ordinary sandal, which is poor protection in cold and rainy weather.

543–45. It is difficult to understand why the hides of firstling kids are recommended for stitching together in order to make a coat. Like firstling lambs, firstling kids were a token of exceptional piety in sacrifices (*Iliad* 4.102). Since animals were almost exclusively slaughtered on religious occasions—much as in modern Greece until very recently—if the farmer follows Hesiod's advice, he can combine virtue with necessity without departing from thrifty habits.

550–53. Hesiod seems to know that mist and rain come from moisture that rises from the earth and not from some body of water in the celestial region. That he does not mention the sea as a source of moisture that turns to mist and rain is remarkable but understandable. Despite his excursus on navigation, the sea is not part of his experience.

559–60. Hesiod recommends a drastic reduction in the rations given to oxen and some increase in the rations given to men. Oxen are idle in their stalls in the heart of winter, but men still work, making wagons, plows, and other implements, and are exposed to cold when they tend their flocks of goats and sheep.

561–63. Strictly speaking, the end of the year for Hesiod would be marked by the summer solstice in June, which also marked the beginning of the new year. Yet, here he seems to have the vernal equinox in mind—roughly March 21—since he speaks of nights and days as no longer unequal. He does not use the technical expression for the vernal equinox. Since threshing starts roughly on the summer solstice when Orion rises (597–98) and therefore well into the third week of June, the advice given here seems hardly useful or appropriate. Thrifty habits can be dispensed with only after the new crop has been harvested and threshed. It is possible that by "end of the year" in 561 Hesiod means the summer solstice and that textual corruption in 562 has left us with a line that now means "when nights and days are no longer unequal" but that in its original form must have meant something like "until the days are more than a match for the nights." M. L. West's translation, "balance the nights and days" (by allowing more food as the nights grow shorter), is probably right on the mark, but the text as we have it betrays that something is either missing or grammatically distorted.

564–70. Sixty days after the winter solstice would take us to February 17 or 18. Hesiod has in mind the acronychal and not the heliacal rising of the constellation of Boötes, of which Arcturus is the brightest star. Arcturus is visible on the eastern horizon in the evening for several days toward the end of February and the beginning of March.

The Athenian king Pandion had two daughters, Procne and Philomela. Procne was married to the Thracian king Tereus, who pretended that his wife died and asked that Philomela be sent to him. When she arrived, Tereus raped her and cut her tongue off to prevent her from revealing his hideous act to anyone. Philomela wove her story into a piece of embroidery and sent it to Procne. Procne took revenge on her husband by killing their son, Itys, and serving his flesh to him. The two sisters were pursued by Tereus, but the gods mercifully put an end to the tragedy by turning all three into birds. Tereus became a hoopoe, Procne a nightingale, and Philomela a swallow. Much like the cuckoo, the swallow is a beloved harbinger of spring in Greece.

Having given the farmer an arithmetic formula and two sure tokens of the imminence of spring's arrival, namely, the acronychal rising of Arcturus and the return of the swallow, Hesiod proceeds to tell him to make sure to prune his vines before the coming of spring. Pruning and hoeing are done at about the same time. Greeks prune their vines in January or February. The area of Askre is still rich in well-tended vineyards. A line of didactic poetry that was passed on to me at the village of Askre counsels: "Prune your vines in January and pay the moon no heed." However, I was told that, despite this admonition, pruning is frequently done in February. I was also told that "pay the moon no heed" means "pay no attention to whether the moon is waxing or waning."

Hesiod and the farmers for whom he sang his compositions must have cared a great deal about their vines. The poet tells them when it is best to prune their vines (570) and gather their grapes (611). One wonders why olive trees are not mentioned and why olive oil is so conspicuously absent in Hesiod's poems. Disciplines other than philology may provide us with answers about this especially intriguing omission. This question is most important in view of the wider, Panhellenic compass of the Works and Days.

571–77. The "house-carrier" is the snail. By referring to the sharpening of sickles for reaping, Hesiod makes a rather spectacular jump. The heliacal rise of the Pleiades is, roughly speaking, in the middle of May, when the heat is so intense that snails seek refuge from it by climbing on plants. His advice is prune and hoe your vines before Arcturus rises and spring is about to arrive; sharpen your sickles

and wake up the farmhands for reaping when the Pleiades rise (see notes on 597–98).

582–89. This is a famous passage that found eager imitators in Greek antiquity. The thistle in question is the golden thistle, which is popularly referred to by Greek peasants as "donkey's thorn." No one who has spent even one summer day in the Greek countryside is likely to forget the sound of the cicadas, which comes to a deafening crescendo at high noon. Hesiod seems to think that the cicada "chirps" or "stridulates" by vibrating its wings. He is actually not far from the truth since the stridulation comes from a vibration of a membrane in the thorax of the insect.

It is not clear why wine should be at its best in the heart of the summer. It is, however, true that oats are fat at this time. Even though men may be parched by the sun and dried up by the heat, Hesiod would probably be nearer the truth if he had said that the summer heat is conducive to increasing the sexual urge in both men and women. His choosing to attribute to women an insatiable sexual appetite in the summer may be a playful, if unfair, way of overdramatizing the plight of men, whose energies are overtaxed both day and night. Yet, the more probable view is that these lines express deep-seated beliefs. R. B. Onians notes that for the Greeks of the archaic period the head was "the seat and source of 'life' and the life fluid" and that much of a man's strength and his seed in the form of fluid resided in his knees (see Onians, *Origins*, 174ff., and especially 177, 187). In a serious sense, therefore, men whose vital life fluid and seed fluid was drained by excessive heat would be a poor match for libidinous women.

The thistle and the chirping cicadas of August may be privy to forgotten ancient secrets. Few people in northwestern Greece now remember that women were advised to bite into the very tart fruit of the cornel tree in order to dull the hurt of their libidinous urges. In Greece, the fruit of the cornel tree ripens in August, and it is extremely tart even when it is at its ripest.

589–96. For wine, Hesiod recommends *Biblinos Oinos*, "wine from Biblos." This may have been a district in Thrace, but be that as it may, the

Works and Days

meaning is "your choice wine," "only the best wine," or something of the sort. There is equal uncertainty as to whether "bread baked in the dusk" may refer to the immediately preceding evening or to the dusk preceding the dawn of the working day—therefore, a very fresh bread. However, what Hesiod means by "milk from goats just as their milk is about to stop" is clear to goatherds who believe that the thick milk goats produce before they stop altogether producing milk is very nutritional and makes men unusually strong. This sort of milk is called *sterphógala* in modern Greek, and it comes in late August when the goats start mating. Meat is richer and tastier when it comes from an animal that has been allowed to graze in open pastures and woodlands where the animal, in addition to grass, also eats small plants, shrubs, and low-lying branches of certain trees. Young kids, especially when roasted on a spit, are a prized delicacy in Greece. Even though the Greeks mixed their wine with water, three measures of water and one of wine would produce a very mildly alcoholic beverage, more suitable for refreshment than for intoxication. This recipe is fitting in a passage that recommends relaxation and fending off the effects of intense heat.

Sheep are very important to the Hesiodic economy. Flocks of sheep are equivalent to wealth: "riches and flocks of sheep go to those who work" (308). Sheep wool was highly valued (516–17). It is rather surprising that Hesiod does not mention cheese anywhere. Homer refers to cheese in *Iliad* 10.638 and *Odyssey* 11.234.

597–98. Hesiod refers to the morning or heliacal rising of Betelgeuse, the brightest star of the constellation of Orion. This rising in Hesiod's time would more or less coincide with the summer solstice. Thus, it is the last third of June and probably the beginning of July that Hesiod recommends as the right time for threshing. That the dates he gives are rough approximations intended as advice the farmer should use when he takes into account the condition of his crops is certain. In 383, Hesiod commands "start reaping when the Pleiades, daughters of Atlas, rise." Now, as has already

been said, the heliacal rise of the Pleiades in Hesiod's day took place in mid-May. The time he recommends for threshing in 597–98 would be more than a month later. Although in the plains of Eleusis and Thebes reaping takes place earlier—sometimes in May—in the area of Askre barley is reaped at the end of May and wheat usually between June 20 and July 10. Threshing may wait as long as a whole month. Although the climate of Askre may have been somewhat different in Hesiod's day, it is entirely possible that his recommendations for reaping and threshing may—even in his own day—have been more applicable to the plains of Boeotia and Attica than to his own village. It is interesting that it is June and not May that is called *Theristés*, "reaper," in modern Greece.

598. The threshing floor must be well-rounded because the yoked oxen that were driven on the sheaves of wheat strewn on it could perform their task easier and more efficiently if they could run in more or less perfect concentric circles. The threshing floor must be in a windy place because winnowing follows threshing.

602–3. Literally, Hesiod says "hire a homeless worker." By this, he means a man without *oikos,* a "household," and therefore a man free of pressing obligations. A childless woman is also ideal as a servant because she is unencumbered and because the master will not have extra mouths to feed.

604. Hesiod's exhortation to keep one's sharp-toothed dog well fed seems to fit the needs of a settled farmer whose animals, including his dog, are domesticated. Cretan and Epirotan shepherds keep their dogs lean and feed them small portions every second or third day. This way, their dogs are alert and dangerous to intruders.

605. The "day-sleeper" is the burglar who sleeps during the day and prowls at night.

609–14. The time indicated here is mid-September. Line 610 is a poetic way of describing the morning rising of Arcturus. September in modern Greek is properly called *Trygetés,* vintage month. Vintage time in the area of Askre nowadays usually begins September 25 and ends October 15.

"The gift of joyous Dionysos" is, of course, wine.

615–17. For the setting of the Pleiades, see notes on 383–87. The constellation of Orion partly sets at the same time as the Pleiades. The Hyades set in the beginning of November.

619–20. The setting of the Pleiades before Orion is here described in terms of flight and pursuit. For the setting of the Pleiades, cf. notes on 383–87.

635. Aeolian Kyme then is the place of origin for Hesiod's family. The city was situated on the coast of Asia Minor, not too far from the river Hermos and, very roughly speaking, across from the islands of Lesbos and Chios. At this point Hesiod offers important information about his own origin. He has nothing good to say about Askre. However, he may be doing what is expected of him. Aversion to living somewhere away from home is very frequent in modern Greek folk songs.

639–40. Askre lay to the northwest of Thespiai and to the south of the Lake Kopais area. It was destroyed by the Thespians, probably at the end of the fifth century. The Askreans who survived the destruction were taken to Orchomenos. When Pausanias visited the site, the only structure he found standing was a solitary tower, no doubt the same tower that still stands on top of the hill Pyrgaki. The Acropolis of Askre must have been located on top of this hill, but the Askreans most likely lived at the foot of the hill and cultivated the fields that lie between it and the foot of Helikon. I visited this area in April 1979 and found it so lovely that I cannot but attribute Hesiod's unflattering comment on Askre to a deep-rooted personal grudge.

651–52. Some scholars understand these lines to mean that the Achaeans "waited through a long winter" before they sailed to Troy. We cannot be sure about the details of the version familiar to Hesiod, but "storm" rather than "winter" is a very definite possibility. Unfortunately, Homer offers no help for the solution of the problem (cf. *Iliad* 2.303).

654–59. Even though there is no independent testimony either for Amphidamas or for the event to which Hesiod refers here, there is no reason to think that we are dealing with fiction. This Amphidamas was most likely a nobleman from Chalkis who fell in a battle against the Eretrians during the long feud over the Lelantine plain. Proclus gives an alternative version for line 657: "I was victor in a song contest with divine Homer." We can be certain that this line should be ascribed to an interpolator who was eager to adduce proof for the historicity of the *Contest of Homer and Hesiod.* Pausanias tells us that when he visited Helikon he was told that the most ancient of the tripods dedicated at Helikon was the one won by Hesiod at Chalkis (9.31.3). Hesiod's statement that "I know nothing about boats and sailing, yet I will teach you what you must know about sailing" contains effective and wry humor.

663–77. Prima facie, Hesiod seems to be suggesting that the best time to sail is the period of fifty days that follows the summer solstice; that is, from about June 20 to August 10. But there are problems with this passage. Line 663 could be translated either "fifty days past the summer solstice" or "for fifty days past the summer solstice." If we take the line to mean that sailing should start fifty days after the summer solstice, we end up with a sailing season that starts very late and does not take advantage of the major part of the summer. If, on the other hand, we understand the meaning of the line to be "for fifty days after the summer solstice," we have a sailing season that ends too soon. In addition to these problems, we also have to come to terms with line 664, which literally says "when the toilsome summer season comes to an end." The summer season does not come to an end either at the end of June or at the beginning of August. Perhaps consideration of some other factors might help us reach a tentative solution. If the dependable winds to which Hesiod refers in line 670 are the Etesian winds, commonly known as *meltémia* in modern Greece, it should be borne in mind that these winds start roughly around July 20, when Sirius rises, and continue roughly until the end of August or the beginning of September. The beginning of the Etesian winds does not come at the end of the summer season. However, we should remember that for Hesiod the summer started with the heliacal rise of the Pleiades (May 11 or so in his day). This rise signaled the beginning of the busy season of summer work. Reaping started then (see notes on 383–84). Threshing started around the summer solstice and the concomitant rise of Orion (see notes on 597–98). Threshing, winnowing, storing, transportation by land, and loading of surplus wheat on boats could well occupy the last week of June and the first two weeks of July. It is, therefore, possible that when Hesiod speaks of the end of the toilsome summer season, he may refer to the period from mid-May to mid-July and mean something tantamount to "when the toilsome part of the summer comes to an end." The key to understanding the passage lies in realizing that Hesiod wants to count the fifty days starting not only after the summer solstice but also after the busy agricultural work more or less comes to an end, and, most likely, after the Etesian winds start to blow. If we count from July 20, we have a sailing season whose height lasts until September 10 or so. Now, one could venture to sail for a longer period, but Hesiod advises sailors to come home "before the new wine and the fall rains" (674). The time of the new wine and of the fall rains is certainly much closer to the end of the specified fifty-day sailing season, if we count the beginning of this season from July 20 rather than from June 20. In this section of the poem, Hesiod may refer to what is usually called "Little summer" in Greece and "Indian summer" in American Indian folklore. Hesiod distinguishes spring sailing from early fall sailing. At all times, he counsels caution and moderation.

678–82. The time to which Hesiod alludes here in this quaint way should be the second half of April.

690–93. Hesiod advises the merchant to overload neither wagon nor ship, but probably for different reasons. In the case of the wagon, the load should not be excessive because it might overtax the strength of the axle, and the merchant might end up with a broken-down wagon and a wasted load of grain and other goods. In the case of a ship's cargo, the poet advises taking to the ship less than what is left behind because the sea is so fickle and perilous and the sea trader should risk no more at sea than he could do without back home.

695–97. This is still considered an ideal age for a Greek man to marry.

698. If we consider the thirteenth year as the year in which girls reach puberty, then Hesiod is suggesting that a girl should marry when she reaches eighteen. His advice seems very sensible but probably does not mirror the practice of his time. Indeed, evidence from various parts of the Greek world suggests that not infrequently girls were given in marriage at much younger ages.

699. "Marry a virgin so you can teach her right from wrong." The emphasis on marrying a virgin here at least seems to have little to do with chastity. The important thing is that a future wife should be so innocent at the time of marriage that her husband could proceed to mold her character according to his own values, and her habits and manners also according to his own. This caution also has to do with the realities of village life. If a young woman was found pregnant before her marriage, questions of morality arose. Hesiod does not say much about Eros. Eros is an unsettling rebellion in so many ways. It defies social convention, social order, and so forth. Frequently, Eros, which comes with passion, may create big problems: sometimes those in love may have to leave the community. Unwanted pregnancies are a huge problem. Only the intervention of third parties may remedy the situation.

700–701. In a small community, a man must guard his reputation and must not risk marrying a girl he does not know because, if she turns out to be a bad wife, he may be ridiculed in the eyes of his neighbors.

702–5. One of the characteristics of a bad wife is that "she is a glutton who reclines to eat." The idea is that it is bad enough for a woman to have a voracious appetite and even worse if she is so lazy and assumes such improper airs as to recline when she eats. Greek men liked to eat half-reclined, supporting the weight of the upper body on one of their elbows, but the women were expected to wait on them. In rural modern Greece until quite recently—and in some remote parts of the country even now—women first served the men and then ate, sometimes separately, especially if guests were present.

When it comes to marriage, Hesiod's advice is practical. He recommends marrying a younger woman from one's own neighborhood or community. We must remember here that there was a high mortality rate among brides. The testimony is overwhelming. Also, there was a high mortality rate for infants. Clearly Hesiod recommends an industrious wife, one who does not expect to have her dinner in bed.

719–20. With these lines, compare *Hávamál* 29.

722. Cf. *Hávamál* 7.

724–26. For ritualistic hand washing, cf. *Iliad* 1.449, 16.230.

727–32. The acts that involve the elimination of human waste are perforce unclean. The concern here is not with cleanliness but with ritualistic propriety. Urinating should preferably be done at night and even then, in some manner that does not offend the night, for the night is also divine. Urinating while facing the sun is tantamount to defiling and perhaps defying not only the source of light and warmth but a celestial body revered as a god. The commandment "Do not piss as you stand facing the sun" goes beyond what is practical. Clearly, Hesiod implies that there are powers in this world that we should respect at all times, because if we fail to do so these powers might be angry with us. The advice to squat before urinating or to urinate against walls seems intended to ensure minimal exposure of the genitals. Temple inscriptions from ancient Greece occasionally contain prescripts against defecation and urination within the area of the temple. These lines are quite similar in spirit to the prescripts given in the *Laws of Manu* 4.45–50. Lines 736 and 757–59 remind me somewhat of a couplet that was recited to me in the Cypriot village of Choulou in the area of Paphos: "If a man farts in church or shits right on the road / or pisses into water, his sins are not forgiven."

733–34. Hestia, the goddess connected with the hearth, was a virgin goddess and as such especially averse to the sight Hesiod describes here. Cf. also notes on *Theogony* 454.

736. The fear that obviously lurked behind this taboo was that contact with death was inauspicious for the procreative act. Death is the enemy of life, and the two must be kept as far apart as possible.

737–41. Rivers were personified and considered sacred. Therefore, a man should be ritually pure before crossing them.

742–43. The "five-branch" is the hand, and these lines are an injunction against cutting one's nails at a sacrifice. Tradition ascribes a similar prescript to Pythagoras. The reason behind this curious taboo is obscure. In the area of Radovyzi, Epirus, formerly people set on taking blood revenge for murder would not cut their nails until they did so. When I asked people from the village of Askre about superstitions concerning nails, they told me that the only knowledge they had of such superstition came from the lines

> Cut not your nails on Wednesdays and
> Fridays,
> and bathe not on Sundays, if you want to
> do well.

744–45. None of the explanations suggested for this superstition is satisfactory.

746–47. Some scholars understand the word that I have translated "carve an auspicious sign" to mean "smooth out" or "polish the roof" and suggest that, if the roof is smooth, crows cannot perch on it. I think this suggestion is quite unlikely, since no roof could be so smooth that crows could not perch on it. I also think that Hesiod suggests the carving of an apotropaic sign or of some sort of figure that could serve as a "scarecrow." Much like owls, crows are considered birds of ill omen in modern Greece.

750–52. "That which is motionless" is most likely a reference to tombs and the dead. We do not know why the number twelve is significant in this connection. That it should be boys and men, rather than girls and women, who can be harmed by sitting on tombs is perhaps easier to

Works and Days

explain. The dead belong to the underworld and, therefore, to powers that are perforce hostile to life and fertility, and it is the man who carries the seed and who is more easily subject to harmful influences. The earth "hides" seeds of all kinds much as it "hides" the dead.

753–54. It is a widespread belief among primitive peoples that contact with the "weaker sex" weakens men. This is the idea that lies behind taboos that forbid men to eat together even with their wives (see Crowley, *Mystic Rose,* London, 1902, 202–30).

These lines suggest the fear of contamination caused by the possible presence of a woman's menstrual blood. In the Orthodox Jewish holy ritual of the mikvah, a woman immerses herself totally in water that is pure and at least partly coming from a natural source. The goal is renewal and reunification with God and with her husband. Relevant to our lines is the stipulation that the mikvah should take place at the end of seven spotless days and seven nights after the completion of the menses. Until a generation ago, Greek shepherds of the Agrapha mountain range did not sleep with their wives on the night preceding the making of cheese. Fear of possible contamination also lay behind this restriction. His advice about cleanliness is very relevant to the necessary culture which preceded the establishment of the first cities.

755–56. The meaning of these lines most likely is that, if a man chances on a sacrifice that is either in honor of a god unknown to him or that is accompanied by rites unfamiliar to him, he should wisely refrain from criticism and disapproval lest he offend some god.

757–60. See notes on 727–32.

761–64. In small homogeneous societies, a man's reputation means everything. This is especially so in a society, such as the Greek, in which shame and social rebuke were and still are extremely powerful forces. Along these lines, a modern Greek proverb says: "It is better to have your eye gouged out than your name tarnished." We find the same feeling expressed in the Edda more powerfully than in the Hesiodic lines:

Cattle die, kinsmen die,
man himself dies.
I know one thing that dies not,
a good name for him who has it.
(*Hávamál* 76, 77)

765–828. *The Days:* This section of the poem has been the subject of controversy among modern scholars, several of whom do not consider it Hesiodic. Whatever the merits of their objections, it should be said that they pit themselves against the weight of ancient tradition. The objections marshaled forth against Hesiodic authorship are: (1) in the "Works," Hesiod reckons time chiefly by means of solstices, equinoxes, risings of well-known bright stars, and the appearance and behavior of certain flora and fauna (the only reference to a month is in line 504); and (2) in the "Works," Hesiod's prescripts are those of a pious but rational and definitely practical man. In the "Days," there is no discernible rational principle, and pure superstition is allowed to run rampant. Other objections concentrate on linguistic and stylistic aberrations from what is considered typically Hesiodic and on certain inherent contradictions between recommendations given in the "Works" for the performance of certain tasks and recommendations given in the "Days" for the performance of the same tasks.

In the "Days," Hesiod refers to the days of the month either by taking the month as a unit of twenty-nine or thirty days, or by dividing it into two halves, the first coinciding with the waxing moon, and the second with the waning moon, or by dividing it into three ten-day periods. These divisions must stem from three different but not incompatible ways of dividing the lunar month, and, allowing for local peculiarities, they are not basically at variance with general Greek practice.

Evidence from some classical sources shows that the ancient Greeks considered some days holy or auspicious and other days inauspicious, but Hesiod's scheme of days that are good or bad for certain tasks or events is unique for classical and preclassical Greece. Examples from Egypt and Mesopotamia are helpful only to the extent that they prove that such schemes existed in ancient times, but no correspondence has been established between them and the Hesiodic list of good and bad days. However, evidence from primitive cultures suggests that the belief in auspicious and inauspicious days is widespread.

One of the best critical assessments of this part of the poem was given by Friedrich Solmsen (1963). He examines some of the most significant views of earlier scholars and, at the same time, gives his own carefully weighed reflections on the incongruities inherent to the "Days." He also considers the original "Days" to have consisted only of lines 770–79, which enumerate the seven auspicious days that come from Zeus; he treats the rest of this portion of the poem as substantial additions and almost haphazard accretions to be credited to rhapsodic elaboration. He condemns all of the "Days" as "a wild growth, proliferating without control and direction and reflecting the equally uncontrolled wild-fire-like spread of the superstition" (313–14). He also condemns lines 724–59 of the poem as rife with the same irrational superstition that characterizes the "Days" (317).

Before addressing these objections, I should like to draw attention to some pertinent details in the "Days." Of the twenty-nine-and-a-half days of the lunar month as well as of the thirty days of the lunisolar month—and Hesiod uses both (cf. line 766)—eleven days are dismissed as insignificant (line 823). The days enumerated in lines 770–79 are good days; for one of them, the seventh, a reason is given for its auspicious character. The good days are the first, the fourth, the seventh, the eighth, and the ninth "of the waxing month," and also the eleventh and the twelfth. Yet as the poem goes on, the reader discovers that Hesiod distinguishes this fourth day—presumably the first fourth of the waxing month—from the middle fourth (794–99), which can bring grief (although it is propitious for the birth of girls). His scheme also includes a third fourth; that is, the twenty-fourth of the month (820–21). The first fourth he calls a

sacred or holy day and then, paradoxically, proceeds to call the middle fourth "the holiest" of all days (819) and the third fourth "best at dawn but not good toward evening"; I say paradoxically because lines 794–99 prove the middle fourth a day of very mixed blessings. In addition to this, lines 797–98 inform us that the fourth of the waxing and waning month is to be shunned as an inauspicious day. How can the middle fourth, which is at best good and bad, be the holiest of all days—holier also than the first fourth, which brings no ills? What are we to make of the belief that the first fourth, an auspicious day, and the third fourth, which is very auspicious in the morning and only not so auspicious toward evening, are, according to lines 797–98, days to be shunned? Surely there are contradictions here, but it is as good as certain that line 798, which is bracketed as spurious by most editors, is indeed spurious, the result of a not too clever interpolation.

Despite these and other contradictions, not all is, by any means, chaotic in the "Days." Most of the auspicious days fall well within the waxing moon, and thus lunar growth is associated with growth and harvesting of crops and with marriage and birth, especially of male offspring. Of the eleven days Hesiod calls "meaningless, untouched by fortune" (823), seven fall after the twentieth of the month, within the phase of the waning moon. The only really bad day within the first half of the month is the fifth (802–3). Indeed, if the lines that refer to it are a non-Hesiodic accretion, then a scheme emerges whereby the first half of the month is preponderantly positive and auspicious, while the second part of the month, although by no means wholly bad, is fraught with more negative possibilities and, besides, contains eight of the eleven days that are insignificant.

The nineteenth is better toward evening, but the twenty-fourth excellent in the morning and not so good in the evening. I am in no position to judge whether this sort of division of a day may ultimately come from Egyptian or Babylonian sources, but I have found lingering traces of this belief in modern Greece. In the summer of 1979, I was told in the village of

Agia (Epirus) by an eighty-five-year-old man that "there is one really bad day in the week, Tuesday, and this day, bad from the start, is worse toward evening."

On the whole, the auspicious birth of boys and girls is assigned to separate days, with the exception of the ninth of the waxing moon, which is "a good day for men and women both to plant offspring / and to be born themselves" (812–13). In the sixth day of the waxing moon, we have a case of contrasting opposition, since this day is good for the birth of boys but bad for the birth of girls. Again, the emphasis is on doing things in a practical way and at the same time keeping an eye on what is sensible and traditional. There is an aspect of the *Works and Days* that leaves us with unresolved questions. For the birth of a boy and a girl as well Hesiod recommends the sixth day of the month. Since there was no method of birth control, how could one observe this recommendation? Perhaps, the answer is that Hesiod simply means that being born on the sixth of the month carried with it a better prognostication for a happy life.

The Hesiodic calendar is neither comprehensive nor entirely consistent, and Hesiod himself is conscious of its inconsistencies and of the uncertainty that surrounds the whole matter:

> Men have days they favor, but few really
> know.
> The same day can be a mother now, a step-
> mother later.
>
> (824–25)

If one takes a conservative view on the matter of interpolated lines—and excises from the text those lines that create glaring contradictions—I think it is unnecessary to go so far as to consider the whole section the result of rhapsodic extrapolation.

The arguments scholars have advanced against the authenticity of this portion of the poem are reasonable but not cogent. In the earlier and major part of the poem, Hesiod is concerned with the right season or the right time of the year for the performance of a task. Having dealt with this, he may indeed feel it

necessary to concentrate on when things should or should not be done from day to day. As for the objection that reason rules "The Works" and superstition "The Days," one can produce abundant evidence of basically contradictory attitudes in our own days. Avowed Marxists insist on having their children christened. Orthodox Jewish scientists may not so much as push the button to turn on the radio on the Sabbath. An otherwise rational nuclear physicist may be afraid to move into a hotel room on the thirteenth floor.

That the practice of attaching special significance not only to various days of the month but also to specific months and years was common in postclassical times is obvious from Paul's injunction to the Galatians: "Ye observe days, and months, and times, and years. I am afraid of you, lest I have bestowed upon you labor in vain" (Galatians 4:10). It is interesting to note the belief that the first of the month (*noumenia*) was, even in Byzantine times, looked upon as a day of special significance during which people would not give anyone fire, vinegar, or almost anything else. Some days were especially observed within the week rather than within the month. Thus, Joseph Bryenios (an Orthodox missionary and teacher at the end of the fourteenth and at the first quarter of the fifteenth centuries) writes that evils befell the nation "because we observe Mondays [second days], Tuesdays [third days] and Thursdays [fifth days]" (*Causes of Grief* 3, 121).

The Hesiodic observation that "men have days they favor, but few really know" (824) is fully supported by modern Greek attitudes. Thus, the Kephallenians consider Saturday an auspicious day, but the people of Gytheion will neither sow, nor reap, nor weave on a Saturday. Occasionally, the prejudice against a certain month seems to have a quasi-logical or folk-etymological association. In Methone, February is not a good month for weddings because there is a fear that children born of parents married in this month will be lame, since February is not a complete month. In the village of Peta (district of Arta), weddings are avoided during the month of June, which is called *Ther-*

istês (The Reaper), because the couple may be "reaped" by Death. (For a full discussion of details, see Koukoules, *Life and Civilization of the Byzantines*, Athens, 1950, 2:150–55).

For modern Greeks, Tuesday is by far the worst day of the week. In the minds of most Greeks, this is connected with the fall of Constantinople to the Turks on a Tuesday, although there is evidence that Tuesdays were considered inauspicious before the year of this national catastrophe in 1453. Thursday was considered an inauspicious day as early as the times of Nikephoros I (patriarch of Constantinople for the years 806–815), who cautions that "you must not observe even Thursdays" (*Patrologia Graeca* 100, 851). In Skopelos of eastern Thrace the Greeks until very recently considered Thursday an inauspicious day "because the Lord died on this day." Many Greeks still consider Wednesdays and Fridays inauspicious days. Wednesday is inauspicious because it was on a Wednesday that "the Jews held council," and Friday because Jesus was crucified on a Friday. The Sarakatsani and other Greek shepherds refuse to shear their sheep or to give them salt on a Friday. Yet Wednesday is an auspicious day for the people of Upper Syros, and both Wednesdays and Fridays are auspicious in Sisanion (Macedonia). Elsewhere in the Greek countryside, Friday is not an inauspicious day but an especially sacred day for the women, who observe it by refraining from work, even from the evening of the Thursday that precedes it. The day, called *Paraskevê* in modern Greek, is personified and identified with St. Paraskevê, who appears as a horrific old woman to those who violate the sanctity of her day (see Kyriakides, *Greek Folklore*, Athens, 1965, 201).

Very interesting is also the belief that people born on Saturdays are favored by the Fates; they are "light-shadowed" and possess the ability to exercise magic powers and to see invisible spirits and especially the *Neráides*, the capricious nymph-like fairies of springs and woodlands (Kyriakides, 195). There are echoes here of such Hesiodic beliefs as the sanctity of the seventh day because Apollon was born on it (771), or the inauspicious character of all fifth days because

"on the fifth the Furies assisted / at the birth of Oath, whom Strife bore as a plague to perjurers" (803–4), or even of "the great twentieth" during which wise men are born (792–93).

There are instructive analogies here, analogies associated with significant religious events. The analogies are limited and they do not suffice to explain Hesiod's scheme, which is probably a mixture of religious and numerological superstition combined with irrational primitive fears and taboos, the reasons for which had sunk into oblivion even by Hesiod's own time. Modern analogies show that frequently a reason is given for the inauspicious character of a day. When it is not given, one may fairly assume that it has been forgotten. The existence of contradictions does not seem to discourage people from observing a day as inauspicious because it is considered auspicious in some other part of the country. Greek farmers who observe the twelve days of August (*hêmeromênia*) as meteorologically significant for the weather of the twelve months of the year do not know the reason for this belief, and they are not bothered by the belief present in some other village that it is the first three or six days of August or of some other month that are significant. If a poet chose to put their beliefs into verse, it is very doubtful that he would change their beliefs so that they would be consistent for the whole country and free of contradictions. I do not believe for a moment that Hesiod constructed a calendar of lucky and unlucky days for his compatriots. I believe that he felt obliged to record as coherently and as faithfully as he could the traditional calendar lore of his birthplace, incorporating at the same time elements known to him from other places, whether they were entirely consistent or not. It should be remembered that Homer built his epics on the heroic legends as they existed, and that to this end he operated within the conventions of the heroic tradition and on his own system of reasoning, leaving his contradictions to scholars. The *Iliad* is a great poem, not a masterpiece of modern logic.

778. "The wise one who piles up his harvest" is the ant.

The *Shield*

Critics who consider the *Shield* at best a mediocre piece of rhapsodic extrapolation feel that our one and only debt to its composer is due him for having preserved in the first fifty-six—or most likely just the first fifty-four—lines of the introduction to his poem our best fragment from the Hesiodic *Catalogue of Women* (the *Eoiai*). The poem may not rival the best in Homer or Hesiod, but I feel that, once the piece was declared un-Hesiodic, the wrath of the critics fell upon it with vehemence greater than it deserves.

The story is simple. The first fifty-six lines tell of Alkmene's marriage to Amphitryon, king of Thebes, and of her giving birth to twin sons, of whom Herakles was the son of Zeus, while Iphikles was sired by Amphitryon. This curious fact is to be traced to Alkmene's having received as lovers on one and the same night both her husband and the irrepressible Zeus.

Fifty-four of the fifty-six lines of the introduction were taken from Hesiod's *Catalogue of Women* by a rhapsode who added two lines in such a way as to be able to start the poem proper with a line referring to Herakles but not naming him. The rest of the poem relates the encounter of Herakles with the bandit Kyknos, who was in the habit of waylaying pilgrims on their way to Delphi. Herakles and his charioteer, Iolaos, are traveling to Trachis, where Keyx, father-in-law of Kyknos, is king. They obviously stop at Pagasai and enter the precinct of the sanctuary of Apollon Pagasaios. It is here that they meet Kyknos, who is asked by Herakles to make way for his chariot, but Kyknos refuses and proceeds to challenge Herakles to combat. Herakles is unarmed and has to don his war gear. It should be said that this is the only instance in which Herakles fights a duel in full Homeric panoply. Kyknos is not alone. He is in the company of his father, the god of war, Ares. Herakles slays his formidable opponent and so brings upon himself the anger of Ares, who hurls his spear at him. The goddess Athena intervenes on behalf of Herakles and staves off the blow. Herakles's spear-thrust, on the other hand, leaves Ares with a gaping wound in his thigh. The wounded god is transported to Olympos, and after Herakles and Iolaos strip the dead Kyknos of his armor, Athena, too, returns to the divine stronghold. Curiously enough, Herakles and Iolaos continue their journey to Trachis, the royal seat of Keyx, who honors his dead son-in-law with a majestic funeral. However, Apollon shows his anger over the misdeed of Kyknos by causing the river Anauros to swell and wash away his grave and burial mound.

The central portion of the poem is devoted to the description of the fabulous shield Herakles bears. The shield is the work of Hephaistos, who has carved on it in gold, silver, bronze, steel, and white and blue enamel, monsters, wild beasts, dragons, vineyards teeming with grapes, hunters pursuing their quarry, legendary battles, and a city—a seven-gated one to be sure—of men celebrating a wedding feast with song and dance, while others of their compatriots are engaged in fierce combat round a golden tripod, obviously the prize for the victorious side.

With the exception of the famous grammarian Aristophanes of Byzantium (257–180 BC), the ancients treated the *Shield* as unquestionably Hesiodic. No less an authority than Apollonios Rhodios considered the poem genuinely Hesiodic, and the poet Stesichorus, probably born no later than 629 BC, did not question its attribution to Hesiod. Modern scholars pit themselves against the weight of ancient opinion on the grounds that, except for the portion that clearly belongs to the *Catalogue of Women,* the poem is rife with repetitious and overexpanded similes and, in general, its structure is unbalanced and uneven.

Some scholars have suggested that the composer might be a Thessalian. The city of Pagasai, where the famous sanctuary of Apollon was built, was most likely founded by Pherai, and it developed into Thessaly's most important port. The powerful local Thessalian kings who came into power after the end of the Sacred War (590 BC), which was waged over the control of Delphi, fought on the victorious side and looked upon their lands as closely allied with Delphi. The prominence given to Pagasai in the *Shield* and the mention of several Thessalian cities may possibly speak for a Thessalian author, or at least for a traveling rhapsode who produced a piece on commission given to him by Thessalian potentates. I myself am inclined to think that the author was a Theban, or at least a Boeotian. It should be remembered that, although the Boeotians were members of the alliance that was bound by oath to protect the Delphic sanctuary and they fought together with the Thessalians in the Sacred War, there must have been tensions and rivalries within this sacred alliance over claims of primacy and prestige. In the Hesiodic fragment that constitutes the proem to the whole composition, it is the Boeotians who, together with the Lokrians and Phokians, battle the Taphians and the Teleboans under the leadership of Amphitryon, father of Herakles and originally a

Theban hero (although he was the son of the king of Tiryns). The city of peace and feasting that is described in lines 270–319 as "ringed by seven-linteled gates" is doubtless Thebes. Also, the hero and demigod Herakles, whose fabulous shield is the subject of the poem, kills Kyknos, a Thessalian robber and son-in-law of a prominent Thessalian king. Such a poem could be easily used as a piece of Theban and thinly masked anti-Thessalian propaganda, especially at a time when other Theban cities, such as Plataea, accepted Theban hegemony with little enthusiasm.

If indeed the *Shield* is not Hesiodic, the prevailing opinion of scholars may come reasonably close to its actual date of composition. The proposed date of 590–560 BC would place the *Shield* roughly one hundred years after the end of Hesiod's floruit. Unfortunately, nothing in the poem helps us fix its date with any amount of certainty.

In most editions and scholarly works, the *Shield* is listed as pseudo-Hesiodic. No matter how scholars understand this term, its pejorative denotation has not made it easy for critics to approach it with an open mind. If the piece were considered by scholars even as one of Hesiod's inferior works, arguments would be invented to defend its weaknesses and extol its virtues. It has been pointed out that the poet does not tell us why Herakles and Iolaos are going to Trachis, or why they stop at the sanctuary of Apollon at Pagasai, or why, for that matter, Herakles reaches the sanctuary unarmed. The place where the duel takes place is absurdly small. Critics find the similes duplicated or overexpanded, and occasionally inappropriate. After Ares is wounded, the poet deals with his hurried removal in just seven lines. Herakles and Iolaos proceed to Trachis as if nothing has happened, although they do not participate in the magnificent funeral by which Keyx honors their victim. The last nine lines on the honors paid to Kyknos and on the manifestation of Apollon's anger are looked upon as a perfunctory conclusion.

However, similar weaknesses can be found in the two undoubtedly Hesiodic poems. Hesiod does not tell us how the quarrel with his brother was settled, or whether his brother profited at all from his moralizing sermons. He includes a section on navigation, which, from a practical point of view, is almost as good as useless. He never explains why Hope remains within Pandora's jar. His digressions are far greater than those of the *Shield,* and he ends both the *Theogony* and the *Works and Days* in a manner that is anticlimactic and not altogether relevant to the scope of the two poems. Usually, inferior poets feel they have to tell everything. Digression, overexpansion, and repetition are so common in epic poetry, whether heroic or didactic, that a poem that does not exhibit these features would be an oddity within this genre. To pick out rather insignificant technical details and treat them as major flaws in the fabric of a poetic work is to resort to a kind of literary casuistry. The aim of the poet of the *Shield* is, as I hope to show, not only to describe a marvelous figment of his imagination, a shield that never existed, but also to use this fabulous piece of armor in order to bring into bold relief the legendary hero in whose hands he places it.

The Hesiodic fragment from the *Eoiai* that serves as an introduction to the poem proper begins too abruptly to satisfy modern taste, but lines 1–56 are, by rhapsodic standards, anything but ill chosen. They not only tell us of the birth of Herakles, but they also dwell on much more that is relevant to the poem. Certainly, the story of Amphitryon attacking and destroying the Taphians and the Teleboans—and doing so in obedience to Zeus's behest—speaks for a rhapsode who chose purposefully. The Taphians and the Teleboans were notorious pirates and robbers, and when Herakles slays the robber Kyknos he does so as heir to a tradition created by his father. Literally translated, the first line of the poem reads "Or such as having left her home and fatherland." In good contemporary poetry, this is surely a poor beginning. However, if one imagines our rhapsode as taking part in a contest in which the pieces recited dealt with the feats of heroes born of gods and mortal women, then he made a choice that should be considered most appropriate and well within the conventions of his art.

Besides the description of the fabulous shield of Achilleus (*Iliad* 18.478–608), we also have the much shorter description of the shield of Agamemnon (*Iliad* 11.32–40). Although our poet was demonstrably familiar with the second one, it is definitely the Homeric shield of Achilleus that served as the model for his inspiration. Great votive shields with fierce-looking beasts portrayed in relief have been found. Also, depictions of personified abstractions, such as Strife, Fear, and Justice, are familiar to us from vase paintings and sculptures of the seventh century BC. To date, no shield that approximates, even on a much smaller scale, the complexity of the shield of Herakles or of the shield of Achilleus has been found. These shields are patently symbolic and allegoric creations of the poetic mind. However, one cannot be altogether sure that we are dealing entirely with exclusively poetic fiction. Certainly, the existence of as elaborate a piece of work as the Chest of Kypselos, dated c. 600 BC and described in great detail by Pausanias, should discourage us from dismissing the existence of real models executed, to be sure, on a less ambitious scale. It is interesting in this connection to observe that the figure of Death (Ker) was depicted on the Chest of Kypselos as a woman with ferocious teeth, like those of a wild beast, and hooked nails on her fingers (Paus. 5.19.6). Yet the literary model for our poet was Homer's shield of Achilleus.

A comparison of the description of the shield of Achilleus and the shield of Herakles shows the sixth-century BC rhapsode far from a slavish imitator.

The differences and the innovations are far more striking than the similarities. Homer begins with a description of the physical cosmos, the universe, and then smoothly graduates into a depiction of the civic world with its two cities—one at peace and the other at war—and then he goes on to show civilized man plowing, reaping, harvesting grapes, and dancing. The ocean (Okeanos) that is depicted on the rim of the shield forms a ring that contains the whole composition. Even a fleeting glance at the Homeric shield shows that our poet borrowed and modified, now expanding, now compressing, several features: the two cities; the scenes on reaping, harvesting grapes, dancing; and a few other details. He also borrowed the somewhat faintly personified Homeric abstractions: Strife, Confusion, and Death (describing the action of Death in words identical to those of Homer).

At the very center of Herakles's shield the poet places Fear, portrayed as a monstrous creature flashing a repulsive array of teeth and casting glances of fire. Perched on his forehead is Strife. This Strife (145–50) is not the same as the Strife of lines 155–56; the former is a personified force, the latter still a borrowed and undeveloped Homeric abstraction. The figures appearing next on the shield are Attack, Counterattack, Battle Din, Murder, Manslaughter, and the Homeric trio of Strife, Confusion, and Death. The first two figures are entirely the poet's own invention, although the second one exists but only as a word in *Odyssey* 12.71; 15.69. Battle Din (*Hómados*) is also first personified here. The figures of Murder and Manslaughter are borrowed from Hesiod's *Theogony*, which makes them children of Strife (*Theogony* 226–31). The poet then invents three of these figures and borrows two from Hesiod and three from Homer. Next on the shield appear twelve gruesome snake heads, and then a herd of wild boars and a pride of lions battling one another like two hostile armies. Then comes the magnificent battle of the Lapiths and the Centaurs. Next, Ares with his horses and his two attendants, Panic and Fear, are introduced. This Fear is not the same as the one who occupies the center of the shield. Fear and Panic are depicted on the shield, and they are the same attendants who carry the wounded Ares away from the scene of the duel (460–65). It is interesting that Fear, as a personified force, appears again in the battle of Perseus against the Gorgons. The trio Gorgo, Panic, and Fear are depicted together on the shield of Agamemnon in *Iliad* 11.32–40, and it cannot be a mere coincidence that our poet first mentions Panic and Fear as a pair and then later on in the poem has one of them whirling and quivering above the heads of the Gorgons. He doubtless borrows these figures from the shield of Agamemnon, but he deploys them in a manner that serves his own purpose. Athena is depicted in full panoply after Ares. It should be remembered that on the shield of Achilleus she and Ares lead the charge of the men who venture forth from the beleaguered city. On the shield of our poem, they are depicted in succession, but in the conflict for which the shield is used they are on opposite sides. The battle of Perseus against Gorgo and her sisters is preceded by two of the loveliest scenes: the sacred dance of the gods and the harbor where dolphins leap in pursuit of fish as a fisherman is about to cast his net.

The battle of Perseus against Gorgo is followed by a depiction of the city at war in which the Death Demons (Kêres), an expansion of Ker (Death), dig their claws into the dead and hurl them down to Hades. This is a variation and a horrific amplification of Death at work in lines 155–60. The poet is aware of Hesiod's *Theogony* 211–32, in which Death and Strife are daughters of Night, and Strife herself the mother of Clashes, Battles, and Manslaughters. It can be no coincidence that, in a passage in which so many of the forces that Strife unleashes are described with blood-curdling vividness, the three Fates—who also occur in the Hesiodic passage that tells us that Death and Strife are daughters of Night—are also mentioned. The Hesiodic parallel becomes even more interesting when one notices that the next personified force, the Deathcloud, nowhere personified in Hesiod or Homer, is given flesh and blood, and portrayed with lurid colors as a fanged, bloodthirsty demon. In Homer, the word *achlys* means the mistlike darkness that covers the eyes of a dying warrior. Here Achlys (Deathcloud) is really a combination of black Night, the mother of Death, and of Death himself. She is the executioner that comes to the warrior when Strife and her evil progeny have done their work. Again, the poet borrows, but he does so with striking boldness of imagination. It is against this gloomy and joyless foil that the splendor and festive glee of the seven-gated city at peace with its torch-lit wedding procession, its dances and wheat fields, its golden vineyard, and its athletic contest for a tripod of gold, is welcomed by the listener as a kaleidoscopic interplay of the sounds and colors of festive and glitter-laden peace. In the ocean that rings the shield, beautiful swans skim the waves. The swans (*kyknoi* in Greek) are harmless and lovely creatures that embellish the peaceful world to which their namesake, the robber Kyknos, is a lawless scourge.

The shield of Achilleus and the shield of Herakles share some thematic similarities, but their differences are such that only a cavalier critic would see in the shield of Herakles a pale and maladroit imitation of the Homeric model. The shield of Achilleus is a small part of a formidably long epic poem. The shield of Herakles is the poem. The shield of Achilleus exudes peace, serenity, order. Through the shield of Herakles, the poet hammers at the listener with terrifying images of repulsive and violent monsters, and despite the presence of the city of peace, which only enhances through contrast the horrors of strife and conflict, the poem is permeated by a nightmarish vision of the powers that man has to battle in order to secure peace.

HESIOD

The approach of the poet is innovative, eclectic, and hardly conventional. Herakles fights this duel not clad in his lion skin and wielding his mighty club, but weighed down with the full panoply of a Homeric warrior. It is interesting that the surviving vase paintings that depict the duel do not show a helmeted Herakles holding the shield of this poem—or any shield, for that matter. The poet's departure from convention cannot be haphazard. Herakles does not set out wearing a Homeric panoply in order to meet Kyknos. He and his charioteer are on their way to Trachis and stop at the temple of Apollon at Pagasai, much as one would stop to pay his respects to a celebrated sanctuary. Although the poet does not say so, it is even conceivable that the panoply they carry, and especially the shield, might be intended as a votive gift to the god. Herakles does not visit the temple in order to battle Kyknos. Actually, battles and killings within sanctuaries were considered sacrilegious by the Greeks. On the other hand, when Herakles encounters the robber, Kyknos refuses to step aside in order to avoid the conflict.

The shield of Herakles bristles with monsters and demons and superhuman warriors such as the hero fought and overcame in his many labors. The Nemean Lion, the nine-headed Lernaean Hydra, the Erymanthian Boar, the Stymphalian Birds, the three-headed Geryon, and the three-headed Hellhound Kerberos may have no exact analogues on the shield of Herakles, but they are creatures of the same monstrous ilk that the hero battled for the benefit of mankind.

It would be unthinkable that a poet set before himself the task of describing a shield for Herakles and somehow ignored his celebrated labors. In a poem so rife with allegory and symbolism, one might even dare suggest that the "twelve unspeakably gruesome snake heads" of the dragons that

> spread fear over the earth,
> among the races of men
> who would fight in close combat
> against the son of Zeus
>
> (160–65)

stand for his Twelve Labors. Given the suggested date for the composition of the *Shield*, it is interesting to point out that the Twelve Labors first appear as a set on the metopes of the Temple of Zeus at Olympia c. 560 BC.

Of course, the peaceful part of the shield, the city at peace with its wedding procession, its reapers and vintagers, its dancers, its splendid vineyard, and its competing horsemen, is not to be dismissed as a mere contrastive device. Herakles fought against grisly monsters and against robbers and warlike giants, such as the Lapiths and the Centaurs, as a protector of man. He did battle so that peace with its manifold blessings might be secured. He even killed the vulture that preyed on the liver of Prometheus, the god who championed the cause of man and stole fire from Sky for him. Herakles's opponent in the contest with Kyknos is not only Kyknos, but Ares as well, the god of war, whom Herakles wounds, thereby dealing a blow to the very god who is an enemy of peace.

The *Shield* could be looked upon as a complex symbol that mirrors all that Herakles stands for. The feats that he performed became an inextricable part of him, and the monstrous powers he subdued were, so to speak, appropriated by him so that he could unleash them upon those who threatened humanity; by fighting demons Herakles became demonified and eventually deified. His victories were the victories of man against man's enemies. This is why in private worship he was hailed as *kallinikos,* demigod of fair victory, and *alexikakos,* warder-off of evils. On yet another plane, the personified powers and monsters that appear on the shield are also symbolic of the warrior's state of mind. They portray fear and anger, and when contrasted with the blessings of peace they also stand for the inner conflict in the hero's mind between the desire to kill and the wish to spare life.

The *Shield* is not a mediocre *pièce d'occasion* but a powerful poem in which the personifications of the gruesome and the macabre interlace in a horrific phantasmagoria of apocalyptic power. The West had to wait for John's Apocalypse and for the terrifying visions of Bruegel and Bosch to meet again with such ghoulish pandemonium. It also is not an exercise in extravagant and morbid teratology. It is a work of a poetic mind that was in tune with such developments in the seventh and sixth centuries as gave us masterpieces in vase painting and sculpture. To judge it by Homeric standards is to place it outside its proper context. It is an impressionistic poem that succeeds in creating a legitimate mood of eerie terror, the terror that is needed to overcome robbers like Kyknos. However fierce this robber was, he perished so ignominiously that, even after he was buried, Apollon saw fit to have the river Anauros wash away his grave and burial mound. The torch in the hands of Herakles's father wiped out the cities of the Taphians and Teleboans; now the water of a river commanded by a god blots out even the memorial tokens of a man who was much like them. The poetic composition is as cyclical and complete as the ocean that flows on the circular rim of the shield.

The *Shield* is a martial poem and, therefore, very different from the *Theogony* and the *Works and Days.* It is for this reason that I felt that a shorter, swifter-moving, and at times even abruptly introduced line might convey the force of the original better. The numbers in my translation do not keep a count of my own shorter lines, but they indicate the five lines of the original to which my text corresponds.

HESIOD

SHIELD

There was another woman,
   Alkmene,
   daughter of Elektryon,
   the people's champion.
She left home and hearth
   for Thebes,
this bride of warlike Amphitryon.
Unrivaled in all the land
   for beauty and stature,
5   she was second to no mortal woman
   whose child was sired by a god,
   in the sharpness of her wit.
Her face and dark eyelids
wafted the charms
   of Aphrodite the golden;
she honored her husband
   from the depths of her heart,
and honored him
10   as no other woman of equal beauty.
Seething with anger over cattle,
Amphitryon, through might and main,
   murdered her illustrious father
   and left the land of his forefathers
   to come to Thebes,
   a supplicant before the shield-bearing Kadmeans.
There he lived in the palace
   with his shy wife,
15   a stranger to the passion of her love,
unable to share the bed

of Elektryon's fair-ankled daughter,
until, for honor's sake,
he took revenge for the murder
   of his wife's kingly brothers
and gave to ravaging fire
   the villages of heroic warriors—
   the Teleboans and Taphians;
this is how he settled the matter,
20   and his witnesses were the gods.
Dreading their wrath,
   he felt the burden of Time
   running out on him
   to accomplish the great deed
   in obedience to Zeus's behest.
   Hungry for war and the din of battle,
the Boeotians, lashing their horses,
and puffing over their shields,
25   the Lokrians, born for battle at close quarters,
and the great-hearted Phokians
all followed him.
Their leader was the noble son of Alkaios,
   glorying in his host.
The father of men and gods
was weaving another plan
   in the loom of his mind,
how to sire for gods
   and men who toil for bread
   a defender against scourges.
30   Contriving a cunning ruse
   in the depths of his mind,
   he sprang forth from Olympos
   through the dark night,
his heart churning in love's longing
   for a wasp-waisted woman.
Wise Zeus reached Typhaonion
and from there he leapt
   to Phikion's loftiest peak.
There he sat and in his mind
   pondered uncanny deeds.

For on that very night
        he fulfilled his desire
        by sharing the passion of love
        as he lay beside Alkmene of the slender ankles.
On that same night Amphitryon,
        —a glorious hero, his people's champion—
        came back to his own home
        richer by one more triumph.
He did not rush to visit his slaves
and his hardy shepherds
        until after he had climbed onto his wife's bed,
so fast was the hold of lust
on the heart of the people's shepherd.
        Unburdened of his toilsome mission,
        Amphitryon welcomed the sight of his own home
        with the loving eagerness
        a man welcomes escape from painful illness
        or from chains of iron.
All night long he lay
        beside his bashful wife
and relished the gifts
        of golden Aphrodite.
Alkmene, overpowered by the passion
of a god and of the noblest man
        of seven-gated Thebes,
        became the mother of twin boys
        not at all alike in mind.
Brothers they were,
but Iphikles was no match
        for his sibling,
        Herakles, the best of all,
        the awesome and mighty.
Alkmene conceived him
wrenched into submission
        by Zeus, lord of dark clouds,
        but Iphikles came from the loins
        of spear-brandishing Amphitryon.
They were not of the same stock;
the one sprang from a mortal's seed,

the other was sired by Zeus Kronion,
who rules over all the immortals.
It was Herakles who slew Kyknos,
    the noble-spirited son of Ares,
    when he found him in the shrine
    of far-shooting Apollon.
Kyknos was there with Ares,
    his war-hungry father,
    and both stood on a chariot,
    shining in their panoplies,
60   like gleaming fire.
Their swift horses pounded the earth,
    digging their hooves
    into the ground,
    and the cloud of dust
    rising from beneath wattled chariot
    and galloping horses
    blazed all about them.
As the horses pressed on,
    the well-wrought chariots and their frames
65   rattled, a joy to blameless Kyknos,
    whose hope was to cut down
    Zeus's warlike son and the charioteer
    with his bronze blade
and strip them of life and fine armor.
Phoibos Apollon
    did not listen to his prayers.
Yet Kyknos lunged
    against the might of Herakles.
70 His own weapons and those of the awesome god
glittered throughout the whole grove
and the altar of Apollon Pagasaios.
    Fire darted from their eyes—
    and what mortal,
    save Herakles and glorious Iolaos,
    could dare forget his mortality
to pit his might against them?
75 Their power was great
    and their arms sprang,
    invincible,

from their sturdy trunks.
Herakles now spoke to Iolaos,
the mighty charioteer:
    "Iolaos, hero beloved of the gods
    more than any man,
    with his misdeeds Amphitryon
    offended the blessed gods who hold Olympos,
80 when, having slain Elektryon for the broad-browed cattle,
he left well-built Tiryns
to return to Thebes, a city that wears
a splendid crown of turreted walls.
He came to Kreon, and to Henioche
    of the trailing garments,
    a guest warmly welcomed;
    and they gave him
fitting gifts, as rightful custom demands,
85 and so honored him from the heart.
He relished his life as husband
of Elektryon's fair-ankled daughter;
but soon, as the years followed their cycles,
    your father and I
    were born unlike each other
    in mind and body.
Zeus deprived him of his senses
90 when he left his home and parents
    set on the course of doing honor
    to Eurystheus, harshness incarnate.
Later he sighed
    the sighs of wistful regret,
    riding his own ruin,
    a ruin no bridle could check.
The god gave me the command
    to follow a path rife with ordeals.
95 Anyway, friend, now quickly hold the purple reins
of our fleet-footed horses.
Let the courage rise bold in your heart
and keep swift chariot and horse mettle
    on a straight course.
Have no fear of the blows and yells
    of man-slaughtering Ares,

now careering in fury
about the sacred grove of Phoibos Apollon,
100   the far-shooting lord,
for strong though he is,
war drives him into reckless folly."
Blameless Iolaos spoke now in turn:
"Dear uncle, the father of gods and men
and bull-like Poseidon the Earth-Shaker,
who holds the turreted crown of Thebes and defends the city,
105   so honor your head
    that they lead into your hands
a man whose might and greatness you shall defeat
    to reap undying fame.
Come, put on your war gear, lose no time!
Let us leap into battle
    and ram our chariot against Ares's chariot.
110   He shall not frighten the son of Zeus.
He will flee the sons
    of blameless Alkides
    who are close upon him
and yearn for the war cry and battle
    they love more than feasting."
115 So he spoke, and mighty Herakles smiled
and his heart throbbed with joy
    for words well spoken;
    his reply came
    in words that were winged:
"Heroic Iolaos, nursling of Zeus,
    the savage clash is pawing us.
Put all the fire you can into your heart
and charge, driving Arion,
120   the great black-maned horse
    in every direction—
    to help now is to do your best."
This said, he put round his shins
    greaves of shining bronze,
    marvelous gifts from Hephaistos;
    then on his breast
    he placed a handsome piece of armor
    laced with intricate design,

125   his golden breastplate.
Pallas Athena, Zeus's daughter,
gave this to him
when he first set out
on the trek of his woeful labors.
Awesome as ever, he covered his shoulders
    with iron gear
      to fend off deadly blows,
        while behind him he slung
a hollow quiver fastened to his breast;
130   it was filled with many arrows,
      killers that bring the shiver of death
      and rob their victims of voice.
On their tips they carried death
    oozing poison tears,
and, long and shaved smooth in the middle,
they had back ends beaming the pride
    of wings borrowed
    from a fiery-red eagle.
135 He grasped the heavy spear
    tipped with gleaming bronze,
and on his noble head placed
his helmet, a well-wrought master craftsman's piece,
    made of steel, with a snug fit at the temples;
    this helmet guarded the head
    of Herakles, the scion of a god.
He lifted the dazzling shield,
    a marvel to the eyes,
    the shield no man's spear-thrust
140   had ever shattered or broken.
On it rings of ivory,
of white enamel and of electrum,
overlaid with folds of blue enamel,
    were a dimmer foil
paling before the gleaming gold.
From its center Fear,
    carved in blue steel,
    unutterable Fear,
145   cast side glances of fire.
White, glistening teeth

filled his mouth
in awesome and repulsive array,
while on his horrid forehead
perched harsh and dreadful Strife,
ever ready to rob of mind and sense
the men who would battle Zeus's son
150   face to face.
Their souls plunge into the nether gloom,
and their bones,
beaten by the Dog Star's scorching heat,
   rot away on rotten skin
   upon the black earth.
On it loomed the figures of Attack and Counterattack,
Battle Din and Murder
and Manslaughter glowering,
155   as Strife and Confusion scuttled about;
   and Death, the destroyer,
   held a man freshly wounded
   and a second one unharmed
   and dragged a dead man by the feet
   and back into the fray.
Strife's shoulder was caked
with the crimson of men's blood
and, glaring terror, she raised the howl
160   of clashing bronze.
From it twelve unspeakably gruesome snake heads
   spread fear over the earth,
   among the races of men
   who would fight in close combat
   against the son of Zeus.
When Amphitryon's son charged into battle
deafening noise rose from their clashing teeth;
165   the craftsman's splendid work was now ablaze.
These dreadful dragons were covered
   with spotted scales,
   dark blue on their backs
   and black all about their jowls.
On the shield herds of wild boars
foaming at the mouth,

and prides of lions
glared unbridled fury at one another.
170 They charged in thick ranks,
their necks bristling with menace,
and neither side flinched for fear.
Between them lay the body of a great lion
flanked by two wild boars
with no life left in them;
killed by the grim-faced lions
there they lay dead
with heads collapsed
175 and blood streaming onto the ground.
This stirred both the foaming wild boars
and the glowering lions
into mounting fury
to do battle.
Depicted on it, too, was
the battle of the Lapith spearmen
rallying round the chieftain Dryas,
all of them—
180 Peirithoos, Hopleas, and Hexadios,
Mopsos, too, and Ampykides,
Titaresios, son of Ares,
and godlike Theseus,
Aegeus's son.
On their silver bodies
they carried weapons of gold.
All the Centaurs gathered against them,
with towering Petraios in their midst,
185 and Asbolos the diviner,
and Arktos and Oureios,
and black-maned Mimas,
and the two sons of Peukeus,
Dryalos and Perimedes.
Their bodies were carved in silver,
but in their hands they carried
golden fir trees;
they brandished spears and trunks of fir,
and they charged into the fray,

190   lifelike.
        On it, carved in gold,
        stood the fleet-footed horses
            of grim-faced Ares,
            and baneful Ares himself.
        Carrying the spoils of war,
        he rode on a chariot
        and, sharp-tipped spear in hand,
        he gave orders to foot soldiers.
        He was coated with crimson blood,
            as if he were slaying living men.
195   Next to him stood
        Panic and Fear, yearning
        to leap amid the battling ranks.
        Depicted on it was also Zeus's daughter
        Athena Tritogeneia, the looter,
            as if she wished to arm for battle.
            Spear in hand,
            golden helmet cresting her head,
            shield slung over her shoulders,
200   she charged into the dread clash. And then one saw
        the sacred dance ring of the immortals,
        and at its center the son of Zeus and Leto
            plucking the strings of his golden lyre
            that rang haunting melodies.
        Sacred Olympos, seat of the gods,
            was there, too,
            and the gods themselves sitting at council,
            crowned by the halo
            of their measureless cheer.
205   The divine Muses of Pieria,
        fashioned to look like clear-voiced singers,
            led them in song.
        On it the unwearying sea
        bent, a horseshoe harbor,
        a haven of blue
        for mooring ships.
        It was made of pure tin,
        and billows rolled over its surface.

HESIOD

In the middle of the harbor dolphins
gave the impression of swimming
210   as they darted about after the fish.
       Two of them, carved in silver,
       were blowing and puffing at the speechless fish;
       the fish, done in bronze,
       quivered with fear before the dolphins,
       while on the beach there sat
       a fisherman, lurking there for fish
       and looking as though he was about
215 to cast the net he held in his hands.
       On it the son of lovely-haired Danae,
       the noble horseman Perseus, stood out;
       he did not touch his shield with his feet,
       and yet he was not far from it,
       hovering above the ground—
       a marvel too great for words.
       Hephaistos, unsurpassed in skill,
       carved his figure with his own hands,
       in gold.
220 The sandals on his feet were winged,
       and his sword was slung over his shoulders,
       a sword fastened by black clasps
       onto a bronze belt;
       he hung in midair
       as winged as man's thought.
       His back was covered
       with the head of Gorgo, the savage monster,
       and this head—what strange wonder!—
225   now wobbled inside a silver bag
       that was fringed with tassels of gold.
       His awesome helmet,
       black like the dread night,
       reeked death
       all about the lord's temples.
       Perseus himself, son of Danae,
       strained in headlong pursuit
       and looked the man
       driven by haste and fear.

Close at his heels
the unspeakable Gorgons charged,
230   glutlusty,
         eager to snatch him.
Under the trample of their feet
the shield rang forth with a loud roar,
         shrill and ear-splitting;
         and on their belts two dragons
         reared heads bent forward,
         and their glare curdled a man's blood,
         as their tongues lashed about
235   and their teeth ground with fury.
On their grisly heads
Fear, the great demon,
         whirled and quivered.
Above these figures were seen
armed warriors clashing in battle:
the one side trying to ward off
ruin from its own city and parents,
240   the other furiously sack-keen.
Many of them lay dead,
and more, not yet worsted,
battled it out with the foe.
And the women standing
on well-wrought bronze towers
         raised shrill cries
         and tore their cheeks,
these lifelike women, the handiwork of glorious Hephaistos.
245   There were also men advanced in years,
         thralls of their old age,
who flocked outside before the gates
         with arms raised in prayer
         to the blessed gods,
fearing for their own children's lives;
they, too, did their share of battle.
Among all these warriors
black Death Demons clattered
teeth that glistened white;
yes, Death Demons war-grim and fierce,

250 glutlusty and dripping, crimson with blood,
       fought over the fallen corpses,
           driven by thirst for dark blood.
    They would dig their great claws
    into the flesh of the first warrior
       they snatched,
           either as he lay dead,
           or as he collapsed, wounded
    by a freshly dealt blow;
    and the souls of such men
    would plummet into the chill
255   of Tartaros.
    When they had their fill
    of a man's blood,
    they tossed him behind over their shoulders,
       only to rush back again
           into the din and toil of battle.
    Klotho and Lachesis stood over them,
    and Atropos was there,
    Atropos, portrayed as the inferior, the lesser goddess,
260   she who was superior and oldest of them.
    All these fought
    a grisly battle over a single man,
    and the glint of anger
       flashed in their eyes,
           and none of them outdid the other
           in fierceness of claw or hand.
    Beside them stood Deathcloud,
       gloomy and eerie,
265   pale and shriveled up;
       subdued by hunger,
       she was swollen at the knees,
       and her fingers were tipped
           with long nails.
    Snot streamed down from her nostrils,
    and from her cheeks blood dripped on the ground.
    There she stood
       with a famished grin,
           wearing on her shoulders a coat of dust
           turned to mud by tears.

Shield

270   There was also a well-turreted
        city of men,
        and the seven-linteled gates that ringed it
        were carved in gold.
    Its men savored the splendor
        of feast and dance.
    Some, on a four-wheeled chariot,
    were escorting a bride to her husband,
        and their wedding songs
        rose loud into the day.
    Far in the distance
275   the light of bright torches
    in the hands of serving maids
        danced in the night,
        and the maids themselves,
        brimming with festive verve,
        pressed on,
    trailed by bands of minstrels and singers.
    All about there echoed
        the men's smooth song
        to the sound of shrill pipes,
    while the girls' voices,
280   filled with longing,
        took up the lead.
    On the other side young men
    reveled to the sound of the flute,
    some playfully dancing and singing,
    while others ran ahead,
        and their laughter rang
        in unison with the trills of the flute.
285   The whole city resounded
    with carousing, and feasting, and singing.
    Others, close by the city,
    charged about on horseback,
    and plowmen, with their clothes tucked up,
        furrowed the divine earth.
    The crop was standing tall,
    and the reapers with sharp sickles
        mowed down stalks

that bent, grain-heavy at the top,
   as if this were to be Demeter's gift,
290 real grain pounded into real flour.
Others with withes bound sheaves
and tossed them down on the threshing floor,
   and still others, with sickle in hand,
   harvested the vines.
Then there were workers
who, in baskets the vintagers gave them,
carried away grapes, white and black,
   picked from rows of vines
295   weighted down by lush leaves and silver tendrils.
Next to them there stretched,
   in gold, a plot of vine rows,
   done by wise Hephaistos with matchless skill.
The workers played to the flutist's tune,
and the vines, tinctured with dark burnish,
bent under the burden of their clusters
and, shivering in the lushness of their leaves,
300   clung to poles of silver.
Some men were treading grapes,
   others drew the liquid;
   and there were fist fights
   and wrestling matches.
Then, too, there were hunters chasing swift hares,
and sharp-toothed dogs running ahead of them;
and the dogs were as eager to catch the hares
as the hares were eager to escape.
305 Close by them horsemen labored and toiled,
   weary with strife,
   for a cherished prize.
Charioteers, standing on chariots
with seats of skillfully wrought wattle,
galloped their horses by slacking the reins;
   and the chariots—snug fits of wooden parts—
   were drawn into thunderous career,
as their hubs gave out a howl.
310 The toil was endless,
   the victory unaccomplished,

the contest unjudged;
and before the assembled throng
there was a great tripod,
 all in gold,
 carved by Hephaistos with matchless skill.
Round the rim of the shield
ran—as if brimming over—
the stream of Okeanos holding together
315 all the complex designs;
and, throughout, flocks of high-soaring swans
 raised a loud song
and skimmed the water's surface
before schools of fish fleeing in confusion.
Even Zeus of the crashing thunder
would have marveled at this sight
on the great and heavy shield
made by Hephaistos, who joined the pieces together
with skill, much as Zeus himself
320 had wished it.
Zeus's mighty son
shook the shield with vigor,
and leaped, light-footed,
on the horse-drawn chariot,
as swift and brilliant as the lightning flash
hurled by his father
Zeus who holds the aegis.
Then Iolaos, the strong charioteer,
 mounted the curved chariot
 and drove it for him
 without ever swerving from his course.
325 Then the goddess gray-eyed Athena
came and, standing close to them,
uttered winged words
aimed at cheering them on:
 "Hail, offspring of Lynkeus
 whose fame reached far and wide.
 Know that Zeus, lord of the blessed gods,
 is now giving you strength to slay Kyknos
 and strip him of his famous armor.

O lord whose power is unmatched
among your people,
330 do listen to what I'll now say:
When you rob Kyknos of sweet life, let him lie in his armor,
and keeping a keen eye
on the charge of Ares, the man-slayer,
watch for flesh left bare
by his intricate shield
335 and stab him with the sharp bronze.
Then you must retreat,
for it lies outside your destiny's compass
to take his horses and famous armor."
These words spoken, the dazzling goddess
swiftly mounted her chariot,
holding in her immortal hands
victory and glory.
340 Then indeed Iolaos of the line of Zeus
howled to his horses a command
that sent them galloping through the plain
as they pulled the swift chariot
amid clouds of dust.
For Athena, the gray-eyed goddess,
waved her shield at them
and filled them with stubborn grit.
The earth gave a loud groan
345 as Kyknos, breaker of horses, and war-hungry Ares
joined their strength and charged forth
speedy as raging fire,
furious like a storm.
The horses now came face to face
and their shrill neighing
echoed all around them.
The first hero to speak
was mighty Herakles:
"Kyknos, my good old friend,
what's the sense of pitting
350 your swift horses
against men who are no strangers
to toil and battle-grief?

Come now, make way!
Turn your trim chariot aside.
   I am riding mine to Trachis
   to visit Lord Keyx,
   who, in power and respect,
   ranks second to none in Trachis;
355   you yourself know this well enough,
since you are marrying Themistonoe,
his dark-eyed daughter.
   Not even Ares, dear boy,
   will be able to ward off death
   from you, if we two clash
   in battle.
For I claim there was a time,
   a time past,
that he dared my spear,
360 when he stood above sandy Pylos—
   face to face with me—
crazed with unslaked longing for battle.
Three times I struck him down
   with my spear,
   and shattered his shield.
   The fourth time I drove my fury
   into his thigh
   and turned it into a gaping sore;
under the thrust of my spear
365 he collapsed headlong onto the dusty ground.
He would have met the scorn of the gods,
if, subdued by my hands,
he had lost his bloodied weapons,
   spoils for me."
These were his words,
but Kyknos, armed with the ash spear,
gave no thought to obeying
and to holding the horses harnessed to his chariot
   in check.
370 Then no time was wasted,
as from beautiful wattled chariots
both the son of great Zeus

and the son of Ares the battle-god
   leapt swiftly upon the ground,
   and the charioteers drove
   the sleek horses close together.
When they charged
the broad earth thundered
   under their feet,
   as when from a lofty mountain peak
   boulders spring loose
375   and roll against one another,
   down the mountainside,
   shattering great numbers
   of towering oaks, pines,
   and deep-rooted black poplars
until they reach the flatlands.
The battlescream of these two
   was no less loud
   when they fell upon each other.
The whole city of the Myrmidons,
380   renowned Iolkos,
and Arne, and Helike, and Antheia
   with its lush grasslands,
   rang with the battlecries
   of the two warriors.
Their shouts, when they clashed,
echoed, broken and uncanny,
as Zeus lord of councils,
rained on them from the sky
the blood tears of his own eyes—
a portent by which the battle
385 of his bold son should be remembered.
The son of Zeus leapt down
from his horse-drawn chariot
   like a tusked boar
   that, hard to spoor
   in wooded mountain glens
   and straining in his mind
   to battle it out with the hunters,
   sharpens his white teeth

when cornered,
        as foam dribbles down
        from his grinding teeth
390   and his eyes gleam fire
and on his neck and back
his bristles stiffen straight.
They fought their battle
at summertime when the loud
dark-winged cicada
begins his song for men,
sitting on a green branch;
395   his food and drink is only sweet dew,
and from daybreak to sundown
he pours his song
        into the dreadful swelter,
        when the Dog Star sears the skin,
and spiked ears of millet
        sown in the summer ripen,
        and green grapes—
Dionysos's bittersweet gift to men—
400   faintly blush with the hue of ripeness.
Yes, this was the hour of their battle,
        and the din that arose
        was deafening.
They were like vultures
—hooked talons, hooked claws—
that, upon some high rock,
405   scream
        as they fight over a mountain goat,
        or a fat deer of the wilds
        struck dead
        by the arrow of some hunter
        who, stranger to the land,
410   has wandered away.
The vultures knew it
        straightway,
        so they swooped down
        to claw one another
        over the dead deer,
        screaming

like our two warriors
when they fell upon each other.
Kyknos,
his heart crying for the death
of mighty Zeus's son,
thrust his bronze spear against
his foe's bronze shield,
the divine gift that guarded the warrior,
415   but did not shatter it.
Amphitryon's son,
rugged Herakles,
put his great strength into the thrust
of the long spear he drove swiftly
into Kyknos's throat,
right under the jaw,
where helmet and shield
420   leave the flesh bare.
The warrior fell
as an oak falls,
or a pine,
struck by Zeus's smoky thunderbolt,
and his fine bronze armor
rattled all over his body.
Zeus's stout-hearted son
let him lie there
425   while he himself kept a keen eye
on Ares the man-slaughterer;
and his gaze was as fierce
as that of a lion come upon a victim
to tear its hide with greedy claws
and rob it of honey-sweet life.
Anger turns his heart black
and, glaring dread from his eyes,
430   he lashes ribs and shoulders
with his tail
and claws the ground;
and the courage to battle him
ebbs away from the hearts
of those who set eyes on him.
This is how Amphitryon's son looked

when, hungry for more conflict,
and with heart waxing steadily bold,
   he rose to challenge Ares.
Now Ares,
435   heartsore with mounting fury,
   approached him,
   and the two sprang upon each other
   with a loud yell.
As when a boulder
sprung loose from a great crag
rolls down with a roar,
   bouncing up high,
   and spends its fury
   as it crashes on some towering rock
440   that blocks its course;
so, too, Ares, the ruin of men,
Ares under whose weight chariots creak,
lunged forth with a loud shout,
and Herakles braced up swiftly
to meet the assault.
Now Athena, daughter of aegis-bearing Zeus,
   stood before Ares,
   dark shield in hand,
   and eyeing him
445   with a fierce scowl,
   spoke to him winged words:
"Ares, hold your anger
and the matchless strength of your hands;
hallowed law dictates it is not yours
to slay Herakles, Zeus's gold-hearted son,
and strip him of his glorious armor.
Come now, end this battle
and do not stand there
before me, like a foe."
So she spoke,
   but she did not sway
450   the proud-hearted Ares,
   who sprang, swift as lightning,
   upon the might of Herakles,

driven by the wish to kill him.
Angry over the death of his son,
he thrust his bronze spear
against the great shield,
455   but gray-eyed Athena
       reached out from the chariot
       and staved off the impact
       of the flying spear.
Bitter grief
       stung Ares's heart,
       who now drew his sharp sword
       and charged against
       iron-hearted Herakles.
Amphitryon's son,
ever yearning for the sound of the battlecry,
stabbed the charging god
where the flesh of his thigh
       was left bare,
460 under the shield of the many designs.
He drove his long spear
and tore a gaping hole
into the flesh of the god,
and then knocked him down
on the ground between them.
Then Fear and Panic swiftly drove
trim-wheeled chariot and horses
close to him, lifted him up
from the wide-pathed earth,
and laid him on the chariot
465 that flashed its intricate patterns.
They quickly lashed the horses
and came to lofty Olympos.
Then the son of Alkmene and noble Iolaos
stripped the shoulders of Kyknos
       of beautiful armor
       and then moved on.
Their galloping horses
speedily carried them
470   to the fastness of Trachis,
         while Athena the gray-eyed

Shield

reached her father's house
on towering Olympos.
Keyx and a huge gathering of people
who lived near the great king's stronghold
buried Kyknos.
They flocked to Trachis
from Anthe, the city of the Myrmidons,
from renowned Iolkos,
and from Helike and Arne;
they flocked in great numbers
475   to Trachis
to honor Keyx,
the hero beloved of the blessed gods.
The river Anauros
swelling with winter rain
ravished both grave and burial mound;
for such was the behest
of Apollon, son of Leto,
because Kyknos,
lying in ambush,
used to fall upon pilgrims
on their way to Pytho
and by brute force plunder
480 their glorious hecatombs.

Notes

1–10. At the very beginning of the *Shield* and also after lines 56–58, it would be natural for the reader to expect an invocation to the Muses, to the goddesses that inspire poetry.

However, there is no such appeal. This in itself may be an indication that the composition is rhapsodic and cannot claim the usual inspiration we find in the opening lines of such great poems as the *Iliad* and the *Odyssey*. The beginning of Hesiod's *Theogony* and the *Works and Days* is the locus classicus for the study of the relationship between poet and Muse in archaic Greece.

Alkmene is the daughter of Elektryon. Most names in the *Shield* are distinctly heroic. Alkmene is the "strong" one. Elektryon is the "amber man," the man who counted his wealth in amber, a precious material imported from the Baltic area. Amber was found in seventeenth century BC shaft graves at Mycenae. The word occurs several times in the *Odyssey*, but not in the *Iliad*. Most likely, Elektryon acquired his amber through acts of piracy. Alkmene is in every way a lovely woman who, unlike the exquisitely beautiful Helen, queen of Sparta, honored her husband as "no other woman of equal beauty." Size and good looks went hand in hand to define the standard of attractive physical appearance in Homeric society (see *Odyssey* 15.428 and *Homeric Hymn to Aphrodite* 5.85).

For the power of Eros wafted from head and dark eyelids, see Ibycus 6 in *Poetai Melici Graeci* by D. L. Page. Sometimes, the formula "head of a person" was used instead of the name of the person. At the beginning of Sophocles's *Antig-*

one Ismene is addressed by Antigone as "head of Ismene" to indicate affection and respect.

10–20. "Anger over cattle" caused a feud between Amphitryon, Alkmene's husband, and Elektryon, her father. Amphitryon killed Elektryon and fled to Thebes, polluted by murder. Unable to share the conjugal bed, he removed the stain of pollution by avenging the murder of Alkmene's brothers and by torching the villages of the Taphians and the Teleboans. We know next to nothing about these tribes, but we can be certain that they excelled in banditry. Etymologically speaking, the Taphians put their enemies to their graves, while the Teleboans frightened people by shouting loudly. It is quite likely that we are dealing with nicknames, or code names, of outlaws. On the cycle of killing and vengeance, compare *Works and Days* 156–64, where the poet informs us that many heroes lost their lives fighting over the cattle of Oedipus while just as many perished fighting at Troy to recover the beautiful Helen. In the cycle of killing and vengeance one should look for the loss of honor and property. Crimes of honor usually involved large herds of cattle. See Athanassakis, "Cattle and Honour in Homer and Hesiod." See also relevant material from Icelandic sagas, especially the Introduction to *Njáls Saga: A Literary Masterpiece* by Einar O. Sveinsson. The ideals of Viking society on honor are beautifully summed up in the immortal lines of *Hávamál* 76 and 77 in the Edda. See notes on *Works and Days* 761–64. In northwestern Greece, until about fifty years ago, among the things that made life worthwhile honor came first, and life and property followed.

Hesiod does not mention the concepts of soul and honor. The omission is deliberate in the *Theogony* and the *Works and Days* and perhaps should be linked with the economy of his age. The one reference to a sacrifice involving an ox is found in the myth of Prometheus (*Works and Days* 42–89 and *Theogony* 507–612). The harsh practices of war involved raiding a place, killing the men, and taking the women captive (see *Iliad* 1.106–129 on Chryseis, 19.282–300 on Briseis, and 24.719–45 on Andromache).

30–60. Herakles and Iphikles are a pair of non-identical twins. Identical twins develop from a single fertilized ovum. They are always of the same sex and also of very similar physical appearance. In the story which involves the birth of twins here Zeus seems to act like a feudal lord taking advantage of the "jus primae noctis," the right to spend the first night with the bride of any man belonging to the estate of which he was master.

Zeus flies from Olympos to Typhaonion (32) and Phikion (33). Both of these are Boeotian mountains. They are "stations" in Zeus's journey to Thebes. From there he proceeds to Thebes to invade Amphitryon's space and sleep with his wife, Alkmene. On the very same night Amphitryon also sleeps with his wife; both Zeus and Amphitryon are driven by passion.

60–85. The poet informs us that it was Herakles who killed Kyknos. The word "Kyknos" seems to be a nickname for this bandit. Kyknos and Ares, his father, stand on a chariot. The Kyknos of the *Shield* must not be confused with the Kyknos of Pindar's *Olympian* 2.81–87. Archilochos of Paros, born sometime in the first half of the seventh century BC, invented the word *tēnella* to imitate the sound of the string of *kithara*. Then he proceeded to compose the following hymn to Herakles and Iolaos:

> Tēnella
> I salute you, Herakles, lord of fair victory,
> Tēnella, lord of fair victory
> in honor both of you and of Iolaos.

> Tēnella,
> kingly Herakles, lord of fair victory.
> (Diehl, *Anthologia Lyrica Graeca*, No. 120)

85–140. Irony and sarcasm frequently precede the clash of warriors. Herakles arms as follows: greaves first, then breastplate, iron gear all around his shoulders, quiver filled with arrows fastened to his breast, heavy spear, and shield. It is peculiar that the bow of Herakles is not mentioned. Instead, his quiver receives an honorable position in the list of his weapons. It may be that the poet of the *Shield* is eager to present Herakles as a spearman and not as an archer. In these lines the poet of the *Shield* presents the iconography of the shield, not so much the order in which Herakles puts his weapons on. For details on armor and arming in Homer, see Wace and Stubbings, 503–30.

140–45. At the very center of the shield of Herakles is Fear carved in blue steel. It may be that the idea here is that Fear is the source of all conflict, that men fight wars because they are afraid of their enemies. Fear is harsh. Because of Fear a man's color turns blue.

145–50. Hesiod's distinction of good and bad Strife in *Works and Days* is relevant here. The good Strife involves effort which leads to competition and productivity. In the *Shield*, the idea of a productive Strife would be an unwelcome intrusion.

150–60. In the sequence Attack, Counterattack, and Battle Din, there is a departure from the visual to the auditory.

Strife, Confusion, and Death succeed one another. "Melee" equals a confused, general hand-to-hand fight between groups or among combatants and might be the word of choice to describe the poet's intention.

160–80. Twelve snake heads leap out of the shield and spread over the earth. These are the twelve labors of Herakles. The idea is that every labor involved a deadly threat to humanity. The number twelve corresponds to the number of the Olympian gods and also to the number of months in one year. It is possible that, originally, each month of the year was given a divine name and that the number attached to the labors of Herakles was derived from this idea. The names of the twelve months in the Athenian calendar are derived from various festivals and agricultural practices. They do not help us determine the connection between the twelve lunar divisions of the calendar to the twelve Olympian gods. In Book 11 of the *Odyssey,* we are told that Odysseus saw the image of Herakles in the underworld and also that he spoke with him. There is no mention of a canon of twelve labors. The evidence we have points to a fixing of the number in the sixth or fifth century BC. So then, the twelve snake heads of line 161 could be used as tentative evidence for assigning the composition of the *Shield* to the sixth or fifth century BC.

180–90. The battle of Theseus and Peirithoos against the Centaurs presents us with some interesting questions. What poetic purpose do the lists of the Lapiths and the Centaurs serve? Every extensive list of names is calculated to show the poet's skill in reciting from memory. In *Shield* the list in lines 178–90 serves an additional purpose. The Lapiths are fierce, heroic warriors; the Centaurs are rough savages. Their names connote a close association with the wilds.

195–200. Olympian gods do not die. After all, they are immortal. However, they may be wounded. In Book 5 of the *Iliad,* we encounter a tearful Aphrodite wounded by Ares, the god of war.

Panic and Fear. The mention of Panic may help us establish a *terminus ante quem* for the composition of the *Shield.* Pan joined the ranks of Greek warriors during the battle of Marathon (490 BC), after which the concept of Panic came into use. The story of Pan as an ally of the Greeks during the battle of Marathon is told by Herodotus in 6.105–6. His appearance caused fear among the Persians. On Pan, see also *Homeric Hymn* 19.

200–205. For Apollon playing the lyre to entertain other gods, see *Iliad* 1.601–4. Here the goddesses and the Muses lead the song. *Iliad* 18.500–508 is the first description of a trial intended to resolve a blood feud. The wise old men who sit in judgment sit within a sacred circle. A Viking outlaw

drew all about himself a circle to establish inviolability. There may be a connection here.

210–15. In these lines we have the description of a beautiful harbor. This is the landscape of leisure and peace. The *Shield* is a poem of restlessness and conflict. The passage about this haven of security and recreational activity plays a central role in the longer poem.

In *Homeric Hymn to Dionysos* (7) we read that the crew turned to dolphins when they saw the transformations of the stranger:

> When they saw this,
> they escaped evil fate by jumping over-
> board into the shining sea
> and turning into dolphins.
>
> (51–53)

> In the middle of the harbor dolphins
> gave the impression of swimming
> as they darted about after the fish.
> Two of them, carved in silver, were blowing
> and puffing at the speechless fish;
> the fish, done in bronze,
> quivered with fear before the dolphins,
> while on the beach there sat
> a fisherman, lurking there for fish
> and looking as though he was about
> to cast the net he held in his hands.
>
> (208–15)

The word for fisherman does not occur in the *Iliad* but it does occur in the *Odyssey* (see *Odyssey* 12.251, 22.384).

215–40. Perseus and the Gorgons. Perseus, son of Zeus and Danae, killed Medousa (see notes on *Theogony* 270–86). Perseus cuts off Medousa's head and Pegasus springs forth. Attention should be paid to details concerning the armor and clothing of Perseus. These details are calculated to show the poet's audience his affection for this popular hero. Although Medousa was a bloodthirsty monster, relating the story of Perseus at this point of the *Shield* is definitely intentional. There were three Gorgons, daughters of Ceto and Phorcys. Two of them, Euryale and Sthenno, were immortal, while the third one, Medousa (also called Gorgo), was mortal.

Shield

The shield of Achilleus portrays the lively and vibrant world Achilleus is prepared to risk in order to avenge the death of his beloved friend Patroklos. The shield of Herakles is a weapon that spreads fear. As a very ancient text, the *Shield* is the first major work on monstrosities and nightmares. In Book 8 of Virgil's *Aeneid*, Hercules—and this is the Latin name for Herakles—is a dark and brooding phantom who wields a deadly club (8.269–98). In Book 11 of the *Odyssey* the mortal part of Herakles is a shade in the underworld, while his immortal part enjoys divine status in Olympos. The Herakles that Odysseus sees among the souls of the dead in the underworld holds a bow and is ready to shoot arrows at his enemies. His bow is slung on a baldrick on which the monsters he subdued are embroidered. The relevant point to make here is that he does not carry a spear.

240–70. When Sarpedon dies his soul departs and Deathcloud is poured all about him (*Iliad* 5.696). Richmond Lattimore translates: "And the mist mantled over his eyes, and the life left him." The image of a misty underworld has survived in certain Greek dirges, almost all of them anonymous. Here is an example:

> I have wandered through all of Hades, all
> of the nether world.
> There is wind blowing, I cannot hear; there
> is fog, I cannot see.
> There is a drizzle, I cannot recognize you.

In lines 258–63 the three Fates are described like bloodthirsty monsters. From Hesiod's *Theogony* we learn that the three Fates are daughters of Themis (see *Theogony* 901–6). Portraying the three Fates as bloodthirsty demons is a deviation from standard ideas about them. In lines 264–69 Deathcloud is personified. She is equipped with long nails, snot is running from her nose, and blood is dripping from her cheeks. The description of this awful creature is followed by the description of a wedding.

270–90. In this city of peace there is feasting and dancing. A bride is escorted to her husband's home. Serving maids dance in the night. Young men dance to the sound of flutes. Plowmen fur-row the earth, others reap. Yet others throw sheaves onto the threshing floor. There is frenetic energy and great potential for fertility everywhere. The section of Book 18 of the *Iliad*, namely lines 590–605, that describes a beautiful celebration at Knossos could well suit a description of a wedding feast in Crete in modern times.

290–300. Harvesting grapes, vintaging, treading on the grapes. In these lines young women and young men carry the sweet fruit of the vine in wicker baskets and in their midst a young man is playing the *kithara* and singing. This scene corresponds to Apollon singing and playing the lyre for the Muses. All these are scenes of exuberant joy and vibrant life. They contrast sharply with the duel between Herakles and Kyknos.

300–320. Okeanos is a stream that girds the earth. *Iliad* 18.606–9:

> He made it on it the great strength of the
> Ocean River
> which ran around the uttermost rim of the
> shield's strong structure.

Compare this with *Shield* 314–15:

> Round the rim of the shield
> ran—as if brimming over—
> the stream of Okeanos holding together
> all the complex designs

Okeanos had a "real-life counterpart" in Acheloos, the great river of the Greek northwest. The root ak^w is reflected in such words as Akarnania, Achaia, and Acheron; then also in Latin *aqua* and then similarly in many other Indo-European languages.

315–20. In these lines the poet makes mention of flocks of swans and schools of fish. Swans are not best known for their vocal skills. What is the point the artist is making here? Perhaps the poet includes the image of swans flying all about and singing a loud song to remind his listeners that the bandit Herakles faces in the duel is named Kyknos, swan. This detail may be important in determining the nature and identity of the *Shield*. There are no swans on the shield of Achilleus.

320–40. Herakles leaps on the chariot. Iolaos mounts the chariot. Athena intervenes. Lines

195–200 of the *Shield* inform us that Athena has joined the battle in full panoply. Here she urges Herakles and Iolaos to kill Kyknos and strip him of his armor. She also exhorts Herakles to wound Ares. In Book 1 of the *Iliad*, lines 205–22, Athena intervenes to persuade an angry Achilleus not to use violence against Agamemnon. In her formal, yet amicable, salutation the goddess addresses Herakles—and by extension Iolaos—as offspring of Lynkeus. Lynkeus was a son of Aegyptos, famous for his powerful eyesight (see Gantz 1.421–23 and Zimmerman under "Lynceus"). Herakles challenges Kyknos and addresses him by saying "Kyknos, you are a nice guy! Why do the two of you stop our swift horses? We are going to Lord Keyx's palace in Trachis. I take it you know who he is. You have married Themistonoe, his daughter. Friend, not even Ares can save you." For warriors leaping from chariot to the ground to indicate their determination to fight, see *Iliad* 3.29, 5.494, 6.103, 12.81. *Iliad* 13.748–53 is a good example:

> Hektor leapt to the ground in full panoply
> and spoke winged words to Poulydamas:
> "Stay your ground, Poulydamas, and summon to it our best warriors;
> I am going over there to get a taste of war;
> I will give orders and I will come back soon."

370–85. Herakles and Kyknos leap on the ground. Kyknos does not reply to the words of Herakles. Note the condescending tone of Herakles's address to Kyknos.

385–400. In these lines the poet of the *Shield* describes the heart of the Greek summer, namely August, when cicadas fill the air with their vibrating and deafening song. See notes on *Works and Days* 582–89. Nothing is said about the lust of women. He also does not give instructions as to how people should seek refuge in shade and refresh themselves with drinking wine mixed with water. There is no rational connection between the heart of summer heat and the time of the duel between Herakles and Kyknos. It seems that our bard seized the occasion to link the heat of the battle with the fierceness of summer heat in Greece.

405–20. Kyknos casts his spear against the shield of Herakles, while Herakles makes his thrust into Kyknos's throat and kills him. The question concerning these lines is why the two combatants use only spears and no bows and arrows. We should not forget that Odysseus killed all the suitors with bow and arrow. Herakles and Kyknos did battle against each other like Homeric warriors in the *Iliad*.

420–50. Herakles is now like a lion. Kyknos falls like an oak. In Homer's *Iliad* only great warriors collapse on the ground like oaks. Examples are found in 13.389, where Idomeneus kills Asios and 16.482, where the great hero Sarpedon is killed by Patroklos. Kyknos may be scary, but he is no hero. In fact, he is a bandit. Athena intervenes again, asking Ares to relent. The god of war is stubborn. Eventually, Herakles drives his long spear and tears a gaping hole into the god's thigh. See notes on 191–200.

460–80. Ares lies on the ground. Fear and Panic lift him up, lay him on the chariot, and bring him to Olympos. Fear and Panic act like his assistants or allies. Herakles and Iolaos strip Kyknos of his armor. They carry him to Trachis. Keyx and a huge gathering of people bury him and build a burial mound for him. Kyknos used to rob travelers to Pytho, and Apollon is angry because Kyknos's actions prevented pilgrims from bringing their gifts to Delphi. Apollon shows his anger by causing the river Anauros to wipe out the burial site and the mound. In one of his labors Herakles drove the rivers Alpheios and Peneios into the Augean stables to wash away the filth that had accumulated over thirty years or so. If there is an analogy here, the grave and the burial mound built in honor of Kyknos are treated contemptuously like dirt.

When the *Shield* comes to an end, Ares is wounded and Kyknos is dead and buried. The author wishes to astonish his listeners and to support the concept of divine justice. Kyknos's outrageous behavior must be punished even after his death. Apollon wipes out his memory. The *Shield* is a puzzle for the classicist as well as for the educated reader. The composer of the poem stitches songs together. After all, he is a rhapsode.

Shield

Select Bibliography

Adkins, A. W. H. *Moral Values and Political Behaviour in Ancient Greece: From Homer to the End of the Fifth Century. Ancient Culture and Society.* London: Chatto and Windus, 1972.

Allen, T. W. "The Date of Hesiod." *Journal of Hellenic Studies* 35 (1915): 85–99.

Andersen, Lene. "The Shield of Heracles: Problems of Genesis." *Classica et mediaevalia* 30 (1969): 10–26.

Arrighetti, Graziano. "Hesiod and the Muses—The Gift of Truth and the Conquest of the Word." *Athenaeum* 80, no. 1 (1992): 45–63.

Athanassakis, Apostolos N. "The Birth of Athena Tritogeneia." *Hellenica* 40 (1989): 7–21.

———. "Cattle and Honour in Homer and Hesiod." *Ramus* 21, no. 1 (1992): 156–86.

———. "Europe: Early Geographic and Mythic Identity." *Dodona: Philologia* 30 (2001): 283–303.

———. "Hesiod's Folk Etymology and the Indo-European Origin of Aphrodite." *Stasinos* 10 (1993): 9–24.

———. "Introduction (Essays on Hesiod 1)." *Ramus* 21, no. 1 (1992): 1–10.

———. "Ōkeanos: Mythic and Linguistic Origins." In *Proceedings of the Tenth Annual UCLA Indo-European Conference, Los Angeles 1999,* ed. Karlene Jones-Bley, Martin E. Huld, Angela Della Volpe, and Miriam Robbins Dexter, 95–116. Washington, DC: Institute for the Study of Man Inc., 2005.

———. "Proteus, the Old Man of the Sea: Homeric Man or Shaman?" In *La Mythologie Et L'Odyssée Hommage à Gabriel Germain: Actes Du Colloque International De Grenoble, 20–22 Mai 1999,* ed. André Hurst, Françoise Létoublon, and Gabriel Germain, 45–56. Genève: Droz, 2002.

———. "Shamanism and Amber in Greece: The Northern Connection." In *Shamanhood Symbolism and Epic,* ed. Juha Pentikäinen, Hanna Saressalo, and Chuner Mikhailovich Taksami, 207–20. Budapest: Akademiai Kiado, 2001.

Baldry, H. C. "Who Invented the Golden Age?" *Classical Quarterly* 46 (1952): 83–92.

Barry, William. "Alone in the Village: Hesiod and His Community in the 'Works and Days.'" *Classical Philology* 111 (2016): 305–29.

Bassanich, John. "A Theoretical Interpretation of Hesiod's Chaos." *Classical Philology* 78 (1983): 212–19.

Beall, E. F. "Hesiod's Prometheus and Development in Myth." *Journal of the History of Ideas* 52 (1991): 355–71.

———. "The Plow that Broke the Plain Epic Tradition: Hesiod 'Works and Days,' vv. 414–503." *Classical Antiquity* 23, no. 1 (2004): 1–31.

Blickman, Daniel R. "Styx and the Justice of Zeus in Hesiod's Theogony." *Phoenix* 41 (1987): 341–55.

Boedeker, D. "Hecate: A Transfunctional Goddess in the Theogony?" *Transactions of the American Philological Association* 113 (1983): 79–93.

Bonner, Robert J. "Administration of Justice in the Age of Hesiod." *Classical Philology* 7 (1912): 17–23.

Brown, A. S. "Aphrodite and the Pandora Complex." *Classical Quarterly*, n.s., 47, no. 1 (1997): 26–47.

———. "From the Golden Age to the Isles of the Blest." *Mnemosyne*, 4th ser., 51, no. 4 (1998): 385–410.

Burkert, Walter. "Hesiod in Context: Abstractions and Divinities in an Aegean-Eastern Koine." In *Personification in the Greek World: From Antiquity to Byzantium*, ed. Judith Herrin and Emma Stafford, 3–20. London: Ashgate, 2005.

Burn, A. R. *The World of Hesiod: A Study of the Greek Middle Ages, c. 900–700 B.C.* 2nd rev. ed. New York: B. Blom, 1966.

Campbell, J. K. *Honour, Family, and Patronage: A Study of Institutions and Moral Values in a Greek Mountain Community.* Oxford: Oxford University Press, 1964.

Carnoy, Albert J. "Hesiod's Description of Winter." *Classical Philology* 12 (1917): 225–36.

Claus, D. B. "Defining Moral Terms in Works and Days." *Transactions of the American Philological Association* 107 (1977): 73–84.

Clay, Diskin. "The World of Hesiod." *Ramus* 21, no. 1 (1992): 131–55.

Clay, Jenny Strauss. "The Generation of Monsters in Hesiod." *Classical Philology* 88 (1993): 105–16.

———. "The Hecate of the Theogony." *Greek, Roman and Byzantine Studies* 25 (1984): 27–38.

———. *Hesiod's Cosmos.* Cambridge Classical Studies. Cambridge: Cambridge University Press, 2003.

———. "What the Muses Sang, 'Theogony' 1–115." *Greek, Roman and Byzantine Studies* 29, no. 4 (1988): 323–33.

Cook, R. M. "The Date of the Hesiodic Shield." *Classical Quarterly* 31 (1937): 204–14.

Crawley, Alfred Ernest. *The Mystic Rose: A Study of Primitive Marriage.* London: Macmillan, 1902.

Daly, L. W. "Hesiod's Fable." *Transactions of the American Philological Association* 92 (1961): 45–51.

Davidson, J. "Zeus and the Stone Substitute (Hesiod, 'Theogony')." *Hermes* 123, no. 3 (1995): 363–69.

Dehousse, M. E. "An Astronomical Determination of the Time of Hesiod." *Mankind Quarterly* 24 (1984): 439–45.

Detienne, Marcel, and Jean Pierre Vernant. *The Cuisine of Sacrifice Among the Greeks.* Chicago: University of Chicago Press, 1989.

Duban, J. M. "Poets and Kings in the Theogony Invocation." *Quaderni Urbinati di Cultura Classica* 33 (1980): 7–21.

DuBois, Page. "Eros and the Woman." *Ramus* 21, no. 1 (1992): 96–116.

Du Boulay, Juliet. *Portrait of a Greek Mountain Village.* Limni Evia, Greece: Denise Harvey, 1994.

Edwards, Anthony T. *Hesiod's Ascra.* Berkeley: University of California Press, 2004.

Falkner, Thomas M. "Slouching Towards Boeotia: Age and Age-Grading in the Hesiodic Myth of the Five Races." *Classical Antiquity* 8 (1989): 42–60.

Farnell, Lewis Richard. *The Cults of the Greek States.* New Rochelle, NY: Caratzas Brothers, 1977.

Feldman, T. P. "Personification and Structure in Hesiod's Theogony." *Symbolae Osloenses* 46 (1971): 9–41.

Finley, M. I. *Ancient Greek Society, Early Greece: The Bronze and Archaic Ages.* London: Norton, 1981.

Fisher, R. "Astronomy and the Calendar in Hesiod." *Echos du monde classique / Classical News and Views* 21 (1977): 58–63.

Fontenrose, Joseph Eddy. "Work, Justice, and Hesiod's Five Ages." *Classical Philology* 69 (1974): 1–16.

Forbes, P. B. R. "Hesiod Versus Perses." *Classical Review* 64, nos. 3/4 (1950): 82–87.

Gagarin, Michael. "Dike in the Works and Days." *Classical Philology* 68 (1973): 81–94.

———. "Hesiod's Dispute with Perses." *Transactions of the American Philological Association* 104 (1974): 103–11.

———. "The Poetry of Justice: Hesiod and the Origins of Greek Law." *Ramus* 21, no. 1 (1992): 61–78.

Gantz, Timothy. *Early Greek Myth: A Guide to Literary and Artistic Sources*, volumes 1 and 2. Baltimore: Johns Hopkins University Press, 1993.

Green, Peter. "A Peasant on Helicon: A Study of Hesiod and His Society." *History Today* 9, no. 11 (1959): 729–35.

Griffith, Mark. "Personality in Hesiod." *Classical Antiquity* 2, no. 1 (1983): 37–65.

Griffiths, J. Gwyn. "Archaeology and Hesiod's Five Ages." *Journal of the History of Ideas* 17, nos. 1/4 (1956): 109.

Guterbock, Hans Gustav. "The Hittite Version of the Hurrian Kumarbi Myths: Oriental Forerunners of Hesiod (Plates III)." *American Journal of Archaeology* 52, no. 1 (1948): 123–34.

Heiden, Bruce. "The Muses' Uncanny Lies: Hesiod, 'Theogony' 27 and Its Translators." *American Journal of Philology* 128, no. 2 (2007): 153–75.

Hirokawa, Y. "On Eros in the Hesiod Theogony." *Journal of Classical Studies* 12 (1964): 13–26.

Hunt, R. "Satiric Elements in Hesiod's Works and Days." *Helios* 8, no. 2 (1982): 29–40.

Hunter, Richard. *Hesiodic Voices: Studies in the Ancient Reception of Hesiod's Works and Days.* Cambridge Classical Studies. Cambridge: Cambridge University Press, 2014.

Hurwit, Jeffrey M. "Beautiful Evil: Pandora and the Athena Parthenos." *American Journal of Archaeology* 99, no. 2 (1995): 171–86.

Jaeger, Werner. *The Theology of the Early Greek Philosophers.* Oxford: Clarendon Press, 1947.

Janko, Richard. *Homer, Hesiod, and the Hymns: Diachronic Development in Epic Diction.* Cambridge Classical Studies. Cambridge: Cambridge University Press, 1982.

———. "The Shield of Heracles and the Legend of Cycnus." *Classical Quarterly* 36 (1986): 38–59.

Kirby, John T. "Rhetoric and Poetics in Hesiod." *Ramus* 21, no. 1 (1992): 34–60.

Kirk, G. S. "The Structure and Aim of the Theogony." *Hésiode et son influence: six exposés et discussions,* ed. Olivier Reverdin, 61–107. Geneva: Fondation Hardt, 1962.

Kirk, G. S., and J. E. Raven. *The Presocratic Philosophers.* Cambridge: Cambridge University Press, 1966.

Koenen, Ludwig. "Greece, the Near East, and Egypt: Cyclic Destruction in Hesiod and the Catalogue of Women." *Transactions of the American Philological Association* 124 (1994): 1–34.

Koning, Hugo H. *Hesiod: The Other Poet. Ancient Reception of a Cultural Icon.* Leiden: Brill, 2010.

Lambert, Wilfred G., and Peter Walcot. "A New Babylonian Theogony and Hesiod." *Kadmos* 4, no. 1 (1965): 64–79.

Lampropoulou, S. "The Status of Women in Ancient Times." *Platon* 32–33 (1980–81): 88–113.

Lardinois, André P. M. H. "The Wrath of Hesiod: Angry Homeric Speeches and the Structure of Hesiod's 'Works and Days.'" *Arethusa* 36, no. 1 (2003): 1–20.

Latimer, J. F. "Perses Versus Hesiod." *Transactions of the American Philological Association* (1930): 70–79.

Select Bibliography

Lattimore, Richmond, ed. *The Iliad of Homer.* Chicago: University of Chicago Press, 1961.

———. *The Odyssey of Homer.* New York: Harper Perennial Classics, 1999.

Lawson, John Cuthbert. *Modern Greek Folklore and Ancient Greek Religion: A Study in Survivals.* New York: University Books, 1965.

Lincoln, Bruce. "On the Imagery of Paradise." *Indogermanische Forschungen* 85 (1980): 151–64.

Loney, Alexander C., and Stephen Scully, eds. *The Oxford Handbook of Hesiod.* New York: Oxford University Press, 2018.

Marquardt, Patricia A. "Hesiod's Ambiguous View of Woman." *Classical Philology* 77 (1982): 283–91.

———. "A Portrait of Hecate." *American Journal of Philology* 102 (1981): 243–60.

Marsilio, Maria Suzanne. "Dependence and Self-Sufficiency in Hesiod's Works and Days." Dissertation. University of Pennsylvania, 1992.

Martin, Richard P. "Hesiod, Odysseus, and the Instruction of Princes." *Transactions of the American Philological Association* 114 (1984): 29–48.

———. "Hesiod's Metanastic Poetics." *Ramus* 21, no. 1 (1992): 11–33.

Merkelbach, R., and M. L. West, eds. *Fragmenta Hesiodea.* Oxford: Oxford University Press, 1966.

Montanari, Franco, Antonios Rengakos, and Christos Tsagalis, eds. *Brill's Companion to Hesiod.* Leiden: Brill, 2009.

Most, Glenn H. "Eros in Hesiod." In *Erôs in Ancient Greece,* ed. Ed Sanders, Chiara Thumiger, Christopher Carey, and Nick Lowe, 163–74. Oxford: Oxford University Press, 2013.

———. "War and Justice in Hesiod." In *War in Words: Transformations of War from Antiquity to Clausewitz,* ed. Marco Formisano and Hartmut Böhme, 13–22. Berlin: De Gruyter, 2011.

Myres, J. L. "Hesiod's 'Shield of Herakles': Its Structure and Workmanship (Plate II)." *Journal of Hellenic Studies* 61 (1941): 17.

Nagler, Michael N. "Discourse and Conflict in Hesiod: Eris and the Erides." *Ramus* 21, no. 1 (1992): 79–96.

Nagy, Gregory. "Authorisation and Authorship in the Hesiodic Theogony." *Ramus* 21, no. 1 (1992): 119–30.

———. "God and the Land: The Metaphysics of Farming in Hesiod and Vergil, (1998) (English) by S. Nelson, D. Grene." *Journal of Religion* 80, no. 3 (2000): 545–46.

———. "Hesiod." In *Ancient Writers: Greece and Rome,* ed. T. James Luce, 1:43–73. New York: Scribner, 1982.

———, ed. *Homer and Hesiod as Prototypes of Greek Literature.* New York: Routledge, 2001.

Nisetich, Frank J., ed. *Pindar's Victory Songs.* Baltimore: Johns Hopkins University Press, 1980.

Northrup, Mark D. "Tartarus Revisited: A Reconsideration of Theogony 711–819." *Wiener Studien* 92 (1979): 22–36.

Notopoulos, James A. "Homer, Hesiod and the Achean Heritage of Oral Poetry." *Hesperia* 29 (1960): 177.

Nussbaum, G. "Labor and Status in the Works and Days." *Classical Quarterly* 10 (1960): 213–20.

Onians, Richard Broxton. *The Origins of European Thought: About the Body, the Mind, the Soul, the World Time, and Fate.* Cambridge: Cambridge University Press, 1951.

Ormand, Kirk. *The Hesiodic Catalogue of Women and Archaic Greece.* Cambridge: Cambridge University Press, 2014.

Page, D. L., ed. *Poetai Melici Graeci.* Oxford: Oxford University Press, 1962.

Pentikäinen, Juha Y. *Golden King of the Forest: The Lore of the Northern Bear.* Helsinki: Etnika OY, 2007.

Perysinakis, I. "Hesiod's Treatment of Wealth." *Métis* 1 (1986): 97–119.

Petropoulos, J. C. B. *Heat and Lust: Hesiod's Midsummer Festival Scene Revisited*. Greek Studies. Lanham, Md.: Rowman & Littlefield, 1994.

Priou, Alex. "Hesiod: Man, Law and Cosmos." *Polis: The Journal for Ancient Greek and Roman Political Thought* 31, no. 2 (2014): 233–60.

Pucci, Pietro. *Hesiod and the Language of Poetry*. Baltimore: Johns Hopkins University Press, 1977.

Rosen, Ralph M. "Poetry and Sailing in Hesiod's 'Works and Days.'" *Classical Antiquity* 9, no. 1 (1990): 99–113.

Rosenmeyer, Thomas G. "Hesiod and Historiography." *Hermes* 85 (1957): 257.

Rowan Beye, Charles. "The Rhythm of Hesiod's 'Works and Days.'" *Harvard Studies in Classical Philology* 76 (1972): 23–43.

Rzach, Aloisius, ed. *Hesiodi Carmina*. Leipzig: B. G. Teubner, 1902.

Sale, W. "Aphrodite in the Theogony." *Transactions of the American Philological Association* 92 (1961): 508–21.

Samuel, A. E. "The Days of 'Hesiod's' Month." *Transactions of the American Philological Association* 97 (1966): 421–29.

Sarno, Ronald A. "Hesiod: From Chaos to Cosmos to Community." *Classical Bulletin* 45, no. 5 (1969): 65.

Scodel, Ruth. "Poetic Authority and Oral Tradition in Hesiod and Pindar." In *Speaking Volumes: Orality and Literacy in the Greek and Roman World*, ed. Janet Watson, 109–37. Leiden: Brill, 2001.

Scully, Stephen. *Hesiod's Theogony: From Near Eastern Creation Myths to Paradise Lost*. Oxford: Oxford University Press, 2015.

Smith, A. H. "The Making of Pandora." *The Journal of Hellenic Studies* 11 (1890): 278–83.

Solmsen, Friedrich, R. Merkelbach, and M. L. West, eds. *Hesiodi Theogonia Opera et Dies Scutum: Fragmenta Selecta*. Oxford: Oxford University Press, 1970.

———. "The Days of the Works and Days." *Transactions of the American Philological Association* 94 (1963): 293–320.

———. "The Two Near Eastern Sources of Hesiod." *Hermes* 117 (1989): 413–22.

Stewart, Douglas J. "Hesiod and History." *Bucknell Review* 18, no. 1 (1970): 37–52.

Sussman, L. S. "The Birth of the Gods: Sexuality, Conflict and Cosmic Structure in Hesiod's Theogony." *Ramus* 7 (1978): 61–77.

———. "Workers and Drones: Labor, Idleness and Gender Definition in Hesiod's Beehive." *Arethusa* 11 (1978): 27–41.

Sveinsson, Einar O. *Njáls Saga: A Literary Masterpiece*. Lincoln: University of Nebraska Press, 1971.

Trever, Albert Augustus. "The Age of Hesiod: A Study in Economic History." *Classical Philology* 19 (1924): 157–68.

Tsagarakis, Odysseus. "On the Question of Priority of Homer and Hesiod." *Emérita* 54 (1986): 189–202.

Van Noorden, Helen. *Playing Hesiod: The 'Myth of the Races' in Classical Antiquity*. Cambridge: Cambridge University Press, 2014.

Vergados, Athanassios. "The Cyclopes and the Hundred-Handers in Hesiod's 'Theogony' 139–53." *Hermes* 141, no. 1 (2013): 1–7.

Wace, Alan J. B., and Frank H. Stubbings, eds. *A Companion to Homer*. New York: Macmillan, 1974.

Walcot, Peter. *Greek Peasants, Ancient and Modern: A Comparison of Social and Moral Values*. New York: Barnes & Noble, 1970.

Select Bibliography

———. "Hesiod and the Didactic Literature of the Near East." *Revue des études grecques* 75 (1962): 13–36.

———. "Hesiod and the Law." *Symbolae Osloenses* 38 (1963): 5–21.

———. *Hesiod and the Near East*. Cardiff: Wales University Press, 1966.

———. "Pandora's Jar, Erga 83–105." *Hermes* 89 (1961): 249–51.

Wallace, Paul W. "Hesiod and the Valley of the Muses." *Greek, Roman and Byzantine Studies* 15, no. 1 (1974): 5–24.

West, M. L., ed. *Hesiod: Theogony and Works and Days*. Oxford: Oxford University Press, 1988.

Wickkiser, Bronwen L. "Hesiod and the Fabricated Woman: Poetry and Visual Art in the 'Theogony.'" *Mnemosyne* 63, no. 4 (2010): 557–76.

Wolf, H. J. "The Origin of Judicial Litigation Among the Greeks." *Traditio* 4 (1946): 31–87.

Zarecki, Jonathan P. "Pandora and the Good Eris in Hesiod." *Greek, Roman, and Byzantine Studies* 47 (2007): 5–29.

Zeitlin, Froma I. "The Economics of Hesiod's Pandora." In *Pandora: Women in Classical Greece*, ed. Ellen D. Reeder, 49–56. Princeton: Princeton University Press, 1995.

Zimmerman, J. E. *Dictionary of Classical Mythology*. New York: Bantam, 1966.

Index

(TH = *Theogony*; WD = *Works and Days*; S = *Shield*)
The letter *n* following line numbers refers to notes.

Achaeans, WD 652
  wait to sail to Troy, WD 651–52n
Acheloios/Acheloos, TH 340
  etymology of, TH 337–70n; S 300–320n
  as possible model of Okeanos, TH
    337–70
Acheron
  etymology of, TH 337–70n; S 300–320n
  omission of, TH 337–70n
Achilleus, TH 1007
  grandson of Aiakos, TH 1005–20n
  grandson of Nereus, TH 233–64n
  son of Peleus, TH 1005–20n
  son of Thetis, TH 1005–20n
  taught by Cheiron, TH 993–1002n
adultery, WD 328–29n
Aegeus, S 180–85
aegis, TH 11, 13, 24, 50, 735, 918, 966, 1022;
    WD 483, 661; S 320–25, 440–45
Aello, TH 267
Agaue, TH 247, 976
  mother of Pentheus, TH 976n
Aiakos, TH 1005
  father of Peleus and grandfather of
    Achilleus, TH 1005–20n
Aidos (Shame), seeking refuge among gods,
    WD 174–201n
Aietes, TH 993
  alternate name
    King Aietes, TH 957
  son of Helios, TH 958
Aigaion, Mount, TH 459–501n, 484
Aineias, TH 1005–20n, 1008
  descent into underworld, TH 721–819n

Alkmene, TH 526, 943, 950; S 35–40, 45–50,
    50–55, 465–70
  daughter of Elektryon, S 1–10, 1–10n,
    10–20n, 30–60n, 85–90
  visited by Zeus, TH 943–44n
Alpheios, TH 338; S 460–80n
Amalthea, and birth of Zeus, TH 459–501n
Amazons, battle of Bellerophon and Pegasos
    against, TH 270–86n
ambrosia, TH 640, 641, 796
Amphidamas, WD 655
  possible historical character of, WD
    654–59n
Amphitrite, TH 243, 252, 930
  one of Nereids, TH 930–33n
  repetition of name in list of Nereids, TH
    233–64n
Amphitryon, TH 316; S 1–55, 10–20n, 415–20,
    430–35
  absent when Zeus visits wife, TH 943–44n;
    S 30–60n
  alternate name
    Alkides, S 110–15
  son of Alkaios, S 25–30
Anauros, S 460–80n, 470–75
Anchises, TH 1009
  affair with Aphrodite, TH 1005–20n
ant, "the wise one," WD 524–25n, 778n
Anthe, city of Myrmidons, S 470–75
Antheia, S 380–85
Aphrodite, TH 16, 196, 197, 822, 961, 975, 979,
    989, 1004, 1014; WD 66, 521; S 5–10,
    45–50, 195–200n
  affair with Anchises, TH 1005–20n

Aphrodite (*cont.*)
  alternate names
    Kyprogenes, TH 199
    Kythera, TH 192, 198
    Kythereia, TH 196, 198, 934, 1008
    Philommedes, TH 200
  attendants of, TH 64–80n
  born from castration of Okeanos, TH
      183–210n
  daughter of Dione, TH 9–21n
  etymology of name and epithets, TH
      183–210n
Apollon, TH 95, 347, 919; WD 771; S 55–60,
      65–70, 460–80n
  accompanies Muses with lyre, TH 64–80n;
      S 200–205n, 290–300n
  alternate names
    Apollon Pagasaios, S 70–75
    Phoibos Apollon, TH 14; S 65–70,
        95–100
  association with laurel, TH 22–34n
  son of Leto, TH 404–8n; S 475–80
  son of Zeus and Leto, S 200–205
apotropaic
  carving against crows, WD 746–47n
  use of kennings, WD 524–25n
Arcturus, WD 565, 610
  in constellation of Boötes, WD 564–70n
  morning rising of, WD 609–14n
  rising as sign of spring, WD 564–70n
Ardeskos, TH 345
Ares, TH 923, 934, 935; S 55–60, 60–85n,
      95–100, 105–10, 180–85, 190–95,
      195–200n, 330–35, 345–50, 355–60,
      370–75, 420–50n, 425–30, 430–35,
      440–45, 445–50, 450–55, 455–60,
      460–80n
Argonauts, story of, TH 993–1002n
Argos (city), TH 12
Argos (dog), WD 68, 78, 85
Argos Panoptes, slayer of Echidna, TH
      295–336n
Argument, TH 229
Ariadne, daughter of Minos, TH 948
Arima, TH 304
Arion, S 115–20
Aristaios, TH 977
Arktos, S 185–90
Arne, S 380–85, 470–75
Artemis, TH 14, 919
  daughter of Leto, TH 404–8n

identification with Hekate and Selene,
    TH 371–74n, 409–52n
  sometimes confused with Eileithyia, TH
      912–29n
ash tree, TH 563; WD 146
  bronze race of men fashioned of, WD
      144–56n
Ash Tree Nymphs, TH 187
  born from Earth after Giants, WD
      144–56n
  born from Okeanos's severed genitals, TH
      183–210n
Asia, TH 359
  as nymph and land, TH 337–70n
Askre, WD 640
  location and history of, WD 639–40n
  threatened by Perses's perjury, WD
      213–85n
asphodel, WD 41
Asteria, TH 409
Astraios, TH 376, 378
Athena, TH 318, 573, 587, 888, 924; WD 65, 73;
      S 325–30, 340–45, 440–45, 455–60,
      470–75
  aids Perseus in slaying Medousa, TH
      270–86n
  alternate names
    Athena Tritogeneia, S 195–200
      explanation of epithet, TH 886–900n
    Pallas Athena, TH 576; WD 77; S 125–30
  born from Zeus's head, TH 912–29n
  daughter of Zeus, TH 13; S 125–30,
      195–200
  intervenes in duel of Herakles against
      Kyknos, S 320–40n, 420–50n
  origin of, TH 886–900n
  Virgin Mary's connection with, TH
      886–900n
Atlas, TH 509, 517, 746, 938; WD 383
  daughters identified with Pleiades, WD
      383–87n
  father of Calypso, TH 507–615n
  house in underworld, TH 721–819n
  lives near Hesperides, TH 507–615n
  role in Herakles myth, TH 507–615n
  supports sky, TH 507–615n
Attack, S 150–55, 150–60n
Aulis, WD 651

Battle Din, S 150–55, 150–60n
Battles, TH 228

bees, TH 594, 596; WD 233, 305
  drones, TH 595, 598; WD 304
  idle man like drone, WD 286–319n
  teeming in middle of oak, WD 233–34n
Bellerophon, TH 325
  battles against Chimaira, Amazons, and
    Solymoi with Pegasos, TH
    270–86n
Betelgeuse
  brightest star in constellation of Orion,
    WD 597–98n
  heliacal rising at summer solstice, WD
    597–98n
Bia (Force), TH 385
  belongs only to Zeus, TH 383–403n
birth, number of nights/men effect on, TH
  56–63n
black poplar, S 375–80
Boeotians, S 20–25
Boreas, TH 380, 870
  as north wind, TH 375–82n
bread, WD 589–96n
bribery, and justice, WD 1–10n

Calypso, daughter of Atlas, TH 507–615n
cart/wagon
  construction of axle, WD 424–25n
  construction of wheels, WD 426–27n
  warning against overloading, WD
    690–93n
castration
  birth arising from Ouranos's, TH 183–210n
  of boars, bulls, and mules, WD 790–91
  explanations of myth of, TH 154–82n
Centaurs, S 180–85, 180–90n
Chalkis, WD 654
Chaos, TH 116, 123, 700, 814
  mingles with Eros, TH 116–25n
  nature of, TH 116–25n
  produces Erebos and Night, TH 116–25n
  produces Night, TH 746–57n
cheese, not mentioned by Hesiod, WD
  589–96n
Cheiron, son of Philyra, TH 1002
  teacher of Jason and Achilleus, TH
    993–1002n
children
  dowry of daughters, WD 376–80n
  number for farmers, WD 376–80n
  patrimony to sons, WD 376–80n
  resemblance to parents, WD 234–35n

Chimaira, TH 319
  battle of Bellerophon and Pegasos
    against, TH 270–86n
  description of, TH 295–336n
Chrysaor, TH 280, 283, 287, 980
Chryseis, TH 359; S 10–20n
chthonic
  character of Hekate, TH 409–52n
  character of Minoan god identified with
    Zeus, TH 459–501n
  character of Pandora, WD 59–105n
  hope of chthonic order in Typhoeus, TH
    820–80n
  powers prayed to by Hera, TH 617–721n
cicada, WD 582; S 385–400n, 390–95
  sound production of, WD 582–89n
city of just men
  description of, WD 234–35n
  peace and prosperity in, WD 220–29n
Clashes, TH 228
cleanliness, and human waste, WD 727–32n
Confusion, S 155–60, 155–60n
cornel tree, fruit as dulling women's
    libidinous urges, WD 582–89n
Counter-Argument, TH 229
Counterattack, S 150–55, 150–60n
crane, WD 448
  migration as sign for plowing, WD
    448–49n
creation, of primordial beings, TH 116–25n
Crete, TH 477, 480, 971
crows, perching on roof, WD 746–47n
cuckoo, WD 486
  song heralds spring, WD 479–90n
cult
  cave cults in Crete, TH 459–501n
  hero, WD 109–25n
  honoring of deity in, TH 22–34n
  of Muses at Pieria, TH 53–55n
  of sun at Rhodes, TH 371–74n
Cyprus, TH 193, 200

Danae, S 215–20, 215–40n, 225–30
  mother of Perseus, TH 270–86n
dance, S 270–90, 270–90n
  dance ring/ring dance, TH 1–4n; S 200–
    205, 200–205n
Day, TH 125, 748
  born from Erebos and Night, TH 116–25n
  house in underworld with Night, TH
    721–819n, 746–57n

days, WD 765–828n

Death, TH 211–32n, 212, 757, 759; S 155–60, 155–60n
  brother of Sleep, child of Night, WD 109–25n
  house in underworld with Sleep, TH 721–819n

Deathcloud, S 240–70n, 260–65

Death Demons, S 240–70n, 245–50

Deception, TH 224

Demeter, TH 454, 912, 969; WD 32, 300, 393, 465, 466, 598, 806; S 285–90
  frequently associated with Hades, WD 465–66n
  identification of Rheia with, TH 133–38n
  mother of Ploutos, TH 969–74n
  union with Iasion, TH 969–74n

Desire, TH 64
  personification of, TH 64–80n

Dione, TH 17, 353
  in song of Muses, TH 9–21n

Dionysos, TH 947; WD 614; S 395–400
  birth of, TH 940–42n
  finds Ariadne on Naxos, TH 947–49n
  wine as gift of, WD 609–14n

disease
  as anger of gods, WD 240–43n
  brought by Dog Star, WD 415–19n

dog, feeding of, WD 604n

Dog Star, WD 417, 586, 609; S 150–55, 395–400
  bearer of heat, disease, and sunstroke, WD 415–19n
  rising of, WD 415–19n

dolphins, S 205–10, 210–15, 210–15n

Doris, TH 250, 350
  daughter of Okeanos, TH 241

Dreams, TH 212
  location of, TH 211–32n

eagle, TH 523, 527; S 40–35
  role in punishment of Prometheus, TH 507–615n

Echidna, TH 297, 304
  daughter of Phorkys and Keto, TH 295–336n
  daughter of Tartaros and Gaia, TH 295–336n
  progeny of, TH 295–336n
  slain by Argos Panoptes, TH 295–336n

egg, primeval, TH 116–25n

Eileithyia, TH 912–29n, 923
  sometimes confused with Artemis, TH 912–29n

Elektryon, S 1–5, 1–10n, 15–20, 80–85, 85–90
  etymology of name, S 10–20n

Eleutherian hills, TH 53
  location at Kithairon, TH 53–55n

elm, WD 435
  recommended for pole of plow, WD 427–36n

Elysian Fields
  identical to Isles of the Blest, WD 157–73n
  Menelaos at, WD 157–73n

Emathion, TH 985
  slain by Herakles, TH 984–92n

Eos, TH 18, 372, 378, 381, 984
  alternate name
    Dawn, TH 451
      in song of Muses, TH 9–21n
  mother of winds and stars, TH 375–82n
  unhappy end of her lovers, TH 371–74n

Eosphoros, TH 382

Epimetheus, WD 86; TH 511
  proverbial for foolishness, TH 507–615n

epiphany, of Muses to Hesiod, TH 1–115n, 22–34n

Erebos, TH 123, 124, 515, 669
  born from Chaos, TH 116–25n
  produces Ether and Day with Night, TH 116–25n
  receives primeval egg from Night, TH 116–25n

Eris, twofold nature of, TH 507–615n

Eros, TH 120, 201
  mingles with Chaos, TH 116–25n
  nature in Hesiod, TH 116–25n
  role in cosmology, TH 116–25n

Ether, TH 125
  born from Erebos and Night, TH 116–25n

Ethiopians, TH 985

Euboea, WD 651

Euenos, TH 345

Europe, TH 357
  as nymph and land, TH 337–70n

Eurystheus, S 90–95
  labors imposed on Herakles, TH 295–336n

Eurytion, TH 293

Famine, TH 227

farmer, priorities of, WD 405–9n

Fates, TH 904; S 240–70n
Fear, TH 935; S 40–45, 140–45n, 235–40,
    460–65
    and Panic, S 195–200, 195–200n, 460–80n
fennel stalk, TH 566; WD 52
fig tree, WD 679
fire, theft by Prometheus, TH 507–644; WD
    42–58n
firs, WD 510; S 185–90
Furies, TH 185; WD 803
    alternate name
        Erinys, TH 472
    born from Ouranos's severed genitals, TH
        183–210n
    as personification of curses, TH 183–219n
    present at birth of Oath Demon, WD
        219n

Gaia, TH 20, 45, 106, 116, 126, 147, 154, 158,
    159, 176, 183, 237, 422, 463, 470, 479,
    494, 626, 644, 821, 883, 889
    alternate name
        Earth, TH 173, 702
            in song of Muses, TH 9–21n
            mating with Sky, TH 133–38n
            produces Giants, then Ash Tree
                Nymphs, WD 144–56n
    mother of Echidna, TH 295–336n
    mother of Okeanos, TH 337–70n
    mother of Themis, TH 901–11n
    origin of, TH 116–25n
Galateia, TH 250
Geryones, TH 288, 309, 982
Giants, TH 51, 185
    born from Earth before Ash Tree
        Nymphs, WD 144–56n
    born from Ouranos's severed genitals, TH
        183–210n
    resemblance to bronze race of men, WD
        144–56n
    in song of Muses, TH 36–52n
Gigantomachy, TH 183–210n
goats
    fattest in summer, WD 582–89n
    milk from, WD 589–96n
gold, significance of, WD 109–25n
Good Law
    daughter of Zeus, WD 275–78n
    sister of Justice and Peace, WD 213–85n,
        220–29n
Gorgo, S 215–40n, 220–25

Gorgons, TH 274; S 215–40n, 225–30
    Euryale, TH 276; S 215–40n
    insignificance of Sthenno and Euryale,
        TH 270–86n
    Medousa, TH 276, 278, 280
        description of, TH 270–86n
        slain by Perseus, TH 270–86n; S 215–40n
    Sthenno, TH 276; S 215–40n
Graces, TH 64, 908, 946; WD 74
    Aglaia, TH 909, 946
        one of Graces, WD 230–31n
    attendants of Aphrodite, TH 64–80n
    connection with Muses, TH 64–80n
    Euphrosyne, TH 909
        one of Graces, WD 230–31n
    names of, WD 230–31n
    names reflect lawful peace, TH 901–11n
    Thalia, TH 909
        daughter of Wide Law, WD 230–31n
        one of Graces, WD 230–31n
Graiai, TH 270
    Enyo, TH 273
    omission of Deino in list of, TH 270–86n
    Pemphredo, TH 273
    as personification of old age, TH
        270–86n
grapes, pressed to make wine, WD 564–70,
    564–70n, 609–14, 609–14n;
        S 290–95, 290–300n, 300–305
Greece, WD 653
Greeks, WD 528
Grenikos, TH 342
guilt, feeling in thief's mind, WD
    359–60n

Hades (god), TH 311, 455, 767, 774, 850; WD 154
    alternate name
        Aidoneus, TH 913
    fertility associations of, TH 969–74n
    frequently associated with Demeter, WD
        465–66n
    in underworld, TH 721–819n; S 240–70n
Hades (place), as usual destination of
        deceased heroes, WD 157–73n
Haliakmon, TH 341
Harmonia, TH 937
    daughter of Aphrodite, TH 975
    daughter of Ares and Aphrodite, TH 937n
    married to Kadmos, TH 937n
Harpies, TH 267
    description of, TH 265–69n

hawk, WD 203, 212
  fable of nightingale and, WD 202–12n
  symbol of kings and Perses, WD 202–12n
Hebe, TH 17, 923
  daughter of Zeus, TH 952
  in song of Muses, TH 9–21n
hecatombs, S 475–80
Hekate, TH 411, 418, 441
  daughter of Perses, TH 375–82n
  daughter of Perses and Asteria, TH
    409–52n
  Hesiod's rehabilitation of, TH 409–52n
  identification with Selene and Artemis,
    TH 371–74n, 409–52n
  origin and powers, TH 409–52n
Helen, WD 166
  wife of Menelaos, WD 157–73n
Helike, S 380–85, 470–75
Helikon, TH 2, 7, 23; WD 639
  location of, TH 5–8
  as sacred location, TH 22–34n
  sanctuary of Muses at, TH 5–8n
Helios, TH 18, 372, 956, 958
  alternate name
    Sun, in song of Muses, TH 9–21n
  Helios Hyperionides, TH 1011
  son of Hyperion, TH 133–38n
Hephaistos, TH 866, 928, 945; WD 61;
    S 120–25, 215–20, 240–45, 295–300,
    310–15, 315–20
  fall to Lemnos, TH 721–25n
Hera, TH 314, 454, 921, 927, 952
  alternate name
    lady of Argos, TH 12
  prayer to chthonic powers, TH 617–721n
  wife of Zeus, TH 328
Herakles, TH 289, 315, 316, 332, 943, 952, 982;
    S 50–55, 55–60, 60–85n, 65–70,
    70–75, 75–80, 115–20, 135–40,
    315–20n, 320–40n, 345–50, 440–45,
    450–55, 455–60
  arming, order of, S 85–140n
  and cattle of Geryon, TH 289–94n
  child of Thebes, TH 530
  connection with Hesperides, TH 211–32n
  descent into underworld, TH 721–819n
  fetching of Kerberos, TH 295–336n
  freeing of Prometheus, TH 507–615n
  offspring of Lynkeus, S 320–40n, 325–30
  role of Atlas in myth of, TH 507–615n
  slaying of Lernaean Hydra, TH 295–336n
  slaying of Nemean Lion, TH 295–336n
  slaying of Emathion, TH 984–92n
  son of Alkmene, TH 526, 950; S 465–70
  son of Amphitryon, S 30–60n, 160–65,
    415–20, 430–35, 455–60
  son of Zeus, S 30–60n, 65–70, 110–15,
    145–50, 160–65, 320–25, 370–75,
    385–90, 410–15, 420–25, 445–50
  twelve labors of, S 160–80
Hermes, TH 445, 939; WD 68
  alternate name
    Slayer of Argos, WD 68, 78, 85
Hermos, TH 343
Hesiod, TH 22
  admonishes brother to choose path of
    virtue, WD 286–319n
  epiphany of Muses to, TH 22–34n
  family from Aeolian Kyme, WD 635n
  perjury of Perses threatens kin of, WD
    213–85n
  subject of Theogony, TH 105–15n
  symbolized by nightingale, WD 202–12n
Hesperides, TH 215, 275, 519
  guard golden apples, TH 211–32n
  live near Atlas, TH 507–615n
Hestia, TH 454
  honored in hymn, TH 22–34n
  virginal nature of, TH 453–58n; WD
    733–34n
  worship of, TH 453–58n
Himeros, TH 201
  attendant of Aphrodite, TH 64–80n
Hippokrene, TH 6
  etymology of, TH 5–8n
  location of, TH 5–8n
holm oak, WD 428, 436
  used for beam of plow, WD 427–36n
hoopoe, transformation of Tereus into, WD
    564–70n
Hope, WD 97
  left in jar, WD 59–105n
  twofold nature of, WD 59–105n
Hubris/Injustice, race against Justice, WD
    216–18n
Hundred-Handers, TH 644
  Briareos, TH 149, 618, 713, 734, 817, 819
  description of, TH 139–53n
  freed by Zeus, TH 139–53n
  Gyges, TH 149, 618, 713, 734, 817
  Kottos, TH 149, 618, 654, 713, 734, 817
  role in Titanomachy, TH 139–53n

Hunger, WD 299, 302
Hyades, WD 615
    setting of, WD 615–17n
Hydra of Lerna, TH 313
    slaying as Herakles's second labor, TH
        295–336n
Hyperion, TH 134, 371
    father of Helios, TH 133–38n

Iapetos, TH 19, 134, 507, 528, 543, 559, 565, 614;
        WD 50, 55
    father of Prometheus, TH 133–38n; WD
        42–58n
Iasion, TH 969
    father of Ploutos, TH 969–74n
    union with Demeter, TH 969–74n
Ida, TH 1010
    location of most important cave cult, TH
        459–50in
incest, of Okeanos with Tethys, WD
        42–58n
Ino, TH 976
invisible divinities, WD 213–85n, 252–55n
Iolaos, TH 317; S 70–75, 75–80, 100–105,
        320–25, 340–45, 465–70
    nursling of Zeus, S 115–20
    offspring of Lynkeus S 320–40n
Iolkos, TH 998; S 470–75
    city of Myrmidons, S 380–85
Iphikles, S 30–60n, 50–55
Iris, TH 266, 784
    daughter of Thaumas, TH 780
    goddess of rainbow, TH 265–69n
Isles of the Blest
    identical to Elysian Fields, WD 157–73n
    ruled by Kronos, TH 133–38n
Itys, son of Tereus and Procne, WD
        564–70n

Jason, TH 992, 996, 1000
    taught by Cheiron, TH 993–1002n
Justice, TH 902; WD 35, 213, 217, 220, 259n,
        279
    daughter of Zeus, TH 256
    daughter of Zeus and Themis, WD
        213–85n
    injured by perjury, WD 213–85n
    nature of, WD 220–29n
    as personification, WD 213–85n
    race against Hubris/Injustice, WD
        216–18n

sister of Peace and Good Law, WD
        213–85n, 220–29n
    surrounded by benign divinities, WD
        230–31n

Kadmeans, TH 327; S 10–15
Kadmos, TH 937, 940, 976; WD 164
    married to Harmonia, TH 937n
Kallirhoe, TH 351
    daughter of Ocean, TH 979
    daughter of Okeanos, TH 287
Kalypso, TH 359, 1017
    affair with Odysseus, TH 1005–20n
Kephalos, TH 986
Ker, TH 211, 211–32n
Kerberos, dog of Hades, TH 311
    fetching as Herakles's twelfth labor, TH
        295–336n
Keres, TH 217
    possible connection with Moirai, TH 211
Keto, TH 238, 270, 295, 333, 336
    mother of Echidna, TH 295–336n
Keyx, S 350–55, 470–75, 475–80, 460–480n
kids
    hides of firstling kids used for winter coat,
        WD 543–45n
    as token of piety in sacrifices, WD
        543–45n
kings
    bribed by Perses, WD 202–12n
    connection with Muses, TH 79–93n
    corrupt, WD 27–41n
    power of from Zeus, TH 79–93n
    symbolized by hawk, WD 202–12n
Kirke, TH 957, 1011
    seduction of Odysseus by, TH 1005–20n
Kithairon, location of Eleutherian hills, TH
        53–55n
Klymene, TH 351
    daughter of Okeanos, TH 508
    daughter of Okeanos and Tethys, WD
        42–58n
    mother of Prometheus, WD 42–58n
Koios, TH 134, 404
    father of Leto, TH 133–38n
Kouretes, and birth of Zeus, TH 459–50in
Kratos, TH 385
    belongs only to Zeus, TH 383–403n
Kreios, TH 133–38n, 134, 375
    insignificance of sons, TH 375–82n
Kreon, S 80–85

Kronos, TH 19, 73, 137, 168, 188, 396, 423, 453,
        459, 473, 494, 534, 625, 629, 633, 646,
        658, 668, 851; WD 18, 70, 112, 139,
        158, 168, 238, 242, 246, 259
    alternate names
        King Kronos, TH 476
        Lord Kronos, TH 485
    as consort to Mediterranean earth
        mother, TH 459–501n
    father of Zeus, TH 133–38n, 459–501n
    least violent of Titans, TH 459–501n
    ruler of Isles of the Blest, TH 133–38n
    swallows stone instead of Zeus,
        TH 459–501n
Kybele, identification of Rheia with,
        TH 133–38n
Kyklopes, TH 139, 144
    anthropophagous, WD 144–56n
    Arges, TH 140, 501a
    Brontes, TH 140, 501a
    description of, TH 139–53n
    Steropes, TH 140, 501a
Kyknos, S 55–60, 65–70, 325–30, 330–35, 345–50,
        365–70, 410–15, 415–20, 465–70,
        470–75, 475–80
    casts his spear against Herakles, S
        405–420n
    Fear and Panic lifting him up, S 460–80n
    grave and burial mound washed away by
        river Anauros, S 460–80n
    and Herakles leap to ground, S 370–85n
    slain by Herakles, collapses like oak,
        S 420–50n
Kyme, Aeolian, WD 635
    location of, WD 635n
    origin of Hesiod's family from, WD 635n

Laistrygones, anthropophagous, WD 144–56n
Lapiths, S 175–90
    names of, S 180–90n
Latinos, TH 1013
    connection with Latium, TH 1005–20n
laurel, TH 30; WD 435
    associated with Apollon, TH 22–34n
    recommended for pole of plow, WD
        427–36n
    symbolism of staff made from, TH 22–34n
law/justice
    difficulty of being just man, WD 213–85n
    lack of respect for, as sign of humanity's
        end, WD 174–201n

natural law imposed by Zeus, WD
        275–78n
    and prosperity of polis, TH 409–52n
    Zeus as highest authority of, WD 1–10n
Lawlessness, TH 230, 902
    born before Oath Demon, WD 219n
Lenaion, WD 504
    time of, WD 504n
Lerna, TH 313
Leto, TH 19, 406, 918; WD 771; S 200–205,
        475–80
    daughter of Koios, TH 133–38n
    daughter of Phoibe, TH 133–38n
    mother of Apollon and Artemis, TH
        404–8n
Lies, TH 229
lies/perjury
    of Hera to Semele, TH 940–42n
    injurious to Justice, WD 213–85n
    Muses' capability of, TH 22–34n
light, production of, TH 116–25n
Lion of Nemea, TH 327
    slaying as Herakles's first labor, TH
        295–336n
Lokrians, S 25–30
Love, born from Night, WD 11–26n
Lyktos, TH 477, 481
    sacred caves in proximity of, TH 459–501n
Lynkeus, S 325–30
    son of Aegyptos, S 320–40n
lyre, TH 94; S 200–205
    Apollon's accompaniment of Muses on,
        TH 64–80n

Maia, daughter of Atlas, TH 938
    etymology of, TH 938–39n
Maiandros, TH 339
mallet, excess wood used for, WD 424–25n
mallow, WD 41
man
    bronze race of, WD 144–56n
    creation in Orphism, TH 617–721n
    descended from Titans, WD 42–58n
    fall of, WD 42–58n
    Five Ages of, WD 106–201n
    golden race of, WD 109–25n
    heroic race of, WD 144–56n, 157–73n
    idle man like drone, WD 286–319n
    industrious man, WD 286–319n
    iron race of, WD 174–201n
    plight in summer, WD 582–89n

reputation of, WD 761–64n
reputation of, affected by wife,
    WD 700–701n
resemblance to Giants, WD 144–56n
silver race of, WD 126–42n
in song of Muses, TH 36–52n
time of marriage for, WD 695–97n
as walking tripod, WD 533–35n
weakened by contact with women,
    WD 753–54n
work on land belonging to,
    WD 405–9n
Zeus's punishment against, WD 59–105n
Manslaughter(s), TH 228; S 150–55
meat
    best, WD 589–96n
    mostly eaten on religious holidays,
        TH 507–615n
Medeia, TH 962
Medeios, TH 1001
    as eponymous hero of Medes,
        TH 993–1002n
Mekone, TH 536
    sacrifice at, WD 42–58n
Memnon, TH 984
    king of Ethiopians, TH 984–92n
Menelaos
    at Elysian Fields, WD 157–73n
    husband of Helen and son-in-law to Zeus,
        WD 157–73n
Menoitios, TH 510, 514
Metis, TH 358, 886, 890, 894
    swallowed by Zeus, TH 886–900n
Mimas, S 185–90
Minos, TH 948
mist/rain, source of, WD 550–53n
Mnemosyne, TH 53, 135, 915
    meaning of, TH 53–55n
Moirai, TH 217; S 240–70n
    Atropos, TH 218, 905; S 255–60
    explanation of names of, TH 211–32n
    Klotho, TH 218, 905; S 255–60
    Lachesis, TH 218, 905; S 255–60
Momos, TH 211–32n, 214
Moros, TH 211, 211–32n
mortar and pestle, construction of,
    WD 423n
Mother of the Gods, identification of Rheia
    with, TH 133–38n
Mr. Boneless, WD 524
    most likely octopus, WD 524–25n

Murder, S 150–155
Muses, TH 54, 93, 95, 97, 100, 114, 916;
    WD 662
    accompanied by Apollon on lyre,
        TH 64–80n
    connection with kings, TH 79–93n
    connection with Graces, TH 64–80n
    cult at Pieria, TH 53–55n
    daughters of Zeus, TH 24, 29, 50, 76, 81,
        104, 1022
    epiphany to Hesiod, TH 22–34n
    Erato, TH 78, 246
    Euterpe, TH 77
    function in proem, TH 1–115n
    Helikonian, TH 1; WD 658
        explanation of epithet, TH 1–4n
        sanctuary at Helikon, TH 5–8n
        significance of their setting out from
            Helikon, TH 9–21n
    Hesiod's list of, TH 64–80n
    invoked at beginning of poem, WD 1–10n
    Kalliope, TH 79
    Kleio, TH 77
    Melpomene, TH 77
    Olympian, TH 25, 36, 50, 75, 965
    Ourania, TH 78
    Pierian, WD 1; S 205–10
    Polymnia, TH 78
    song of, TH 9–21n, 36–52n
    Terpsichore, TH 78
    Thaleia, TH 77
Myrmidons, S 375–80, 470–75

Nature, WD 388
Naxos, where Dionysos found Ariadne,
    TH 947–49n
nectar, TH 640, 641, 796
Neilos, TH 338
Nemea, TH 329
Nemean Tretos, TH 331
Nemesis, TH 211–32n, 223
    seeking refuge among gods, WD
        174–201n
Nereids, TH 233–64n
    Amphitrite one of, TH 930–33n
Nereus, TH 233, 240, 263, 1003
    father of Thetis, TH 1005–20n
    grandfather of Achilles, TH 233–64n
    origin of name, TH 233–64n, 1005–20n
    Proteus as another version of, TH
        233–64n

Night, TH 20, 107, 123, 124, 211, 213, 223, 744,
     748, 756, 758; WD 17
  born from Chaos, TH 116–25n
  daughter of Chaos, TH 746–57n
  grandmother of Oath Demon, WD 219n
  house in underworld with Day, TH 721–
       819n, 746–57n
  lays primeval egg in Erebos, TH 116–25n
  produces Ether and Day with Erebos, TH
       116–25n
  produces Old Age, WD 109–25n
  produces Sleep and Death, WD 109–25n
  produces Strife and Love, WD 11–26n
  in song of Muses, TH 9–21n
nightingale, WD 203
  fable of hawk and, WD 202–12n
  symbolizes Hesiod, WD 202–12n
  transformation of Procne into, WD
       564–70n
Nike, TH 383–403n, 384
Notos, TH 380, 870
  as south wind, TH 375–82n
number
  of nights/men influencing childbirth,
       TH 56–63n
  significance of 9, TH 721–25n
nymph(s), TH 130, 298

oak, WD 233, 436, 486, 510; S 375–80, 420–25,
     420–50n
  acorns eaten, WD 233–34n
  middle teeming with bees, WD 233–34n
  significance of "oak and rock," TH 35n
  used for share of plow, WD 427–36n
oath
  breaking as injurious to Justice, WD
       213–85n
  explanation by Styx, TH 383–403n,
       775–806n
Oath, TH 231; WD 804
  as personification of perjury, TH
       211–32n
Oath Demon, WD 219
  born after Lawlessness and Ruin, WD
       219n
  Furies present at birth of, WD 219n
  grandson of Night and son of Strife,
       WD 219n
  as personification, WD 219n
  punisher of perjurers, WD 213–85n
Oblivion, TH 227

Odysseus, TH 1012, 1018
  affair with Kalypso, TH 1005–20n
  descent into underworld, TH 721–819n
  seduction by Kirke, TH 1005–20n
Oedipus, WD 163
  and Sphinx's riddle, TH 295–336n
Oizys (Distress, Woe), TH 211–32n, 214
Okeanids
  catalogue of, TH 337–70n
  companions of Persephone, TH 337–70n
Okeanos, TH 20, 133, 215, 241, 265, 274, 287,
     337, 363, 364, 368, 383, 960; WD 171,
     566; S 310–15, 300–320n
  alternate name
     Ocean, TH 282, 291, 294, 389, 695, 776,
       789, 816, 841, 907, 956, 979
     in song of Muses, TH 9–21n
  child of Gaia and Ouranos, TH 337–70n
  description of, TH 133–38n
  father of Klymene, WD 42–58n
  Hesiod's conception of, TH 337–70n
  husband of Tethys, TH 133–38n
Old Age, TH 225
  child of Night, WD 109–25n
old age, and care of parents by youngest
     son, WD 376–80n
olives, not mentioned by Hesiod, WD
     564–70n
Olmeios, TH 5–8n, 6
Olympians, TH 408
  gods Kronos sired, TH 646, 668; WD 140
  gods of Olympos, WD 257
  in song of Muses, TH 9–21n
Olympos, TH 37, 42, 52, 62, 68, 101, 113, 114,
     118, 391, 398, 634, 680, 689, 783, 793,
     804, 842, 855, 953, 963; WD 82, 110,
     128, 199, 257, 474; S 30–35, 75–80,
     200–205, 465–70, 470–75
omen, crows as sign of ill, WD 746–47n
Orion, WD 597, 609, 615, 619
  Betelgeuse as brightest star in constella-
       tion of, WD 597–98n
  as lover of Eos, TH 371–74n
  partly sets at time of Pleiades, WD
       615–17n
  rise marks summer solstice, WD 561–63n
  setting of, WD 619–20n
orphan, harsh lot of, WD 328–29n
Orthos, TH 293, 326
  dog of Geryones, TH 309
Othrys, TH 632

Ourania (Okeanid), TH 350
Ouranos, TH 45, 106, 126, 133, 147, 154, 157, 176, 207, 422, 463, 470, 503, 617, 644, 889
  alternate name
    Sky, TH 702
      mating with Earth, TH 133–38n
  castration of, TH 183–210n
  as consort to Mediterranean earth mother, TH 459–501n
  description of, TH 126–32n
  father of Okeanos, TH 337–70n
  father of Themis, TH 901–11n
oxen
  age for plowing, WD 437–40n
  as priority for farmer, WD 405–9n

Pallas, TH 376, 383
  as father of Moon, TH 375–82n
Pandion, WD 568
  father of Procne and Philomela, WD 564–70n
Pandora, WD 82, 100
  etymology of, WD 59–105n
  as punishment, TH 507–615n; WD 59–105n
Panic, TH 935; S 460–65
  and Fear, S 195–200, 195–200n, 460–80n
Parnassos, TH 499
Parthenios, TH 344
Peace, TH 902
  sister of Justice and Good Law, WD 213–85n, 220–29n
Pegasos, TH 281, 284, 325
  aids Bellerophon against Chimaira, Amazons, and Solymoi, TH 270–86n
  and origin of name *Hippokrene*, TH 5–8n, 270–86n
Peirithoos, S 180–85, 180–90n
Peleus, TH 1007
  father of Achilleus, TH 1005–20n
  son of Aiakos, TH 1005–20n
Pelias, TH 994
  sends Jason in quest of golden fleece, TH 993–1002n
Peneios, TH 343; S 460–80n
Pentheus, son of Agaue, TH 976n
Permessos, TH 5, 5–8n
Perseis, TH 356
  daughter of Ocean, TH 956
Persephone, TH 768, 774, 913
  Okeanids as companions of, TH 337–70n

Perses, brother of Hesiod, WD 10, 27, 213, 274, 286, 298, 397, 611, 633, 641
  admonished by Hesiod to choose virtuous path, WD 286–319n
  bribes kings, WD 202–12n
  perjury threatens Askre and kin, WD 213–85n
  symbolized by hawk, WD 202–12n
Perses, son of Eurybie and Kreios, TH 377, 410
  father of Hekate, TH 375–82n
Perseus, TH 280
  slayer of Medousa, TH 270–86n
  son of Danae, S 215–20, 215–40n, 225–30
  son of Zeus and Danae, TH 270–86n
personification
  of curses by Erinyes, TH 183–210n
  of desire, TH 64–80n
  of justice by Justice, WD 213–85n
  Oath Demon, WD 219n
  Okeanos, TH 337–70n
  of old age by Graiai, TH 270–86n
  of perjury by Oath, TH 211–32n
  of rivers, WD 737–41n
Persuasion, WD 74
Petraia, TH 357
Petraios, S 180–85
Phaethon, TH 987
  usually son of Helios, TH 984–92n
Phikion, S 30–35, 30–60n
Philomela
  daughter of Pandion, WD 564–70n
  transformation into swallow, WD 564–70n
  violated by Tereus, WD 564–70n
  weaves message to Procne, WD 564–70n
Philyra, TH 1002
Phoibe, TH 136, 404
  mother of Leto, TH 133–38n
Phokians, S 25–30
Phokos, TH 1005
  eponymous ancestor of Phokians, TH 1005–20n
Phorkys, TH 238, 270, 333, 336
  father of Echidna, TH 295–336n
  occasionally identified with his father, TH 233–64n
Pieria, TH 54; S 205–10
  cult of Muses at, TH 53–55n
  location of, TH 53–55n; WD 1–10n
pine, S 375–90, 420–25
pipes, S 275–80

Pleiades, WD 572, 615, 619
    daughters of Atlas, WD 383
    heliacal rising of, WD 571–77n
        as start of summer for Hesiod, WD
            663–77n
    identified with daughters of Atlas, WD
        383–87n
    partly set at time of Orion, WD 615–17n
    rising and setting of, WD 383–87n
    setting of, WD 619–20n
Ploutos, TH 971
    son of Demeter and Iasion, TH 969–74n
plow
    description of advanced, WD 427–36n
    types of, WD 427–36n
plowing and reaping
    age of oxen for plowing, WD 437–40n
    migration of crane as sign of plowing,
        WD 448–49n
    plowing at winter solstice, WD 479–90n
    prayer before plowing, WD 467n
    with rising and setting of Pleiades, WD
        383–87n
    sickles sharpened for reaping, WD 571–77n
    stripping down for, WD 388–93n
    time of reaping at beginning of summer,
        WD 663–77n
poet, self-reference to, TH 1–115n
Ponos (Pain), TH 226
Pontos, TH 107, 131, 233, 237
    progeny of, TH 233–64n
Poseidon, TH 15, 278, 732, 930; WD 667;
        S 100–105
    alternate names
        Earth-Shaker, TH 441, 456
        Shaker of the Earth, TH 818
poverty, virtuous poverty better than cor-
        rupt wealth, WD 27–41n
Procne
    daughter of Pandion, WD 564–70n
    kills son Itys and serves his flesh to
        Tereus, WD 564–70n
    transformation into nightingale, WD
        564–70n
Prometheus, TH 510, 521, 522, 533, 536, 546;
        WD 48, 87
    as creator of men, WD 42–58n
    comparisons with Christ, TH 507–615n
    freed by Herakles, TH 507–615n
    myth explains harsh lot of man, WD
        42–58n

punishment of, TH 507–615n
    son of Iapetos, TH 133–38n, 528, 543, 559,
        565, 614; WD 50, 55
    son of Iapetos and Klymene,
        WD 42–58n
Proteus, as another version of Nereus, TH
        233–64n
Proto, TH 243, 248
    repetition of name in list of Nereids, TH
        233–64n
public performance, effect of, TH 94–104n
punishment, of Prometheus, TH 507–615n
Pylos, S 360–65
Pytho, TH 499; S 460–80n, 475–80

Quarrels, TH 229

Retribution, WD 197
Rheia/Rhea, TH 135, 453, 467, 625, 633
    identification with Demeter, Kybele, and
        Mother of the Gods, TH 133–38n
    mother of Zeus, TH 133–38n, 459–501n
Rhodes, sun cult at, TH 371–74n
ritual
    cleanliness and propriety of, WD 727–32n
    copulation on plowed field, TH 969–74n
    purity at crossing of rivers, WD 737–41n
rivers, TH 337–70n
Ruin, TH 230
    born before Oath Demon, WD 219n

sacrifice
    dishonoring unknown god at, WD
        755–56n
    explained by Prometheus myth, TH
        507–615n
    firstling kids as token of piety at, WD
        543–45n
    injunction of cutting nails at, WD 742–43
    at Mekone, WD 42–58n
    not offered by silver race of men to gods,
        WD 126–42n
sailing
    best time for, WD 663–77n
    done only out of necessity, WD 236–37n
    warning against overloading of ship, WD
        690–93n
Sangarios, TH 344
Seasons, TH 901; WD 75
    names reveal character of Zeus's new or-
        der, TH 901–11n

Selene, TH 18, 372
  alternate name
    Moon
      as daughter of Pallas, TH 375–82n
      in song of Muses, TH 9–21n
      identification with Artemis and Hekate,
        TH 371–74n, 409–52n
Semele, TH 976
  birth of Dionysos by, TH 940–42n
  daughter of Kadmos, TH 940
Shame, WD 197
shame, in manual labor, WD 286–319n
sheaf, cross-binding of, WD 479–90n
Simoeis, TH 342
Skamandros, TH 345
Sky Dwellers, TH 461
Sleep, TH 212, 757, 759
  brother of Death and child of Night, WD
    109–25n
  house in underworld with Death, TH
    721–819n
smithy, as gathering place, WD 493–94n
snail, as "house-carrier," WD 524–25n,
    571–77n
Solymoi, battle of Bellerophon and Pegasos
    against, TH 270–86n
Sorrows, TH 227
sowing
  job of slave women following oxen, WD
    405–9n
  stripping down for, WD 388–93n
Sphinx, TH 326
  riddle of, TH 295–336n
spring
  heralded by song of cuckoo, WD 479–90n
  rising of Arcturus as sign of, WD 564–70n
  swallow as harbinger of, WD 564–70n
  time of pruning of vines, WD 564–70n
  vernal equinox, WD 561–63n
stone, disgorged by Kronos, TH 459–501n
Strife, TH 211–32n, 225, 226; WD 11, 15, 24,
    28, 804; S 145–50, 145–50n, 155–60,
    155–60n
  daughter of Night, WD 11–26n, 17
  in Empedoclean doctrine, WD 11–26n
  mother of Oath Demon, WD 219n
  twofold nature of, WD 11–26n
Strymon, TH 339
Styx, TH 361, 397, 806
  connection with Arcadian Styx, TH
    775–806n

daughter of Ocean, TH 776
daughter of Okeanos, TH 383, 389
explanation of oath by, TH 383–403n,
    775–806n
origin of, TH 775–806n
in underworld, TH 721–819n
succession myth, TH 459–501n
summer
  beginning as time for reaping, WD
    663–77n
  effects on men and women, WD 582–89n
  end of, WD 663–77n
  goats fattest during, WD 582–89n
  solstice, WD 561–63n
    and best time for sailing, WD 663–77n
    signaled by heliacal rise of Pleiades, for
      Hesiod, WD 663–77n
    signaled by rise of Betelgeuse, WD
      597–98n
    signaled by rise of Orion, WD 561–63n
    time of threshing, WD 561–63n, 663–77n
    wine best during, WD 582–89n
sun
  omniscience of, WD 267n
  winters in Africa, WD 527–28n
swallow, WD 568
  as harbinger of spring, WD 564–70n
  transformation of Philomela into, WD
    564–70n
swan, S 315–20, 315–20n

Taphians, S 10–20n, 15–20
Tartaros, TH 119, 683, 721, 725, 726, 737, 808,
    822, 851, 868; S 255–60
  father of Echidna, TH 295–336n
  location in underworld, TH 721–819n
  origin of, TH 116–25n
Teleboans, S 10–20n, 15–20
Telegonos, TH 1014
Tereus
  transformation into hoopoe, WD 564–70n
  violates Philomela, WD 564–70n
Tethys, TH 136, 337, 362, 368
  mother of Klymene, WD 42–58n
  origin of name, TH 1005–20n
  wife of Okeanos, TH 133–38n, 1005–20n
Thaumas, TH 237, 265, 780
Thebes, TH 530, 978; WD 164; S 1–5, 10–15,
    10–20n, 30–60n, 45–50, 80–85,
    100–105
Theia, TH 133–38n, 135, 371

Themis, TH 16, 135, 901
  daughter of Gaia and Ouranos, TH
    901–11n
  etymology of name, TH 901–11n
  mother of Justice by Zeus, WD 213–85n
  mother of Fates by Zeus, S 240–70n
  second consort of Zeus, TH 133–38n
Theseus, son of Aegeus, S 180–85
  abandons Ariadne on Naxos, TH 947–49n
  descent into underworld, TH 721–819n
Thetis, TH 244, 1006
  daughter of Nereus, TH 1005–20n
  mother of Achilleus, TH 1005–20n
  origin of name, TH 1005–20n
thistle, golden, WD 582–89n
Thrace, WD 507, 553
threshing
  floor, WD 598n
  time at summer solstice, WD 561–63n,
    597–98n, 663–77n
thrift
  habit dropped after new crop harvested
    and threshed, WD 561–63n
  with wine, WD 368–69n
Time, S 20–25
Tiryns, TH 292; S 80–85
Titanomachy, TH 617–721n
  role of Hundred-Handers in, TH 139–53n,
    617–721n
Titans, TH 208, 393, 424, 629, 632, 646, 649,
    662, 668, 674, 676, 697, 698, 717, 730,
    814, 820, 851, 882
  alternate name
    Overreachers, TH 208
  and creation of man, TH 617–721n; WD
    42–58n
  etymology of, TH 183–210n
  nature of those born of Earth and Sky,
    TH 133–38n
  object of Hera's prayer, TH 617–721n
  in song of Muses, TH 9–21n, 36–52n
  in underworld, TH 721–819n
Tithonos, TH 984
  as lover of Eos, TH 371–74n
tombs, prohibition of men and boys sitting
  on, WD 750–52n
Trachis, S 320–40n, 350–55, 460–80n, 470–75,
    475–80
transformation
  of Philomela into swallow, WD 564–70n
  of Procne into nightingale, WD 564–70n

of Proteus, TH 233–64n
of Tereus into hoopoe, WD 564–70n
tree, world, TH 726–39n
Tritogeneia, TH 895
Triton, TH 930–33n, 931
Troy, WD 166, 653
  Achaeans wait to sail to, WD 651–52n
truth, Muses' capability of, TH 22–34n
Tyche, TH 360
Typhaonion, S 30–35, 30–60n
Typhoeus, TH 821, 823, 837, 858, 868,
    869
  alternate name
    Typhaon, TH 307
  battle against Zeus, TH 617–721n
  born from Hera, TH 820–80n
  as primordial serpent, TH 820–80n
  relation to Norse World Serpent, TH
    820–80n
  in underworld, TH 721–819n
Tyrsenians, TH 1005–20n, 1015

underworld
  descent into (Katábasis), TH 721–819n
  geography of, TH 721–819n
  lack of souls of dead in, TH 337–70n,
    721–819n, 775–806n
  place of in poem, TH 721–819n
universe, tripartite division of,
    TH 721–819n

vines, pruned at beginning of spring,
    WD 564–70n
virginity
  emphasis on marrying virgin girl,
    WD 699n
  of Hestia, TH 453–58n; WD 733–34n
virtue, path to, WD 286–319n

wealth
  sheep as, WD 589–96n
  virtuous poverty better than corrupt
    wealth, WD 27–41n
Wide Law, mother of Thalia,
    WD 230–31n
wife, characteristics of bad, WD 702–5n
wine
  best in summer, WD 582–89n
  from Biblos, WD 589–96n
  cut with water, WD 589–96n
  gift of Dionysos, WD 609–14n

winter
cloth used for clothing during,
WD 538n
coat of firstling kids worn during, WD
543–45n
rationing of food to oxen and men dur-
ing, WD 559–60n
sandals worn during, WD 541–42n
time of solstice, WD 479–90n
women
distrust of, WD 373–75n
insatiable sexual appetite in summer, WD
582–89n
libidinous urges dulled by fruit of cornel
tree, WD 582–89n
men weakened by contact with, WD
753–54n
as priority for farmer, WD 405–9n
as punishment for men, TH 507–615n;
WD 59–105n
task of grinding corn belonging to, WD
423n
thievish nature of, WD 373–75n
time of marriage for, WD 698n
twofold nature of, TH 507–615n
woodcutting, time of, WD 420–22n
work
golden race enjoys fruits of earth with-
out, WD 109–25n
value of manual labor, WD 286–319n

xenia, breaking as sign of humanity's end,
WD 174–201n

Zelos, TH 384
as personification, TH 383–403n
Zephyr, WD 594
Zephyros, TH 380, 870
as west wind, TH 375–82n
Zeus, TH 4, 29, 47, 54, 76, 81, 96, 141, 316, 386,
399, 479, 498, 513, 537, 550, 568, 571,
600, 613, 615, 687, 707, 784, 815, 820,
857, 868, 886, 899, 908, 912, 918,
938, 940, 944, 949; WD 3, 7, 9, 47,
49, 51, 106, 144, 180, 228, 252, 256,
267, 273, 276, 280, 333, 465, 661, 724,
765; S 30–35, 50–55, 65–70, 85–90,
195–200, 200–205, 325–30

alternate names
Father, WD 84
lord of councils, S 380–85
lord of Olympus, WD 474
Olympian, TH 529, 884; WD 88, 245
Olympian hurler of lightning, TH 390
Zeus Chthonios, WD 465–66n
Zeus Ephestios ("Zeus of the Hearth"),
TH 453–58n
Zeus Kronion, WD 259; S 55–60
battle against Typhoeus, TH 617–721n,
820–80n
birth of, TH 459–501n
birth of Athena from head of, TH 912–29n
destruction of iron race of men by, WD
174–201n
father of Good Law, WD 275–78n
father of Herakles, S 30–60n
father of Justice by Themis, WD 213–85n
father of Perseus, TH 270–86n; S 215–40n
father-in-law of Menelaos, WD 157–73n
frees Hundred-Handers, TH 139–53n
as highest authority, WD 1–10n
identified with chthonic Minoan god, TH
459–501n
imposition of natural law by, WD 275–78n
kingly power from, TH 79–93n
Kratos and Bia belong only to, TH
383–403n
omniscience of, WD 267n
protector of suppliants and strangers,
WD 327n
punishment against man, WD 59–105n
punishment against Prometheus, TH
507–615n
punishment for injured Justice, WD
213–85n
relation to Thor, TH 820–80n
in song of Muses, TH 9–21n, 36–52n
son of Kronos, TH 133–38n, 423, 450, 534,
624, 658; WD 18, 70, 139, 158, 168,
238, 242, 246
son of Kronos and Rheia, TH 459–501n
son of Rheia, TH 133–38n
swallows pregnant Metis, TH 886–900n
Themis as second consort of, TH 133–38n
visits Alkmene while husband absent, TH
943–44n